D1523402

Evaluating Higher Education

Higher Education Policy Series 6

Evaluating Higher Education

Papers from the *International Journal of Institutional
Management in Higher Education*, Centre for
Educational Research and Innovation,
Organisation for Economic Co-operation
and Development

Edited by Maurice Kogan

Jessica Kingsley Publishers
London

First published in 1989 by
Jessica Kingsley Publishers Ltd.
13 Brunswick Centre
London WC1N 1AF

Copyright © 1989 Organisation for Economic Co-operation and Development

British Library Cataloguing in Publication Data

Evaluating higher education. - (Higher education
   policy series).
   1. Higher education. Assessment
   I. Kogan, Maurice II. Series
   378'.01

ISBN 1 85302 510 0

ISSN 0954-3716

Printed and bound in Great Britain by
Biddles Ltd, Guildford and King's Lynn

Contents

III EVALUATING INSTITUTIONS

IV EVALUATING FACULTY, COURSES AND DEPARTMENTS

V EVALUATION OF RESEARCH

Preface

This book contains a selection of essays published in the *International Journal of Institutional Management in Higher Education* between 1979 and 1986. It was felt that these contributions to thinking about the evaluation of higher education, some of which are now out of print, represent many different perspectives and come from many different OECD countries, and could usefully be brought together and made available to a wider audience.

The articles are mainly reproduced in the form in which they were first published by the OECD's Programme on Institutional Management in Higher Education. For the most part, in order to keep this book to a reasonable size, the considerable body of writing in the *Journal* specifically concerned with performance indicators has been omitted.

Maurice Kogan.
Brunel University, July 1988.

The Evaluation of Higher Education: An Introductory Note

Maurice Kogan,
Brunel University
United Kingdom

This book contains articles drawn from the *International Journal of Institutional Management*, (now known as *Higher Education Management*) which display the wide range of possible approaches to the evaluation of higher education that can be found at different levels in different systems. The experiences described are drawn from many countries represented in the Organisation for Economic Co-operation and Development (OECD) but raise issues which concern higher education in all countries where questions of quality control and of accountability have become prominent.

At no time has higher education been faced with such strenuous demands, from its political paymasters and its sponsoring publics, to demonstrate its work and account for its share of national resources. Nor have the challenges come only from the outside. Partly on the basis of long established impatience, but also taking the opportunities presented by external challenges, higher education administrators have been shaking off the 'academic veto' and increasingly feel able to demand demonstration of worth. The 'drive towards managerialism, powerfully reinforced by those governments which cannot abide the thought of beneficent public institutions with freedom to create their own missions and style, at least at public expense, has made managers more anxious to find rational bases upon which their judgements can be justified. Hence the demand for more specific and objective forms of evaluation which might convert the private judgements of academics into public truths.

As many of the essays reproduced here imply, the change in emphasis from practitioner self evaluation to external and managerial assessment can bring with it certain problems. There is the temptation to apply techniques developed within industry which may be of limited value to higher education. Higher education is concerned with essentially process-orientated activities in which, in the last analysis, the output is the same as the input, that is, the students themselves. Parallels to productive functions should therefore be made with caution. At the same time, however, there are growing and legitimate social pressures for knowledge of what are the outcomes of higher education.

The main issues divide broadly into questions of power, or what should be the institutional mechanisms for evaluation, and questions of technology, or how evaluation might convincingly and acceptably be performed. The expert contributions which follow can be considered within a frame of the following issues: the range of approaches to the evaluation of higher education; the institutions and mechanics for evaluation; and the impact of evaluation. These thematic issues are pursued or illustrated in the expert contributions which discuss evaluation undertaken at different levels systems; institutions; basic units and individuals in different national settings.

In several important senses, there is already a great deal of evaluation in higher education. At the level of the individual academic, appointments and promotions follow evaluation of research or other scholarly activities. Higher education teachers are constantly evaluating each others' work, within institutions and across the invisible colleges. Academics are exigent in determining academic merit; in most systems the process of securing tenure is amongst the most rigorous of any profession. At the institutional level, whilst some national systems have sought to reduce the power of traditional institutional pecking orders, in most there remain steep hierarchies based on private endowments, access to other forms of funding, research reputations and the extent to which able students compete to seek entry. The academic reputation of an institution feeds into the evaluations made by national systems which determine levels of grant. The evaluations are usually made for them by co-opted academics, and then placed within a frame of political and social criteria which institutions ignore at their peril.

The question is, therefore, not whether there should be evaluation, but who will do it, and on what basis. Academics undoubtedly fear that evaluation might be taken out of their hands and for purposes which they do not themselves determine. Moving the criteria from those of excellence determined by 'internalist' criteria, by those intrinsic to the academic profession, towards criteria related to discernible economic or other social outcomes inevitably moves the control of evaluation away from the academics towards managers. They are as capable as are academics of manipulating criteria and indicators which need not depend largely or wholly upon academic judgements, or which may start as academic judgments but become more easily controlled because stated numerically.

Before these issues of power are taken up, it will be appropriate to glimpse the range of evaluative approaches frequently noted in the main literature. It will be readily seen that, in fact, these are not easily separable from each other.

THE RANGE OF EVALUATIVE APPROACHES

Evaluating involves the use of techniques which entail different assumptions about the purposes to which evaluation will be put. It is not possible or necessary here to attempt to provide more than a brief glimpse of approaches that might be followed, all the more because several excellent discussions of evaluative practice, theory and research in general are available (for example, House (1980), Cronbach (1982), Stufflebeam and Shinkfield (1984), the Evaluation Studies Review Annual, and, directly relating to higher education, Adelman and Alexander (1980)).

In practice, whilst dichotomies are set up for purposes of describing the field of evaluation, actual evaluations tend to contain mixed approaches.

The mode of evaluation varies according to the motives underlying it. For the most part, evaluation is likely to involve the notion of change. The evaluation may be called upon to make judgements about changes already installed or changes in prospect or to ascertain whether changes are needed. The nature of the evaluation will vary according to whether an intervention is primarily directed to, for example, improvements in quality, reduction in cost, equalisation of access, or improvement in working conditions; and it will also vary according to its sponsors whether they be managers, political leaders, client groups, or the workers who are subject to the evaluation.

It is thus possible to note several important dichotomies, or ranges containing dichotomous extremes, in the approaches adopted. Some of them are: scientific experimental as against qualitative or non-controlled; formative as against summative, and process as against product related evaluation.

The first group of distinctions are essentially concerned with the scientific base of the different approaches. It is possible to conceive of them as a continuum, at the extremes of which there are two principal modes. There is the classic, experimental, 'scientific approach' which primarily depends upon the establishment of a strict control group against which comparative observation over time can be made. Thus, the nature of an existing state can be assessed, the effects of a clearly specified intervention can be evaluated and hypotheses tested. This mode is at the extreme of the spectrum but is, nevertheless, important in practice. It encompasses, for example, clinical trials of new drugs and such large scale social experiments as the Rand study of alternative national health insurance programmes (Freeman and Rossi, 1981) or much of the assessment of the conditions under which horticultural developments will be profitable. (Lawton, 1980).

There is, in fact, a massive American literature concerned with the evaluation of large scale experiments which are undertaken under controlled conditions in order to note the effects of systematically introduced change. Anything is possible in this era of heroic ministers, but attempts at. large scale change of that kind, within scientific controls, are unlikely to concern at least our present generation of readers.

In some areas of social policy, but hardly in education, the 'scientific clinical model' has become an ideal, even in areas where it is unattainable, against which other forms of evaluation now tend to be judged. At the other extreme there is evaluation addressed to a situation where there is no control that is or can be specified and no testable hypothesis rigorously established. Here there can be no attempt to compare equivalent states over time. The evaluation rather involves collecting as much information as possible with a view to making judgements based upon impact as perceived by those involved and attempting to derive patterns and trends of action and impact or the internal logic of the activity which might or might not have explanatory force. It is this style which some would regard as evaluation but not evaluation research.

Most inventories of evaluative frames include components of the two extremes. For example, Dennis Lawton makes the case for evaluation being more than a measurement of the success of a particular intervention (1980). We might consider, for example, whether that intervention was valuable as well as whether it was successful.

In educational studies at large, the scientific approach has been strongly challenged by 'illuminative' research. This emphasises the importance of context, system and milieu from which the individual should not be divorced. Human nature is dynamic and cannot be pinned down. Subjective experience is both varied and important. It is therefore unrealistic to identify particular and finite numbers of outcomes of interventions. Nor should one generalise them. It will be readily seen that such an approach would not sit easily with such calculative techniques as performance indicators.

Scriven (1967) advances a key distinction, that between formative and summative evaluation. Summative evaluation involves an independent evaluator rendering a judgement of an object based on the accumulated evidence about how it compares with similar objects in meeting the needs of consumers. In formative evaluation, however, an evaluator collects and reports data and judgements to assist the development of an object. This distinction is particularly important in new or innovative programmes where built in evaluation may become an integral part of the innovation itself. Evaluation may then be used formatively as a tracking mechanism so that the innovation itself can be redirected as progress on the earlier steps is evaluated.

A further dichotomy is whether the evaluation is directed to judgements on the quality of the process or of the product (Stufflebeam, 1969). If education is seen to produce important outcomes which are not easily measured or defined, evaluation is more meaningfully directed towards the processes of education so that the satisfaction enjoyed, the experiences received, and the style used, become more relevant.

A further distinction has been made (Becher and Kogan, 1978) between instrumental, interactive and individualistic evaluation. The instrumental style is employed by professional evaluators and aspires to impartiality and universality by using measures for comparison and control. In this it counts people as objects whose behaviour is in principle explicable in terms of a series of natural laws. The interactive style is based on the anthropological paradigm and emphasises the uniqueness and untidiness of educational contexts and those who work within them. This views people as social animals conforming to no absolutes and obeying their universal rules and incapable of being understood within their own terms. Individualistic evaluation is near to narrative history. It insists on the uniqueness of the particular instance. The evaluator's task is to create a careful case study. It may serve to point a moral but not to prove a rule. It is a romantic value position.

COMPONENTS OF EVALUATION

The notion of a continuum of evaluation does not, however, adequately encompass the ways in which many different approaches can be combined in any single evaluative exercise. The following list draws broadly on some of the authorities and attempts to identify the range of issues, substantive and methodological, which evaluators must face.

(1) Who sets the criteria for evaluation?

(2) What are the criteria?

(3) Who is intended to benefit from the evaluation?

(4) What is its focus: input; process; output; impact?

(5) Is the evaluation made over a time series?. And does it start before any intervention?

(6) Are there formal controls (e.g. are they randomised)?

(7) What sources of information and data are employed?

(8) Is change measured quantitatively?

(9) Are there predefined hypotheses?

(10) Is either replicability or generalisability an objective?

(11) Is the evaluation intended to be:

    (a) summative or formative;

    (b) to allow for full participation of those involved, or to be 'objective' and 'external'?

In considering the 11 points listed above, the main concern would be with making distinctions between the accountability or authority consequences of different kinds of evaluations. The evaluation would vary in terms of who evaluates whom and between external appraisals, which derive authority from objectivity, and expressing the aims and activities of those evaluated in such a way that they can learn from it. In the latter case authority is derived from sensitivity and powers of communication as well as from critical analysis. And these can be further distinguished from activity helping those evaluated to achieve change.

EVALUATIVE TECHNIQUES

In approaching their task, higher educational evaluators could draw upon a large range of techniques but must first decide which dimensions to pursue. They must also make their selections from the intellectual disciplines being used, whether they are economic, or derived from curriculum studies perspectives, or social psychology, organisational studies or political science. There would also be differences according to the level at which the evaluation is being pitched: whether it is the individual teacher with the pupil, a whole institution, or, indeed (and perhaps not before time) the functioning of a central government department. The kinds of techniques which might be used would depend on the following range of data:

(a) various measures of input or resources used;

(b) descriptive measures of activity, such as an analysis of the extent to which an institution achieves a balance between its different functions, or portfolio analyses (Sizer **(11)**);

(c) descriptive measures of throughput, such as the numbers of students recruited from different ability groups and socio-economic classes and their ultimate destinations;

(d) descriptive measures of outcome (for example, employability of students, published refereed work, research results, performance tests such as those described by Bogue **(2)**, the value added by undergraduate study. See the accounts of Northeast Missouri State University and the University of Tennessee by McClain and Banta and colleagues **(3,4)**, and Bauer's critique **(5)** of computerised statistics on student performance (Premfors, 1985);

(e) cost based analysis relating cost measures to outcomes for national systems on, for example, the residual factor in economic growth studies (Premfors, 1985);

(f) techniques for establishing experimental control such as randomisation, matching and double blind;

(g) surveys of attitudes of students (see Miller **(15)**) or employees;

(h) interviews with participant and non participant observers;

(i) analysis of content of meetings observed;

(j) analysis of organisations or formal organisational modelling.

MECHANISMS AND INSTITUTIONS FOR HIGHER EDUCATION EVALUATION

If experimental evaluation based upon the scientific model is an unlikely event in the life of a higher education institution, evaluation of the quality of present performance is not only part of the academic way of life under any circumstances, but is now reinforced by pressures from the political and social environment. Much writing on evaluation, including some in this volume, evinces the values of the academic community, but there is a growing body of writing intended to assist the introduction of new forms of management in higher education. The first group mostly expresses the need for professional self evaluation and cautions about external evaluation attempting to repeat the attitudes and techniques of standardised testing now treated with suspicion in many school systems. However, in some systems results related evaluation are being attempted. The movement towards performance indicators (Sizer 1979 and 1982, Cave et al., 1988) is getting stronger in many countries. For example, in the United Kingdom, a series of governmental and quasi governmental reports have pressed for their introduction (e.g. Jarratt, 1985, Croham, 1987, the White Paper, 1987).

The range of devices will be best considered when we describe examples of evaluation at the different levels. In the meantime, the relationship between different approaches and institutional mechanisms should be briefly explored.

The institutions for evaluation can be described in terms of three analytic categories: the authority or power or influence which they exercise; the level of the system from which they operate and to which they address their evaluative efforts; and, harking back to the previous section, the techniques and styles which they adopt in making their evaluations. Different aspects of all three dimensions emerge in the contributions to this book; only the briefest enumeration of the main points will be necessary here.

Evaluation can be highly authoritative in the sense that consequences in terms of the flow of resources or institutional futures may depend on it. The decision of a central ministry or of a body consisting of co-opted academics to enhance or reduce institutional status is authoritative of that kind. So are the decisions of appointments or promotions boards determining the futures of individual academics. Such authoritative decisions may be made by bodies which have no direct managerial line with those being evaluated. For example, professional bodies accrediting programmes make evaluations which have far more than influence; they carry authority. Further along the spectrum there are non authoritative evaluations which carry power to affect the normative judgements made about academic work or institutional performance. Many peer judgement evaluations are of this order: public reviews of written work, for example, affect reputations. Reputational evaluations may or may not be converted into judgements leading to authoritative decisions. Indirectly, however, they are certain to affect them. National bodies such as that described by Staropoli (12) recently established in France and certain aspects of the British HM Inspectors' work, are of this order. The influence is normative rather than authoritative. Finally, there are evaluations which overtly and deliberately carry no authority: they can be self evaluations or evaluations made on a consultancy or colleague basis to enhance self improvement. This does not mean that self evaluations may not be used authoritatively. They may be the basis, as in the CNAA example described by Brennan (14) for authoritative judgements.

It would be tempting to assume that the spectrum of authority is coterminous with the spectrum of levels. The levels from which evaluation might be made are those of central authorities (whether internal to government or appointed by government); institutional; and judgements made by basic units. There are also intermediate levels (such as local authorities in some countries) and individual evaluators who might be acting on behalf of one level or the other or contributing to the system of peer judgements.

It is possible for a central authority to attempt to act non-authoritatively by providing advisory services (which may or may not be called inspectorial) and, equally, as has already been remarked, self evaluation by a basic unit may form the basis for authoritative judgements elsewhere. A great deal of writing from the liberal perspective assumes that central authorities must always be authoritative in their actions. This is often so, but this is not a logical necessity. Nor, for that matter, should it be assumed that 'democratic' evaluation (the misnomer for evaluation of teachers by teachers) does not lead to judgements that affect individual futures.

Thirdly, there is the question of evaluative techniques and their relationship to authority and levels of evaluation. Again, it is too easily assumed that national authorities will always be 'hard nosed' in the evaluations which they sponsor whilst 'grass root' evaluation will always be soft and liberal. But the history of higher education evaluation in some countries, and particularly in the United Kingdom, has been that in the past central authorities as represented by the University Grants Committee and HM Inspectorate have been impressionistic and interactive in their modes of working, at least until retrenchments and determined ministerial changes of policy caused change, whereas evaluating bodies lower down the system have been more authoritative. Central governments can sponsor self evaluation and can continue to encourage formative, interactive, process orientated evaluation as against summative, quantitative and product related evaluation if they so choose. Liberal objections to national interventions can too easily script national authorities into adopting harder styles than are necessary for the performance of their task.

With these general points in mind, it is now possible to consider the discussions of evaluation at the different levels.

SYSTEM LEVEL

The present anxiety is to make sure that institutions are performing well, rather than that national systems and policies should be evaluated. Yet there can hardly be a democratic country where Parliamentary scrutiny of the way in which central ministries deal with higher education problems would not be possible. In almost all OECD countries there have been *ad hoc* exercises in evaluation. The Swedish U68 and the Dutch Contours exercises are obvious examples.

In the United Kingdom, the Robbins Report (1983) was the first and perhaps only comprehensive attempt to evaluate the demand and need for higher education and to specify the institutional and educational provisions that should then be made. The drastic readjustments to the Robbins policies which the UK witnessed in 1979 certainly led to reappraisal of individual institutions. These were contestable in themselves yet based on no systematic evaluation of the total system in terms of its costs and benefits, inputs and outcomes, student access and flows to the labour market, which a true evaluation would require (Kogan and Kogan, 1983).

Central administrators might reasonably protest that they do nothing but evaluate the performance of the system. But the essence of evaluation in a democracy is that the evaluators will show their working to those who are being evaluated. The UGC is evidently attempting to meet criticisms on this score, by being far more open and consultative as it moves towards a second review of research ratings in 1989. In Britain a recent report of the National Audit Office (1985) raised questions about the efficiency and accountability of the central departments in making cuts over the last five years.

Interesting normative propositions have been elaborated on the accountability of educational national authorities in general. (Gray, McPherson and Raffe, 1983). McPherson and his colleagues envisage a government which is accountable in terms of 'rational democracy'. This means that the basis of government's legitimacy is its claim to be acting rationally. It does not follow that the government's actions are rational, merely that, if required to defend its legitimacy, government could in principle be forced to do so in terms of the criterion of rationality. Accountability would be discharged through 'the telling of stories' or 'the rendering of account'. Electors might then have the means for evaluating the quality and accuracy of an account that is independent of government. Citizens must be able to evaluate their accounts and provide other ones. 'The effectiveness of such pressure and sanction must figure in a normative definition of accountability'.

Most governments do not render account in such terms. But for those concerned with rationality, the stewardship for a whole system would involve the creation of data and judgements related to the central issues of operating the system. Such an evaluation would be concerned not only with the effectiveness of the system in terms of its primary objectives but also in terms of how well it is administered: does it respond to the good administrative norms of equity, reasonable predictability and efficiency, and openness? Administrative audit of government and the way in which it visits its policies upon its client groups are still a weak zone in evaluation.

INSTITUTIONAL EVALUATION

On the evaluation of whole institutions, however, the literature is extensive. Institutions may be evaluated by themselves by state authorities or by peer review bodies. Kells (10) describes how all three are present in institutional evaluation in the USA. Self regulation remains dominant and Kells argues, by reference to organisation theory, as well as from the US experience, that 'for purposes of enhancing institutional effectiveness and management capabilities, the self regulatory scene at its best is far more effective over time than an external inspectorial control or planning scheme'. Moreover, the US market oriented mode produces 'far more and more useful institutional and programmatic evaluation' than do centrally planned systems.

Specialised program accreditation in the USA now covers over 50 areas. Peer accreditation of institutions, too, has enabled standards to be ascertained within the widely diverse American system. But since the 1960s, 'long dormant' state co-ordination and control have come to life, as have institutional attempts to plan and monitor their own developments, in response to retrenchment and demands for accountability. Most states now have institutional licensing and review incorporating processes which range widely in intensity and range. Voluntary accreditation is carried out by non governmental systems. And alongside these external evaluations are the growing practices of institutionally initiated evaluations. At the same time programs are evaluated from their specialist perspectives.

Kells records how in spite of state initiatives the trend is towards increasingly formalised external review by non-governmental bodies and self review. Against this background of institutional development Kells maintains that whilst the 'goals ends plus analysis of functioning' evaluation model may be relevant it does not sufficiently reckon with the potential benefits that self assessment and self study can bring to the task of institutional improvement. Moreover, state agencies can secure evaluation adequate for their purpose by relying on self evaluation which is beneficial in other ways.

That assumption underlies the experience, too, of the British Council for National Academic Awards (CNAA) as described by Brennan (14). Yet the British case is, indeed, shot through with paradoxes. Until recently, the British universities enjoyed a well celebrated freedom. Their money came from the public purse in the form of five year grants recommended by the University Grants Committee on the basis of a most unoppressive form of peer evaluation. But now a political judgement seems - it has never been explicit - to have been made that the universities cannot be trusted to perform either their academic or their social functions without exigent external evaluation. Performance indicators, including the secondary school examination results of students on entry, the research grants and contracts earned; citation indices and other quantitative measures, have been proposed and are being installed. Classic peer evaluation of a more subjective kind will continue to be applied but more rigorously, and with overt criteria of selectivity between institutions. At the same time, the public sector institutions, the polytechnics and other colleges, whilst being equally rigorously assessed for resource allocation purposes by the proposed Polytechnic and Colleges Funding Council (P.C.F.C) are likely to be evaluated under increasingly liberal regimes administered by the Council for National Academic Awards (CNAA). Both universities and public sector institutions will soon come under new funding bodies whose resource offers will be tied to the completion of contractual undertakings. The evaluation is likely to become more insistent and authoritative. So British higher education enters the bracing world of explicit evaluation in a cultural and moral confusion in which traditional academic values remain highly valued but in which even the more prestigious institutions are likely to be subject to some increasingly 'external' and 'objective' evaluative procedures.

One feels that Kells would approve of the 'trustful' developments towards self evaluation described by Brennan. The CNAA has, in fact, been a force for the liberalisation of the non university institutions in the UK. It does not yet accredit institutions, which would mean validating them to the point where they might award their own degrees. But the process of external evaluation of courses, which is the CNAA's primary function, has produced, in Brennan's view, several beneficial effects. It has helped institutions find increased freedom from the local authorities which own and control most of them; it has made serious progress in the business of encouraging collegial forms of self evaluation, through its Partnership in Evaluation Scheme, and it has helped prepare the way for some institutions to take on de facto whole institutional accreditation in line with the recommendations of the Lindop Report (see Brennan), a judgement upon which is, however, awaited from the British government. In arguing for assessment of responsiveness to the external environment through a portfolio approach, Sizer also urges the case for self evaluation.

Yet there are critics of self evaluation. One set of criticisms concerns the obvious difficulty of securing objective judgements which are useful to the clients as well as the inmates and receivers of salaries from institutions. Certainly, a great deal of writing about 'democratic' evaluation in education has been unashamedly normative in its assumption that professionals constitute the democracy for which evaluation must be fashioned (Kogan, 1986). But objections come, too, from the liberal or 'soft' end of the theoretical spectrum. 'Internal validations may tend to exist not so much because they are seen as educationally desirable but because they are a proven device for maximising the chances of success in external evaluation. This may distort the judgmental criteria so they are less about the educational quality of the proposal than about its chances of being externally validated They may display disproportionate concern with documents and claims (rather than actions) and the ability to present a convincing case: performance and pre-packaging skills may count for more than the case itself.' (Adelman and Alexander, 1982).

Both Brennan and Adelman and Alexander are concerned with self evaluation as a process enabling an institution to give assurances to the outside world of its probity and quality, though both are also concerned with the formative or self developmental aspects of evaluation. Others, including Sizer (11), have taken up the latter issue more directly. Sizer offers an evaluative frame in which the institution is able to assess its own potential 'in terms of its responsiveness to the needs of a complex and rapidly changing society.' It would analyse its historical and current performance against 'a continuous examination of the future environment to enable it to consider what courses and research to best market.' Management must also motivate academics to join this quest for renewal which will help institutions to survive. Furumark (8) describes an institutional self evaluation project carried out by the Swedish National Board of Universities and Colleges. This was seen as an aid to greater autonomy at a time of financial restriction through strengthening the capacity for self renewal. The paper draws attention to some critical issues in self evaluation.

Sizer and others concerned with portfolio analysis (for example, Doyle and Lynch, 1979) bring us closest to evaluation that has clear functional outcomes. It could be criticised, however, for not taking much account of what has been called the high culture of higher education, namely, scholarship, research and teaching for the sake of sustaining the progress of human thought and the capacity to provide society with critique.

At a time when national systems are becoming tougher in their relationships with universities and evaluation is becoming more explicit it is perhaps paradoxical to note how the mode adopted in the centralised systems is becoming more tender to the susceptibilities of the institutions. Kells observes that governments of some centrally controlled systems are seeking to encourage some deregulation and institution based evaluation. The duty of government is to promote the welfare of the people and to safeguard the appropriate distribution of tax money. Government has a legitimate stake in higher education's production of manpower, the maintenance of cultural values, innovation and individual development. The government must therefore evaluate by both process and output directed evaluation. In Holland an Academic Council lays down development plans for the disciplines to be evaluated by the institutions and the ministry. There is also a recently created inspectorate for higher education and directives to universities about the structures of their annual reports.

Anxiety about the narrowness of system evaluation of institutions has led to thought about the allocation of public funds on instructional performance and quality indicators. Bogue (2) describes a performance funding policy implemented in 1979 in the State of Tennessee. This is an attempt to get away from allocating funds on an enrolment based model or formula in which activity or size rather than achievement is the principal criterion of funding. Growth is not a good measure of achievement and enrolment levels are maintained at the expense of standards. Accordingly, an instructional evaluation schedule was developed, and since modified, which allocated two per cent of appropriations on the evaluation of instructional performance on five variables: numbers of programmes accredited; performance of graduates on general educational outcomes; performance of graduates on major field outcomes; evaluation of institutional programmes and services by enrolled students, recent alumni, and community employer representatives; evaluation of institutional programmes by peers from other institutions. In 1979, 23 institutions submitted data on these five variables. The peer evaluation variable has since been replaced with a variable giving credit for evaluation planning. The project is intended to encourage re-examination of intentions and content. It provides several indicators of educational effectiveness of both process and outcome. It allows for different measures of effectiveness as selected by institutions. And it is claimed that it preserves the 'basic integrity and meaning' of academic degrees and credentials as a basic responsibility of an institution.

Reports of increased evaluative activity have emerged from several countries in recent years. In France, in 1985, the national authorities set up a National Committee for Evaluation. The Committee reports directly to the President, and not the Minister of Education. It decides for itself which institutions to review and will have freedom to publish its conclusions. Its Secretary General, Staropoli, (12) emphasises that its function is not to verify administrative policies: that task remains with the Ministry if it chooses to exercise it. It will rely on peer judgements and will respect the fact that academic responsibility remains with the universities themselves. He emphasises that the committee is not an inspectorial body. Its remit includes evaluation of the whole system as well as universities and their component units. The evaluators will be appointed after consultation with the university to be evaluated. They will get information not only from the central administration and from major research bodies but also from the institutions themselves. Their evaluation will cover all aspects of institutional life as well as research and teaching including the origins and destinations of students, the social life of the university and its administration.

EVALUATION OF TEACHING STAFF

Implicit in the growth of evaluation by systems and their components is the issue of teacher evaluation. This practice is gaining ground in many systems. The UK, for example, seems likely to find most of its universities following the prescription of the Jarratt Report (1985) in making this a general practice. With this development, the university teacher becomes more explicitly part of a line management hierarchy and moves away from the role of the freestanding practitioner nurtured within a publicly funded institution. Miller (15) describes how over the last 10 years there has been a significant increase in faculty evaluation in the USA; perhaps between two-thirds and three-quarters of higher education institutions evaluate their teacher members. The range of data contributing to evaluation is wide and becoming wider. Whilst evaluation may be linked with staff development, institutions may not use evaluation well for this purpose. Procedures are, however, becoming more systematic. Survey instruments have improved and procedures generally have improved partly under the pressure of court cases brought by faculty members.

Miller well draws attention to the dangers implicit in over-strenuous evaluation activity. Judgements can be acted on too hastily. There is resistance to subordinating individualistic activity to evaluative formulae. Excessive reliance on quantification can be detrimental.

EVALUATION OF BASIC UNITS

These fears are echoed by Premfors (16) writing about the evaluation of basic units partly from the perspective of the Swedish experience. He asserts the need for evaluators to be explicit about the reasons for and the methods to be adopted in the evaluation. Not only are basic units exceedingly various but the purposes of evaluation, too, are various and may be aimed at accountability or at the not easily reconciled purpose of organisational learning. Self evaluation leading to self improvement does not sit easily with summative and external evaluation intended to reinforce the power and policies of the hierarchy. Furumark (8) writes of Swedish attempts, encouraged by the central authorities, to use self evaluation as a developmental process free of managerial connotations. Drenth and colleagues (6) describe a technical development (AMOS) which provides a model for the analysis of study progress at the level of the discipline which, internally administered, might cause 'the issue of external evaluation [to] lose much of its saliency.'

Basic units have many functions and attempts to assess them for particular functions, though legitimate and perhaps useful in themselves, may do violence to the fact that the basic unit's problems and merits result from the interaction of its teaching, research, administrative and social functions. Similarly, the criteria and methods of evaluation have to straddle the opposing criteria of authoritativeness and consensus, in default of hard scientific theory and knowledge. Certainly the measures and techniques available are of varying usefulness, and formalised and quantitative methods must be used with great caution. Some of the complexities involved in evaluating a single course or program have been outlined by McIntosh (1978). Balderston's account (13) of attempts at program review across the nine campuses of the University of California relates the anxieties and fears of loss of academic autonomy engendered by the attempt.

Premfors reminds us of the essentially conservative nature of higher education evaluation. It looks to past performance, or, even worse, to past global reputations of whole institutions. It rarely can or does concern potential, a point reinforced by Henkel's account (20) of the evaluation of government sponsored research in the UK.

EVALUATION BY STUDENTS

In spite of the significant increases in their power within higher education institutions, students have no universally accepted part in the evaluation of the education which they receive. Talbot and Bordage (7) give an illuminating account of an experiment in course evaluation undertaken at Laval University. It is based on directed small group discussions and is student centred in that the evaluations are generated directly by the students rather than based on questionnaires prepared by the teachers. The method is derived from the nominal group technique which was found to require too much work on the part of both teachers and students. Talbot's article discloses, unsurprisingly, that there are discrepancies in the objectives attributed to evaluation as between students and professors; one objection concerned the objectivity of methods that depended upon a high level of interaction among those evaluating and being evaluated. Talbot's conclusion that further research is needed in order to clarify the disparities of perception between students and professors can be addressed to the whole field of study of evaluation by students and other clients of higher education in terms of both the appropriate methodologies and of the resulting power relationships.

EVALUATION OF RESEARCH

On the face of it, research is an area in which evaluation should be the most feasible. Its products are published for all to see and are susceptible to multiple and public review. Yet evaluation produces severe problems many of which are reviewed by Gibbons (17). Archambault (19) describes a pilot exercise in Quebec which sets evaluation of research quality alongside resource planning within a university, as does Fransson in his Swedish example (18), and Rouban (23) in her analysis of how evaluating must be related to the economy of complex systems, and how in this process sociology, economics and political science have a part to play.

Rasmussen (22) reports an evaluation at the departmental level carried out at the Technical University of Denmark. This distinguished between input material, estimations of research activity and productivity and evaluation of the relevance of the research to teaching, international research and to society. Gibbons notes the limitations of peer review and argues for a 'methods mix' and contrasts the benefits of monitoring ('What is is happening?' or 'What happened?') with those of evaluation ('Has it made any difference?'). He also notes developments in the evaluation of strategic research and the institutional relationships surrounding it. Spaapen's (24) account moves into the territory of government and its increasing control of university research programmes. A principal motive behind the Dutch conditional finance system, introduced in 1982, was to make explicit the distribution of research effort and to ensure deference to the criteria of scientific excellence and social relevance. It gave rise to changing power relationships both between the state and the universities and within institutions.

One of the themes in Henkel's article (20) is that the range of science which might be required by a government department varies widely in its style, methodologies and objectives and that, correspondingly, the range of evaluative criteria must be wide. For example, some of the least paradigmally certain science, concerned with urgent social problems, might be evaluated as much according to its usefulness and the reality which it conveys to practitioners as by the canons of classic experimental science. Her case study of the application of the Rothschild experiment in a British central department shows how evaluation, usually undertaken by highly reputable health service and social science scientists, is mainly, if not wholly, conducted on classic scientific criteria, which do not easily or necessarily match those of policy makers. It also gives cause for scepticism about the concept of 'peer review', a concept to be modified in the light of observation of the power relationships between those evaluated and those evaluating.

The issue of the evaluation of science raises several policy issues. Many institutions will become increasingly dependent upon government sponsored contract research in their attempt to keep their level of resources and academic activities high. They, too, may find themselves caught between the criteria of policy makers and those of high quality science which remain dominant in most higher education systems.

Moed and colleagues (21) pursue the central technical theme of outcomes evaluation through their account of quantified bibliometric indicators as a tool for research policy.

THE IMPACTS OF EVALUATION

Some of the impacts of evaluation have been discussed earlier in this article. Adelman and Alexander (1982) express concern about the cosmetic nature of activities that can result from anxiety to make the right impression. In assessing likely impacts, several dimensions might be noted. By whom will the impact be felt: academics, their clients, the wider society as represented through the economy and the political system? Different modes of evaluation might be assessed against broad criteria to include: academic self confidence and the ability to sustain their independence; institutional and unit responsiveness to external needs and wants; the system's ability to assure itself that skills are being learned and good research outcomes achieved within reasonable resource constraints. For the most part, anxiety is expressed about the effect of rigorous evaluation on academic well being and social legitimacy. Another aspect is the issue of privacy and visibility. The process of giving an account has been described as dramaturgical (Grey, 1981). In such a performance the actor seeks to avoid embarrassing and revealing incidents by adopting devices protective of performance and this may also elicit protective participation from the audience. A further point developed by Black et al. (1984) as they describe the potential effects on school science teaching of testing performance is that expectations created by testing may lead to a reduction in variation of actual performance because norms are being promulgated through the very mechanisms of the testing. Certainly there is a long tradition of anxiety about the effect of focusing on measurable attainments and the narrowing of curriculum and activity that this might produce. Romney et al. **(9)** enumerate the 'political, economic and philosophical concerns which arise in assessing institutional performance'.

A further question of impact concerns costs. The American experience of evaluation requirements for federal research and development projects is that they have 'become issues of permanent concern' (Alkin and Solmon, 1983). Alkin and Stecher (1983) quote estimates of as much as 10 per cent of programme costs being devoted to evaluation. Henkel's article points out that preparing for the evaluation of a research unit might take up to six months of researcher time and concern.

Yet evaluation has a clear moral basis and some documented benefits. The moral basis is that of fairness; it enables those institutions which otherwise would stand no chance in a reputational system where subjective impression plays a large part to achieve public acknowledgement of the standards reached. It might cause long lingering reputations to be tested and perhaps adjusted in the light of more recent achievements. At a time when institutions are undergoing large changes and reorganisation both the public and the academic systems need accounts of the effects of change which systematic evaluation can provide. The cautions expressed in the articles in this book are, however, clear. Evaluation which pays no proper heed to the nature of higher education's tasks, individualistic and dependent upon creativity as they are, but instead looks for outcomes which can be easily quantified, will be doing violence to the activities being evaluated.

REFERENCES

Clem Adelman and Robin J. Alexander, *The Self Evaluating Institution: Practice and Principles in the Management of Educational Change,* Methuen, 1982.

M. C. Alkin and L. C. Solmon (ed.), *The Cost of Evaluation,* Sage Publications, 1983.

M. C. Alkin and B. Stecher, 'A Study of Evaluation Costs', in Alkin and Solmon, op.cit.

T. Becher and M. Kogan, *Process and Structure in Higher Education*, Heinemann, 1980.

P. Black, W. Harlen and T. Orgee, *Standards of Performance and Reality*, Chelsea College, University of London, 1984.

M. Cave, S. Hanney, M. Kogan, and G. Trevett. *The Use of Performance Indicators in Higher Education: A Critical Analysis of Developing Practice.* Jessica Kingsley Publishers, 1988.

Croham Report (1987). DES, *Review of the University Grants Committee* Cm 81, HMSO.

Lee J. Cronbach, *Designing Evaluations of Educational and Social Programs*, Jossey Bass, 1982.

Department of Education and Science, White Paper (1987), *Higher Education. Meeting the Challenge.* HMSO, Cm 114.

P. Doyle and J. E. Lynch, 'A Strategic Model for University Planning', *Journal of the Operational Research Society,* 30.7:60- 609, 1979.

Evaluation Studies Review Annual, Sage Publications.

A. Gray, *Codes of Accountability and the Pattern of an Account*, PAC Annual Conference, 1981 (mimeo).

J. Gray, A. F. McPherson and D. Raffe, *Reconstructions of Secondary Education Theory: Myth and Practice Since the War,* Routledge & Kegan Paul, 1983.

Jarratt Report (1985), Committee of Vice Chancellors and Principals, *Report of the Steering Committee for Efficiency Studies in Universities.*

E. R. House, *Evaluating with Validity,* Sage Publications, 1980.

M. Kogan, *Education Accountability*, Hutchinson, 1986.

D. Lawton, *Politics of the School Curriculum*, Routledge & Kegan Paul, 1980.

Naomi E. McIntosh, 'Evaluation and Institutional Research: The Problems Involved in Evaluating One Course or Educational Programme,' *International Journal of Institutional Management in Higher Education,* Vol. 2, No. 1, May, 1979.

M. Miles, 'Qualitative Data as an Attractive Nuisance: The Problem of Analysis', *Administration Science Quarterly,* 24, 1979, pp 590-601.

Rune Premfors, *Evaluating Basic Units in Higher Education,* University of Stockholm, Group for the Study of Higher Education and Research Policy, Report No. 33, February 1985.

P. Rossi and H. Freeman, *Evaluation: A Systematic Approach*, Sage Publications, 1982.

M. Scriven, 'The Methodology of Evaluation', in *Perspectives on Curriculum Evaluation*, AERA Monograph No. 1, 1967.

D. L. Stufflebeam, 'Evaluating as Enlightenment for Decision Makers' in *Improving Educational Assessment,* Association for Supervision and Curriculum Development, 1969.

D. L. Stufflebeam and A. J. H. Shinkfield, *Systematic Evaluation: A Self Instructional Guide to Theory and Practice,* Luwer Nijhoff Publishing, 1984.

R. Y. Yin, 'The Case Study Crisis: Some Answers', *Administrative Service Quarterly,* 26(1), March 1981, pp 58-65.

Allocation of Public Funds on Instructional Performance/Quality Indicators[1]

E. Grady Bogue
Louisiana State University
in Shreveport
United States

ABSTRACT

In the United States, funding of public colleges and universities is almost entirely dependent on previous funding history and on the enrollment patterns of higher education institutions. If questions of performance are asked of colleges and universities, these are inevitably answered in terms of process, size, and activity levels rather than outcomes and effectiveness. A performance funding policy implemented in the State of Tennessee links 2 per cent of state funding for higher education to achievement rather than activity, to outcomes rather. than size. The policy has major implications for linking funding for higher education to achievement rather than activity, to outcomes rather than size. The policy has major implications for linking funding and performance in colleges, and in service-based institutions in both government and private sectors.

THE PERFORMANCE FUNDING CHALLENGE

In the United States, public sector managers and scholars of public administration have long sought closer links between funding and results in governmental activity. Lay trustees having governance responsibility for colleges and universities have likewise yearned for better ways of relating funding to performance in government.

For the past five years a major developmental venture to do just that has been underway in the State of Tennessee. The outcome of that venture is a performance funding policy implemented in the fall of 1979. This policy allocates some state dollars to colleges and universities on a criterion of accomplishment rather than activity, rewards qualitative outcomes rather than size of growth. Implemented in the higher education sector of government service, the policy has potential for management of service enterprise in both government and profit sectors.

---

1.   An earlier version of this paper was presented at the Fifth IMHE General Conference held in Paris on 8th-10th September, 1980.

We turn now to a description of the policy, the history of its development, and examination of its potential for management of service-based institutions.

ACHIEVEMENT VERSUS ACTIVITY IN FUNDING

An introductory note on higher education funding in the United States will prove useful in understanding the performance funding policy adopted in the State of Tennessee. In most American states, funds for public higher education institutions are generally requested and allocated on an enrollment-based model or formula. In other words, activity or size rather than achievement is the principal criterion of funding.

Allocating tax funds to a public institution based on how many students come to study there, and what they study, constitutes an improvement on earlier models of state higher education funding. These earlier models (circa 1950, 1960) relied heavily on analyses which failed to consider the complexity of institutional mission.

For example, the pattern of degree programmes at a small liberal arts institution or community college is certainly different from those at a major research university. Contemporary funding models recognize this diversity by providing funds based on size, degree level, and programme field of student enrollments. The essential principle of this funding model is "equivalent funding for equivalent programmes". Objectivity and equity are nicely served by this approach to funding.

Other principles are not so well served, however. Among the more prominent criticisms of enrollment-based funding are these:

1. *It emphasizes growth as a measure of achievement.* To obtain significant additional dollars, an institution has to add students.
2. *It encourages a displacement of purpose.* Since growth is the principal achievement rewarded, serving students is displaced with the goal of obtaining more students.
3. *It provides no incentive for qualitative improvements.* A programme with mediocre performance record is funded at the same level as one with a better performance record.
4. *It encourages a lowering of educational standards as a means of maintaining enrollment levels.*

These are not the only difficulties. Readers interested in a more thorough treatment are referred to resources by Gross (1973), Moss and Gaither (1976) and Bogue (1977).

Public funds will be allocated among colleges and universities every year by some type of allocation policy or model. Enrollment driven funding, or any other policy, will satisfy some goals and evaluation criteria and not others. The choice of funding policy is a choice of goals and a choice of satisfaction – but always less than optimal on both counts.

The probability of continued imperfection in state funding policy is not an excuse, however, from seeking improvements. We move now to a description of the performance funding policy adopted in Tennessee, a policy which rewards achievement rather than activity.

THE INSTRUCTIONAL EVALUATION SCHEDULE

The Tennessee Higher Education Commission is a state planning agency for higher education. Similar to companion agencies in the United States, the Commission is responsible for developing a master plan for higher education, evaluating proposals for new programmes in higher education, and recommending to the Governor and Legislature the annual budget for the twenty-five public colleges and universities in Tennessee.

In August of 1979, the Commission adopted a performance funding policy inserting into the basic enrollment-driven funding model a performance-based schedule entitled the *Instructional Evaluation Schedule.* This policy permitted institutions to earn an additional *two percent* of their appropriations based on evaluation of institutional instructional performance on five variables as follows:

1. *Number of academic programmes accredited* – such as accreditation of professional programmes in law, engineering, education, business, etc.
2. *Performance of graduates on a measure of general education outcomes* – such as ability to communicate, analyze, evaluate, and familiarity with major modes of intellectual inquiry, etc.
3. *Performance of graduates on a measure of major field outcomes* – such as performance on nursing exams, engineering exams, etc.
4. *Evaluation of institutional programmes and services by enrolled students, recent alumni, and community-employer representatives.*
5. *Evaluation of institutional programmes by peers from other institutions.*

An institution could earn a maximum of 20 points on each variable, for a total award of 100 points. Here is how the schedule would function for a hypothetical institution known as First Rate University.

ILLUSTRATION 1

First Rate University has a basic funding recommendation for $20 M, based on the enrollment-driven funding model. The maximum amount available to First Rate University for the Instructional Evaluation Schedule would be 2 percent of its basic funding recommendation or $400,000.
First Rate University receives the following evaluation and point allocation on the five performance variables.

Variable	Maximum Points	Allowed Points
Accreditation	20	10
General Education Outcome	20	15
Specialty Field Outcomes	20	5
Peer Evaluation	20	10
Evaluation by Enrolled Students, Alumni, Employers	20	15
	100	55

Added to the funding recommendation for First Rate University would be an amount equal to 55 percent of $400,000 or $220,000, making the total recommendation for First Rate University $20,220,000.

In the fall of 1979, twenty-three public institutions submitted performance data on these five variables. The total performance scores ranged from a low of 0 to a high of 67. Participating in the schedule were nine universities, ten community colleges, and four two-year technical institutes. The maximum amount that these institutions might have earned was just a little over $4 million. The dollars actually recommended for the institutions were just over $2 million.

Commentary and criticism of the initial performance funding policy have been solicited and an initial set of comments has been used to revise the Instructional

Evaluation Schedule. The performance standards have been improved and the "peer evaluation" variable has been replaced with a variable emphasizing evaluation planning. An outline of the performance standards and definitions for one of the variables – the General Education Outcome variable – can be found in Illustration 2.

Among the important assumptions on which this policy is built are these:

1. An emphasis on the outcomes and effectiveness of educational programmes encourages a re-examination of programme intent and content. Looking at "ends" forces an examination of "beginnings".
2. There is no single indicator of educational effectiveness that cannot be criticized for some theoretical or practical frailty. Thus, the policy makes use of multiple indicators – both process and outcome – and multiple evaluators – faculty, student, employers, etc.
3. One of the important historical strengths of American higher education is its diversity. Diversity is preserved by providing for different measures of ·
    effectiveness as selected by institutions.
4. Many variables, some external to the control of colleges and universities, can affect learning. However, the basic integrity and meaning of academic degrees and credentials remains a basic responsibility of an institution and is under its active control.

We believe that this revised policy will have a constructive impact at the campus level, that it will encourage the renewal uses of evaluation, and that it will involve campus communities not as a bureaucratic add-on but as a part of activity that flows naturally within the educational process.

There are important risks to this venture. Data and results may be misused and misinterpreted. The policy may result in a "teaching to the test" syndrome, with surface effects but little disturbance in deeper waters. These risks we count relatively modest, however, with the potential for achievement. It is now appropriate to say a word about policy origins.

THE PERFORMANCE PROJECT

Work on development of the Performance Funding Policy in Tennessee began in the fall of 1974, with the implementation of a major developmental project entitled The Performance Project. *The purpose of this project was to explore the feasibility of allocating some portion of state funds on a performance criterion.* This project anticipated growing dissatisfaction with enrollment driven funding models and emerging public concern with educational standards and accountability in higher education.

Among the difficulties anticipated by project staff were these frequently heard concerns:

a) Evaluation of effectiveness requires an assessment, methodology not well developed. Measurement is not the same as judging the goodness or worth of an event, activity, or product.
b) Consensus on standards of evaluation is difficult to obtain. A performance criterion on which agreement is obtained may turn out to be trivial.
c) Not all variables related to student performance effectiveness are under direct higher education control.
d) Some programme effectiveness indicators – licensing examinations, for example – are subject to external manipulation.
e) Narrow definitions of effectiveness may cause perversions in educational processes.

ILLUSTRATION 2

INSTRUCTIONAL EVALUATION VARIABLE
GENERAL EDUCATION OUTCOMES

Performance Standards	Points Awarded
1. The institution has assessed the performance of a representative sampling of graduates for its major degree – associate or bachelor's – on a measure of general education outcomes at least once during the past four years	5
2. The institution has, during the past four years, assessed the general education performance of a representative sampling of a majority of its graduates by major field or college, and has begun a programme of inter-field or inter-collegiate analyses of the data	10
3. The institution has an ongoing programme to assess the performance of its graduates on a measure of general education outcomes and has available data, preferably on the same measure, for representative samples of two or more classes of graduates during the previous four years	15
4. The institution meets the requirements of standard (3) and can further demonstrate for the most recent or one of the two most recent assessments that the development of its graduates – that is, the change in performance from freshman to graduation – is equivalent to or greater than the development of students from at least one institution whose freshman performance is at a comparable level	20

Definitions, Commentary, Procedures

1. "General Education Outcomes" are generally defined as those knowledges and skills expected of graduates earning the major degree of an institution. These may include communication, problem solving ability, reasoning skill, analytic and synthesis skills, familiarity with major modes of inquiry, etc. The specific definition of these outcomes is expected to reflect the mission, philosophy, and special character of each institution.

2. The "measure of outcome" must be an assessment instrument having norms beyond the institution. Examples would include the ACT, COMP battery, the ETS GRE Aptitude tests, and ETS Undergraduate Assessment Programme, the Adult Proficiency Level Examination, elements of the National Assessment of Education Progress[2]. This list of examples is not intended to be exhaustive.

3. A "representative sampling" is defined as a sample of graduates chosen so that the sample statistically represents the population of graduates. The population of graduates is presumed to include all those receiving the institution's major degree for a given year.

4. An "ongoing programme" of general education assessment is defined as a programme described in formal institution policy and published in appropriate academic policy documents.

5. Information supplied in support of performance on this variable and its standards should include:
   a) A brief description of the instrument employed and the agency or company publishing the instrument. The general education outcomes assessed by the instrument should be concisely described.
   b) The dates of administration.
   c) A description of the population or sample assessed – including size of the sample and other evidence of how the sample was chosen to represent the population.
   d) A concise presentation and analysis of results for each administration.
   e) An analysis of those institutions and /or referent student populations judged to be comparable for those institutions attempting to qualify on standard (3). The analysis should include the data for concluding that the institution's graduates developed at a rate equivalent to or greater than students from comparable institutions.
   f) *A description and analysis of instructional policy or practice changes made as a result of institutional review of the data obtained from the general education assessment after two years' data have been collected.*

---

   2.   *ACT COMP Battery:* American College Testing Program, College Outcome Measures Project Battery. *ETS GRE Aptitude Test:* Educational Testing Service, Graduate Records Examination Aptitude Test.

f) There is a tendency to believe that what can be measured is all that is important.

g) There is potential for misuse of data.

Believing that meaningful achievement on the project was more likely to come from an alliance of thought and action, the project staff adopted the motto, "Acting on the Possible While Awaiting Perfection".

Convinced that those affected by a potential change in policy, especially one of this complexity, should be involved in shaping that policy change, project staff constructed a partnership plan of involvement – a plan calling on the intelligence and initiative of both professional and lay colleagues. The partnership involved institutions, their governing boards, and executive and legislative officers.

Securing external funding support was an early activity of the project. During 1974-76, funds exceeding a half-million dollars were secured from the Fund for the Improvement of Postsecondary Education (as a Health, Education and Welfare agency), the Kellogg Foundation, The Ford Foundation, and one Tennessee-based foundation desiring to remain anonymous. *Thus, the funding support for this initiative came not from state funds but from federal and foundation funds sought specifically for this purpose.*

These funds were used to support planning activities and project staff at the Higher Education Commission. In addition, twelve major campus-based pilot projects were sponsored over a two-year period from 1976 to 1978. The purposes of these campus-based pilot projects were to have participating institutions develop institutional goals, identify associated performance indicators for those goals, and acquire initial performance data on those indicators. Thus, the performance funding project had a "grass roots" involvement at the campus and governing board level from its very inception. In addition, two advisory panels – state and national panels – guided develoment and implementation of the project.

One of the more distracting aspects of human achievement is that we tend to see more the arrival than the struggle. We see the final forms of an idea – but not the ambiguity, the mistakes, the false starts from which the idea was fashioned. There is no time to describe here all the hurdles encountered in the project or the many questions and concerns encountered: 1) Will public officials take the performance ratings and attempt to establish some sort of qualitative ranking of institutions? 2) Why should institutions be deprived of allocations on quality under current appropriations levels? 3) Will the rich get richer and poor get poorer? Will the large universities make out better on these variables than the smaller community colleges? 4) To what extent do the performance variables and standards adequately recognize the wide variation in mission among the state's institutions? Nor is there time to recount the pleasures of achievement realized.

Those interested in a more complete story of the project are invited to contact the Tennessee Higher Education Commission, Nashville, Tennessee for a complete report on the project from its inception in 1974 to the adoption and revision of the policy in 1979-1980 (Bogue and Troutt, 1980).

The outcomes of the performance funding project are concrete and positive. A specific policy for recognizing and rewarding performance, for linking government dollars and institutional performance has been designed, implemented, evaluated, and revised for implementation again. This is the primary outcome.

There are other outcomes. There is a set of ideas, some of immediate and practical utility and others of stimulative value. There is an extended concern for instructional evaluation and improvement. There is a model of change – a model which knows the uncertainty of risk, the discomfort of dissent, the inventing force of action and initiative, the necessity for patience, and the pleasure of accomplishment. There is, finally, a community of faculty and staff who had the qualities of mind and heart, and who now have the experience to take the next steps,

March 1982 Vol. 6 No. 1

REFERENCES

Bogue, E. Grady (1977). "Formula Funding in Higher Education". In *Allocating Financial Resources to Higher Education.* Proceedings of an Invitational Conference, The University of Alabama, College of Education (December).

Bogue, E. Grady and Troutt, William D. (1980). *Allocation of State Funds on a Performance Criterion: The Performance Funding Project of the Tennessee Higher Education Commission.* Nashville: Tennessee Higher Education Commission.

Gross, F.M. (1973). *A Comparative Analysis of the Existing Budget Formulas Used for Justifying Budget Request or Allocating Funds for the Operating Expenses of State-Supported Colleges and Universities.* Knoxville.Tennessee: University of Tennessee, Office of Institutional Research.

Moss, C.E. and Gaither, G.H. (1976). "Formula Budgeting: Requiem or Renaissance?" *Journal of Higher Education,* Sept.-Oct.

Northeast Missouri State University
Value-Added Assessment Program:
A Model for Educational Accountability

Charles J. McClain, Darrell W. Krueger and Terry Taylor
Northeast Missouri State University
United States

ABSTRACT

The Northeast Missouri State University Value-Added Student Assessment Program developed from the proposition that an educational institution should be able to determine the value added to a person as he or she proceeds through the educational system. This value added is demonstrated through student output performances, which serve as a system of accountability to the university's students, faculty, staff, and its external constituencies.

While traditional evaluation practices in United States higher education have tended to assess only through individual's competitive output differentials, NMSU's Value-Added Program attempts to measure gains in the total person – knowledge, analytic ability, skills, values, cultural awareness, and other personal development – by measuring changes within the individual. The program has evolved over a period of twelve years and impacts, today, nearly every managerial function at the university, including tactical, strategic, and long-range planning; student, faculty, and curriculum development; university funding and fiscal resource allocations and reallocations; participative management; formal accreditation reviews of the university; and the university's organisational culture and climate.

The university has received the prestigious G. Theodore Mitau Award for Excellence and Innovation in Higher Education for its Value-Added Program. The program's design, implementation, and value for management are described in this article.

The purpose of this article is to revitalise the pragmatists and practitioners among us, as well as the theorists, through an examination of the Value-Added story of Northeast Missouri State University (NMSU), a story of thirteen years of continuing active implementation. Dr. Alexander Astin, a scholar expert in American higher education studies, considers the longevity and proven record of the assessment program to be one of the major factors that distinguishes Northeast Missouri State University from all the other universities in the USA. The implementation of the Value-Added Program (VAP) over the past thirteen years was reflected in the title of an address given recently, "Northeast Missouri State University's Value-Added Program: It Works in Practice; Will It Work in Theory?"[1] The answer is partly revealed by the enthusiastic, numerous, and diverse inquiries concerning the program. The VAP has been studied in detail by nearly a dozen statewide governing and coordinating boards of higher education, by nearly 300 individual colleges and universities in the USA, by the United States Army Reserve Officers Training Corps, by a number of corporations, and by several prominent education, business, and economic publications including *The Chronicle of Higher Education*[2], *Money*[3], and *Today's Manager*[4].

These diverse sources present a common appraisal, i.e. the VAP not only discovers problems within an organisation, VAP becomes part of the managerial solutions. It should be noted that the VAP also uncovers organisational successes, important for an organisation's internal and external environments.

It needs to be understood that the VAP is but one approach to ensuring educational effectiveness and accountability through assessment. There are a number of valid approaches to assessment that can help an institution become more effective. Each institution must select the evaluation or assessment model which is most relevant to its individual institutional mission and which will maximise its own achievement levels.

Some of the basic assumptions for VAP came from the Valued-Added Tax System implemented in several western nations. The VAT economic proposition states that a commercial enterprise should be accountable, for tax purposes, for the value it adds to the finished goods or services it helps to produce, and an assessment of the actual value added must be made to determine this real growth.

In a similar fashion, beginning in 1973 at NMSU, it was believed the university should be able to determine the value added to a student as he or she proceeded through his/her years of study at the institution, and thus have a record of accountability for individual, programmatic, and institutional growth levels. Just as many economists argued that the VAT is too complicated to implement, so, too, did most educators attempt to discourage the value-added educational assessment and accountability model as being too complicated to implement in higher education. However, the university plunged ahead with the implementation of the first phase of such a program fully realising it was pursuing a goal in virtually uncharted waters.

Although early aspects of the program could have been called a "competency-based student outcomes measurement program" or any one of a number of other titles common to educational assessment jargon, the emerging implementation and refinement of the program led to the title, Value-added Program, since that reflects an accountable result and positive outcome.

The program is a performance assessment plan that has impact upon all of the ingredients usually considered important for a healthy college or university: 1) students, most importantly; 2) faculty, who have the most direct intellectual impact on the students; 3) the academic curriculum, the intellectual substance the faculty expose and convey to the students; 4) student development services which assist in developing the whole person; 5) fiscal support which funds the entire enterprise and is becoming more closely linked to a demonstrable record of accountability; and 6) organisational culture within which the many activities of an institution of higher education flourish or fail to flourish.

The foundation of the VAP is a comprehensive student data base which was initially quite simple but has evolved through the years into a rather sophisticated set of performance measurement instruments. This comprehensive student data base continues to expand with the evolution of the program.

The cornerstone of the comprehensive student data base is an external national examination developed by the American College Testing Program (ACT) that measures the effects of the liberal arts and sciences component of a curriculum. This examination is administered as a pre-test to all students prior to their enrollment at the university, and later as a post-test to the same students upon completion of their first two years of study, the period of time in which the curriculum focuses almost exclusively upon the liberal arts and sciences. The difference between the pre-test and post-test scores, statistically adjusted, is the "value-added". In recent years, a sampling of students who have just completed their freshman year of study are tested in a like manner so that even more discriminant patterns of learning can be observed.

In order to ascertain equally important assessments of affective learning changes in the students and to provide information on growth factors such as cultural awareness, interpersonal skills, self-esteem, problem solving, and functioning in the larger society, surveys were developed to measure changes in the individual along a pre-applicant to long-time alumni continuum. Students in some instances, are first surveyed as early as the pre-applicant stage concerning their image of the university. All freshmen are then surveyed at their initial orientation activity at the university. Samples of students are surveyed at intermediate points in their student experience. All students then complete the Graduating Student Questionnaire (GSQ) at the conclusion of their programs of study. A sample of alumni are also surveyed each year in order to better ascertain the longer term effects of the university experience. The specific survey instruments used are a combination of national and local measurement techniques developed to determine changes in individuals' apperceptions and affective learning.

By lengthening the measurement time period on such surveys in both directions, the university has helped to diffuse two common value-added assessment criticisms: 1) How does a college or university really know what the attitudes and abilities of its students are before that college or university began to affect them? (the pre-college influence question); and 2) How can pre-test/post-test systems measure the more subtle, yet extremely important influences a college or university hopes to have on the careers, personal development, and life experiences of its graduates? (the post-college influence question).

The final critical element in the comprehensive student data base is the evaluation of student performances in their major fields of study. It is extremely important that external nationally normed examinations be the basis for these assessments; thus the primary test instruments utilised are the entrance examinations commonly used in the USA for admission to post-baccalaureate study in graduate and professional schools. In these assessments of students' standings in their academic disciplines, there is still a subtle adherence to the "value-added" pre- and post-test format. In this instance, academic programs are themselves being measured along a historical continuum. Collective performances on such external national examinations, when factored for student ability levels at the time of admission to the university, serve as a general index of progress within specific academic disciplines, departments, and individual majors. Such longitudinal comparisons become, in a sense, pre-tests and post-tests of programmatic effectiveness.

Why nationally normed examinations? There seem to be significant drawbacks, generally, in relying on locally-designed examinations. The threat exists that an academic department or an individual institution may design a curriculum which meets only localised strengths and interests. The evaluation and assessment of such curriculum, based only on local criteria, faces the danger of being little more than an exercise of self-indulgence.

The advantages in using nationally normed examinations are threefold and interrelated. First, the graduates of the university enter a national and international world. The majority of the graduates will not be found in the immediate locale or the general region of the USA. Some will even find themselves within the world community. In such a situation where one has global dispersion of graduates, what good does it do to produce graduates who have been versed in a curriculum that is indigenous to the narrow locale of the site of the university? There is, after all, an academic, technological, and professional world "out there" that is constantly changing, and student performance results and faculty reviews of national examinations alert an academic department or institution of some of its academic shortcomings, including obvious weaknesses in local curriculum. One of the most highly regarded of faculty members, working in a traditional discipline, has evaluated VAP as follows:

> Our Value-Added Program leads each faculty member into the broader reaches of his or her academic discipline. We can no longer be content with only a narrow focus in isolation from the rest of the world. Instead, we examine our academic disciplines with a wide-angle lens, much more aware of the world around us in our academic fields. Most of my colleagues will attest that they are better faculty members as a result of this examination and reexamination of our disciplines and curriculum as active members of the assessment and, thus, management team at the university.

The second reason for external nationally normed examinations is that they are designed by the two foremost examination development organisations in our country, i.e., The American College Testing Program, and the Educational Testing Service. Their staffs consist of some of the top psychometrists, cognitive and affective learning experts, and higher education research experts in the nation. The resources they bring to bear in their test development efforts greatly exceed any individual institution's available resources.

The third reason for nationally normed examinations is the most important for any university. One of the most important university-wide objectives at NMSU, part of its official state-mandated goals, is to produce graduates who are nationally competitive. How else does one demonstrate accountability and meet such a critical institutional goal without national instruments of assessment? What alternatives are there for effective and immediate national comparisons? These external national examinations are an important vehicle for developing institutions such as NMSU, institutions that wish to demonstrate their progress and comparative worth. Such worth is oftentimes a given at certain historically prestigious colleges and universities that have a long history of "excellence" as the "evidence" of greatness. But old excellence, however it was defined, real or not, is not necessarily new excellence. Old excellence can, in fact, be remote from current realities. Nationally normed examinations are *one* highly legitimate way of competing on more even terms in overviews of worth and accountability by funding sources, potential students, the greater academic community, and the general public. When NMSU's accounting graduates, for example, led all colleges and universities in the USA on the National Certified Public Accounting Examination three years ago[5], it was no surprise that the university received more attention from the business community and potential accounting students than ever before in its history.

One other point must be made in concluding this description of the assessment program. NMSU's Value-Added Program is not merely a snapshot or still-life portraiture of currently enrolled students. Much of the university's success comes from being a part of a dynamic rather than a static process. Judgements are based not only on where individual students or the university might be at a given point in time, but also where they have come from and what their potential is for reaching the goals they have set for themselves in the future.

Although the descriptive portion of this article has focused on the student learning effects of the VAP, it needs to be made clear that the VAP has a pervasive effect on the management functions of the university. The VAP is inexorably linked to the faculty; curriculum; student development; tactical, strategic, and long-range planning; fiscal resources, the monitoring function of management; and organisation environment. It has made decision making purposive and given direction to changes that are considered. The comprehensive VAP data system has been the catalyst for change and has created an environment that stresses the essential mission of higher education, namely, the education and achievement of students. It has increased attention and the commitment in the campus community to increasing the quality of the educational experience.

To illustrate the influence of VAP upon university management, a number of examples could be given. For the sake of brevity, a single case study involving mathematics and business majors now follows.

A CASE STUDY FOR IMPROVING THE MATHEMATICS FOUNDATION FOR BUSINESS MAJORS

Prior to and during 1979, the sophomore test results of the ACT liberal arts and sciences examination achieved by business majors indicated an increase in all subject areas with the exception of mathematics. Likewise the senior tests results of business majors taking the Graduate Management Admissions Test (GMAT), the graduate school admissions examination for M.A. and Ph.D. programs in business, also revealed a comparative weakness in mathematics. Students perception of unpreparedness in mathematics began to appear in the survey results.

The utility of the VAP model as a technique for management diagnoses now becomes evident. One might dismiss one set of low performance results on one examination, but when a second set of completely different examination results reveals the same performance shortcomings, reinforced by students' self-assessments, it is apparent there is a problem. When at least three independent indicators point to the same performance result, there is a "triangulation effect" (Cf. Figure 1). This points to a problem or a success, depending upon whether or not the performance is positive or negative.

The data in this case study prompted concern among the business faculty. They concluded that the lack of quantitative skills could have a devastating impact on the performance of business majors in various upper division courses, on GMAT scores, which might preclude graduates from admission to prestigious graduate schools of business, and eventual career performances and life satisfactions.

Curriculum committees within the various business disciplines of accounting, business administration, and business education discussed several alternatives for improving the mathematical skills of their business students. They also involved the mathematics faculty in these deliberations. In May, 1979, the curriculum committees recommended that a much stronger mathematics foundation be required of all four-year business majors in the liberal arts and sciences core of the curriculum. The recommendation was approved and became effective during the 1979-1980 academic year. In addition, the division of business subsequently set escalating outcome goals in mathematics performance and satisfaction for its majors. Since the university's internal budget requests are driven by student outcome performance goals, these changes of the business faculty translated into fiscal resources to assist in attaining the goals.

Figure 1
"TRIANGULATION"
(using multiple measurement technique)

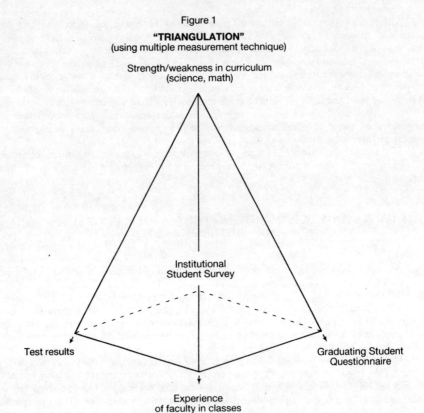

Strength/weakness in curriculum
(science, math)

Institutional
Student Survey

Test results

Graduating Student
Questionnaire

Experience
of faculty in classes

What was the result of this added focus on improving the mathematics foundation for business majors? Sophomore test results in 1979-1980 and each subsequent year have shown gains in all areas, including mathematics, even after factoring in the increases that have occurred in the ACT scores of entering freshmen business majors (Cf. Figure 2). Students in business have a higher satisfaction with their mathematics preparedness, and although it is too early to have conclusive results, it appears that alumni satisfaction is much improved (Cf. Figure 3).

This one case study demonstrates a number of managerial benefits of the VAP. It began with diagnosis through the commonly defined *control* function of management. Through *participative management* and *leadership* of the business faculty, required changes in the organisation were introduced. The curriculum committees deliberated and introduced *strategic planning* to *re-organise* the curriculum in order to accomplish long-range goals. The entire process was driven by highly specific performance outcome *objectives* which have been linked to the internal *funding* process. The impact of the entire process is *accountable* through future performance results. Thus, nearly all of the critical elements of management are contained in the VAP model.

Figure 2

MATH ACT PERCENTILE CHANGE STUDY
Freshmen vs. Sophomores
University Total vs. Business Administration

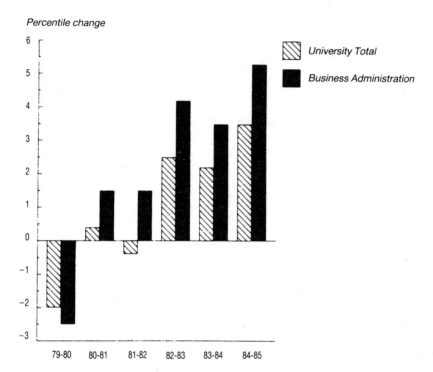

The central strength of the VAP model and management approach is that the faculty are at the heart of the whole endeavor. They have internalised both the positive and negative assessments of their students at all academic levels. The faculty genuinely provide their own leadership in fine-tuning their curriculum, resource materials, and even teaching styles, to try to turn negative results into positive ones. They have welcomed VAP because it is defined in a way that is understandable and demonstrable to their students, themselves, and the public. Faculty are not leaving the university because of the implementation of VAP; on the contrary, VAP has helped attract and employ more top-notch faculty than possible in the past.It seems that a penchant for quality begets even more quality.

The VAP not only causes curriculum modification as shown in the case study but also assists student development as well as resource allocation. Student development is partly shown as the instructors required more research and writing.That emphasis in turn brought about a 30 per cent increase in student use of the library with the average student making 48 visits to the library in 1979 as compared to 62 visits in 1985. The increase usage in turn put

Figure 3

**INSTITUTIONAL STUDENT SURVEY
WEIGHTED MEANS ON STUDENT SATISFACTION
UNDERSTANDING AND APPLYING MATHEMATICS**

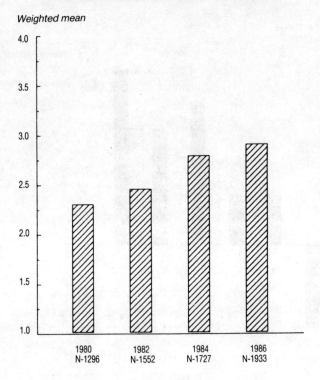

pressure upon the aging facilities of the library which brought about a 10 per cent decline in student satisfaction with the quality of the library. These two factors, growing student use of the library and a growing dissatisfaction with the library, gave impetus to the recent funding by the State of Missouri for a $15 000 000 renovation of the library.

Perhaps the most dramatic evidence of the extent to which VAP has pervaded the curriculum and student development efforts at the university is shown in the recent comprehensive accreditation review. The accreditation self-study prepared by the university achieved a historical first when the faculty, staff, and students developed an assessment document constructed completely of outcome performance measurements as the documented record of institutional accountability.

The impact of VAP on the university's fiscal resources and funding levels has been just as significant. Peter Ewell (1983) describing the fiscal power of VAP made this statement:

... a distinctive attribute of Northeast Missouri State University's approach is that explicit criteria derived from the assessment program are made the concrete basis for funding requests to the board and legislature... student-outcomes information represents a powerful collective resource for restoring higher education to its former priority in the public mind[6].

An additional observation could be added to Ewell's depiction of the assessment program's fiscal power: instead of the maximisation of the budget as the "end" itself, the budgetary process and budget become the *means* to maximise student outcomes. Improved student outcomes are rewarded by appropriate monetary sources with increased funding, in order to perpetuate the momentum toward quality. Such a reward is crucial. If improved educational quality goes unrewarded, there is little to sustain the improvement that has been made. With VAP, the budget is not tied in a remote or mysterious fashion to quality educational outcomes. On the contrary, with VAP, the budget is directly connected to projected educational outcomes as specified in the budgetary requests of the various academic and administrative units of the university.

Northeast Missouri State University's Value-Added Program has brought major financial dividends for the university. Governor John Ashcroft of Missouri, chairman of the U.S. National Governors' Association Task Force on College Quality, reiterated his belief that for too many years institutions have been rewarded for the wrong reasons, and he called upon other colleges and universities in Missouri and throughout the nation to follow NMSU's lead, and apply quality controls based upon academic performance to their educational systems.

Finally, contemporary management theory and practices are focusing more than ever before on organisational culture and climate. The VAP seems to have become a rallying symbol for addressing qualitative issues on all fronts. The university community is spurred toward excellence by its Value-Added Program.

While some education research writers have voiced concerns about the potential for misuse or abuse of certain components of VAP (and such warnings must be taken seriously), Dr. Clifford Adelman of the National Institute for Education, writing in the recent NIE and AAHE (American Association of Higher Education) publication, *Starting with Students: Promising Approaches* of the VAP model on the university's organisational culture:

> ... But there is a different – and perhaps more valuable – type of learning that takes place at NMSU. A learning which the examinations stimulate, but do not control. Because the assessment process permeates the institution, departments are in a perpetual state of self-reflection, refining instructional objectives and teaching methods. NMSU was wise to add a set of attitudinal surveys to assist the process, surveys that follow the student body through the University and into life. For the students, knowledge that the University cares about their perceptions as much as their performance is extraordinarily important, and perhaps accounts for their acceptance of what might be regarded as a very intrusive program of pulse-taking. For the faculty and administration, student and alumni assessments are goads to the improvement process, and have resulted in changes such as the raising of admissions criteria, revision of audit and course withdrawal policies, the improvement of the academic advisement system, the hiring of new faculty, and the purchase of instructional equipment. There is no question that all of this evolves naturally from an institutional culture dominated by a commitment to documenting what happens to students in college[7].

The Northeast Missouri State University model may not be for every institution. Indeed, it probably is not. However, it is a model that fits the purposes and mission of the university and has served well in achieving those purposes and the mission. NMSU is a better institution because of the thirteen year experience with VAP, and the data support this conclusion. More importantly, students are reaching higher standards of educational performance, and the data support that conclusion.

The naysayers have said students will feel oppressed; overwhelmingly the students seem enlightened in knowing where they stand. The naysayers have said the faculty will boycott VAP, if not leave the university; instead, the faculty have led the way in expanding and improving the system of assessment. The naysayers have said the program is too costly in terms of money, possible loss of potential students and governmental support; on the contrary, the university has been rewarded in its increased appropriations for the risk taking with accountable results, and currently, the university is nearly 100 per cent ahead of any previous year in applicants for the freshman class. Further, the university receives so many accolades from legislators and the Governor that it is almost (but not quite) embarrassing.

This article has made a strong case for assessment and accountability. Assessment provides the road map to the attainment of quality in education and educational administration and management. Without assessment and accountability, universities don't know where they are and have little direction as to where they need to go. Ultimately each institution of higher education must answer two questions: 1) What maximum contribution can the institution make to those individuals who are directly or indirectly affected by its functions? and 2) How effectively is the institution meeting its maximum potential? Northeast Missouri State University's Value-Added Program brings one very close to the answers to these two questions. The potential greatness of the Value-added Program model for assessment and accountability is its promise for even greater future achievements, far beyond the walls of a single university.

November 1986 Vol. 10 No. 3

REFERENCES

1. McClain, C. J. (April 1986), "NMSU's Value-Added Program: It Works in Practice; Will It Work in Theory?", Fourth Regents' Conference on Higher Education, Nashville, Tennessee.

2. Jachik, S. (1985), "As States Weigh 'Value-Added' Tests, Northeast Offers Model", *The Chronicle of Higher Education*, XXXI. October 2.

3. Stickney, J. (1986), "Ten Public Colleges with an Ivy Twist", *Money*, XV: 196-198. May.

4. Huffman, L. (1986), "Preparing for the Business World: Valued-added Assessment in Higher Education", *Today's Manager*, I :12-16. January.

5. National Association State Boards of Accountancy (NASBA) (1982) *National Report. Uniform CPA Examination Statistical Report.* (November).

6. Ewell, P. (1983), *Information on Student Outcomes: How to Get it and How to Use it.* Boulder, Colorado: National Center for Higher Education Management Systems : 66.

7. Adelman, C. (1984), *Starting with Students: Promising Approaches In American Higher Education.* Washington, D.C., National Institute of Education, December : 83-84.

Assessment of Institutional Effectiveness at the University of Tennessee, Knoxville

Trudy W. Banta, Homer S. Fisher and C. W. Minkel
Tennessee, Knoxville
United States

ABSTRACT

The University of Tennessee, Knoxville has successfully integrated a program for assessing student outcomes in the on-going institutional processes of peer review, strategic planning, and internal resource allocation. At this research-oriented land-grant university with an enrollment of 25.000, students are tested in general education and in their major field and participate in evaluative surveys designed to assist in the assessment of curricula and instruction. Outcome information from the exams and surveys is combined with more traditional data on resources in the peer reviews process. Recommendations from the reviews are used in planning and budgeting.

Public colleges and universities, like other social and cultural institutions, periodically must adjust philosophy and policy in response to changing societal influences. During the 1960s and early 1970s, when both enrollment growth and public recognition of the value of higher education were at peak levels, the flow of federal and state resources to colleges and universities in the United States was almost directly proportional to the size of increases in enrollment. But in the 1980s, increasingly scarce tax dollars must be allocated among a variety of services with the potential to improve the quality of life. Throughout society there is mounting concern about the quality of products and services as international competition increases. Acceptance of the inherent worth of a college degree is no longer as strong or as widespread, and consumers of public services are demanding evidence of quality in return for investments in higher education. As much as educators might like to justify what they do on the basis of its being right and good, they must begin to demonstrate their accountability as the public schools and many social service agencies have been doing for two decades.

With increasing competition both for tax dollars and for students, each post-secondary institution must assess its internal strengths, determine what it can do best, and husband its resources for those programs. Having defined its unique mission, the institution must effectively communicate that mission to those it seeks to serve, then deliver its programs and services in ways designed to retain as many as possible of those students who can both contribute to, and benefit from, the institution's offerings.

PLANS FOR ENHANCING INSTITUTIONAL EFFECTIVENESS
AT THE UNIVERSITY OF TENNESSEE, KNOXVILLE

The University of Tennessee, Knoxville (UTK) is Tennessee's comprehensive land-grand and state-assisted research university, with an enrollment of approximately 25 000 students, including 5 500 graduate students. Some 1 200 faculty in fifteen colleges and schools offer more than 270 undergraduate, graduate and professional degree programs.

In 1982, at the conclusion of his tenth year of service, UTK Chancellor Jack E. Reese asked the President of the University of Tennessee System to appoint a task force to assess the status of essential University functions. The task force, which included members of the Board of Trustees, business and community leaders, deans of several UTK colleges, faculty and students, was asked to evaluate the institution's mission, organisational framework, key personnel, planning activities and responses to major changes in the institutional environment.

Observations and recommendations of the task force were transmitted to Chancellor Reese and made public during the spring of 1983. These recommendations have contributed to a number of positive actions since that time.

The task force report called for a more precise and current mission statement for UTK, improvements in the program of selective admissions, qualitative improvements in teaching and research, significantly enhanced state support, better communication to the state concerning the nature and significance of the University, and organisational and other changes needed to accomplish these and related goals. The task force endorsed the UTK approaches to strategic planning, comprehensive program (peer) review, and outcomes assessment.

Since the release of the task force report, UTK has acomplished the following:

- Implemented through more selective admission standards a calculated reduction in enrollment (from 30 000 to the current 25 000 students), with the principal reduction being made in undergraduate students so that the proportion of graduate students will increase;
- Initiated an aggressive program to recruit outstanding undergraduate and graduate students;
- Gained the necessary approvals for requiring more rigorous high school preparation for admission to the University (to become effective Fall 1989);
- Upgraded advising and counselling activities;
- Expanded an existing undergraduate honors program to provide access to students in all colleges;
- Made the decision to convert from a quarter to a semester calendar, effective Fall 1988;
- Implemented plans to strengthen the general education component of the undergraduate curriculum in the process of revamping curricula in every college to fit the semester format;
- Established several centers of excellence and chairs of excellence in selected units, using combinations of state and private funds;
- Undertaken a number of cooperative ventures with the federally-supported Oak Ridge National Laboratory and private businesses and industry in the Technology Corridor between Knoxville and Oak Ridge, including the formation of the Science Alliance, a center of excellence that links a number of University programs with the National Laboratory.

INCORPORATING OUTCOMES ASSESSMENT
IN THE EVALUATION OF INSTITUTIONAL EFFECTIVENESS

By the beginning of this decade it had become quite clear that state funding formulas for higher education based on historical program costs and enrollment growth were inadequate to address the exigencies presented by the growing inflation of costs and precipitous decline in the number of students of the traditional age for entering college. Tennessee became the first state to base part of the funding for higher education on the ability of public colleges and universities to demonstrate performance on a specified set of outcome measures. In 1982-83, as the Chancellor's task force was completing its overall assessment of the institution, UTK faculty and administrators were trying to decide how to adapt to the state's new performance funding policy.

The Tennessee Higher Education Commission (1983) proposed to offer an annual supplement of up to 5 per cent of the instructional component of each institution's formula-generated education and general budget if the institution demonstrates in an annual report that it has met five performance standards. These standards include:

a) The percentage of programs eligible for accreditation that are accredited;
b) The percentage of programs that have undergone peer review, administered a comprehensive exam to majors within a five-year period, or both (maximum-credit is awarded if the mean student performance of an exam in the major improves over time or exceeds that of students in similar programs at comparable institutions);
c) Value added by the general education component of the curriculum, as measured by the difference between mean scores for freshmen and seniors on the American College Testing (ACT) College Outcome Measures Project (COMP) exam (maximum credit is awarded if the mean score gain from freshman to senior year exceeds that of a group of comparable institutions);
d) Positive opinion concerning the quality of academic programs and services as measured by surveys of students, alumni, employers, or community members; and
e) Implementation of a campus-wide plan for improvement of programs and services based on the findings derived from the procedures just described as well as from other sources.

Motivated in part by the substantial financial supplement (more than $3 million annually for UTK) associated with the performance funding initiative, UTK faculty and administrators decided in late 1982 to undertake a systematic outcome assessment program for the purposes of: 1) establishing the level of effectiveness of programs in meeting their objectives for student development; 2) providing direction for improving and strengthening campus programs; and 3) improving the quality of information used by faculty and administrators in making decisions about the relative priorities of activities and related resource allocations. More specifically, procedures were developed for incorporating the results of a variety of surveys and comprehensive exams for students in each of the following:

a) Development of the University's mission statement and related planning documents;
b) Conduct of comprehensive academic program reviews; and
c) Evaluation of the University's effectiveness in achieving its planning goals.

Since 1983 substantial progress has been achieved in making systematic outcomes assessment an integral part of these on-going institutional activities.

MISSION STATEMENT AND STRATEGIC PLANNING

At UTK a central planning group of administrators and faculty leaders continually seeks the best match between internal program strengths and weaknesses and external opportunities and constraints in determining strategies for the institution. Areas of strategic decision-making include: mission; goals and objectives; number and diversity of institutional clientele; size, quality, and content of programs and services to be provided for the clientele; geographical service areas for offering programs/services; and areas of comparative advantage to be sought (see Figure 1).

In 1985, the UTK Statement of Mission was modified to include the assurance that the institution provides "a rigorous system of program review and assessment". The results of testing students in their major and in general education and of surveying students, alumni, and employers, have contributed to the evaluation of strengths and weaknesses of existing programs and to the determination of needs for new programs. They have also used to set planning goals related to enrollment and marketing; student/faculty/staff development; and improvement of equipment, physical facilities, and the library.

Frequently institutional resources are provided by the central administration to strengthen programs for which assessments reveal qualitiative concerns that additional resources can help to correct. Programs assessed to be capable of achieving or sustaining national or international distinction also may receive additional funds. Outcomes information is among the determinants of programs to be designated centers of excellence or awarded chairs of excellence. Finally, assessment results are factors considered in making decisions concerning the long-term retention or elimination of programs, the potential for merging small programs, and the need to reduce program size or scope.

COMPREHENSIVE ACADEMIC PROGRAM REVIEWS

Since 1974, UTK has utilised teams of external consultants (usually two) in the discipline and internal reviewers (most often three) from units outside the one being reviewed, to combine the information contained in a departmental self-study with that obtained during a 2½-day visit with program faculty, administrators, and students in making judgments about departmental progress toward meeting its objectives and realising its full potential and in offering recommendations for improvement. In 1981, reviews that had focused only on programs at the doctoral level were expanded to include assessment of baccalaureate and master's degree programs as well.

Prior to 1983, the guidelines for the self-study to be prepared by the faculty during the year preceding the peer review had suggested that the document include assessments of resources such as faculty credentials; quality of incoming students; size of the library collection; and adequacy of salaries, physical facilities, and operating budget. With the implementation of a systematic outcomes assessment program, the self-study guidelines were expanded to include a statement of instructional objectives for students and evidence of effectiveness in achieving these objectives obtained both from student test scores and external recognition of accomplishments, and from surveys of students, alumni, and employers (See Figure 2).

Achievement in general education

The ACT College Outcome Measures Project (COMP) exam with its six subscales, Functioning in Social Institutions, Using Science, Using the Arts, Communicating, Solving

Assessment of Institutional Effectiveness at the
University of Tennessee, Knoxville

Figure 1
UTK STRATEGIC PLANNING PROCESS

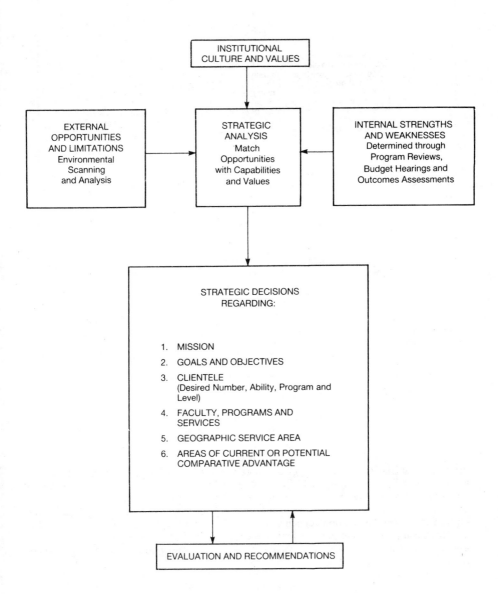

Figure 2

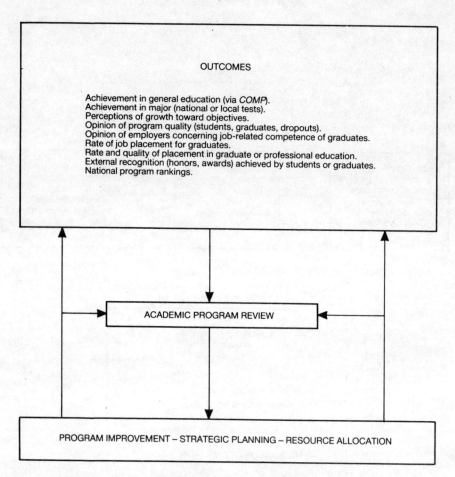

Problems, and Clarifying Values, is given annually to a sample of the entering freshman class and is required of all seniors at UTK. This test of effective adult functioning provides a measure of growth over the four years of the college experience in the ability to apply in situations encountered in daily life some of the knowledge and skills acquired in the University's general education curriculum. The COMP exam is administered by staff at the Student Counseling Center and students' mean scores for the subscales, as well as an overall growth score, can be provided for each department that is engaged in self-study prior to peer review.

Achievement in the major field

Each department at UTK must administer to students preparing to graduate a comprehensive examination in the specialised subject matter of the student's major. For approximately half of the University's academic programs, primarily those offering degrees in professional fields, a nationally standardized exam in the field is available. Examples of the standardized tests for majors that used to provide evidence of a department's success in achieving its instructional objectives for students include:

Student Major	*Examination Used by the Faculty*
Elementary and secondary education	National Teacher's Exam
Engineering	Engineer-in-Training Exam
Nursing	National League for Nursing State Board Exam
Chemistry, physics, history, psychology, sociology, economics	Graduate Record Exam Advances Tests

For approximately 40 departments, no standardized exam is available, so the faculty must develop its own test for the purpose of curriculum evaluation. A partial listing of programs for which the faculty, in consultation with two external consultants, have constructed their own exams includes:

Adult Education (Master's degree level)
Animal Science
Anthropology
Art History
Broadcasting
Child and Family Studies
Communications (Master's level)
Dance
Ecology (Master's level)
Food Technology and Science
Geography
Nutrition
Polymer Engineering (Master's level)
Ornamental Horticulture and Landscape Design
Textiles and Clothing.

Whether the comprehensive exams in the major field are nationally standardized or developed on campus, the faculty examine mean scores on subparts of the exams to determine areas of relative strength and weakness in students' preparation. This study often suggests the need for changes in curriculum and in methods of instruction.

Opinion of program quality

Faculty with expertise in survey research have worked with students, faculty, department heads and directors of student services units to develop a series of survey instruments that provide measures of opinion about the quality of academic programs and related student services. Four questionnaires, each containing a core of common items for comparative purposes, have been prepared for administration by mail to samples of enrolled undergraduates, enrolled graduate students, alumni, and students who have dropped out of the University.

For each department engaged in self-study prior to peer review, a survey of enrolled students is conducted. Program majors, as well as students from other disciplines who are taking classes in the department, are asked questions about the quality of instruction and related services such as advising. Survey results are presented in tables that permit the department to compare its student ratings with those of its parent college and with those of the University as a whole.

Each department is encouraged to use a variety of methods for assessing outcomes (see Figure 1) because no single method can begin to measure all the outcomes of a university education. A combination of methods, though still inadequate to assess all desirable outcomes, provides valuable guidance for those seeking direction for improvement. As the comprehensive program reviews at UTK are presently structured, the thinking of peer reviewers is informed by data on program goals, processes and resources applied toward accomplishing those goals, and outcomes. Peers in the discipline, but external to the campus, can compare the department with similar ones across the country, while campus reviewers can assess the program by comparing it with others in the institution. The factor of human judgment in peer review makes this the most comprehensive method of assessing overall program quality.

ACHIEVEMENT OF PLANNING GOALS

The University is continuously engaged in the process of evaluating its progress in meeting stated goals, and the peer reviews and results of outcomes assessment activities play an important role in that process. In annual budget hearings conducted by central administrative officials, department heads are strongly encouraged to use the recommendations from academic program reviews and the results of outcomes assessment in making their case for resource needs in the coming year. The University's planning and budgeting committee uses these sources of information in evaluating the status of progress toward the broad institutional goals of:

- Recruiting more highly qualified and better prepared students;
- Increasing the percentage of students who persist to graduation at UTK;
- Enhancing the quality of student advising;
- Improving the effectiveness of teaching and learning;
- Increasing faculty-student interaction;
- Improving essential student services such as counseling, career planning, and placement;
- Improving procedures for faculty workload assignment and evaluation for promotion and salary increases;
- Providing appropriate faculty development experiences as needs are determined;
- Increasing public understanding of the University's mission and knowledge of its accomplishments in teaching, research, and services.

IMPACT OF ASSESSMENT ACTIVITIES
UPON INSTITUTIONAL EFFECTIVENESS

In the three years since the University of Tennessee, Knoxville undertook a systematic outcomes assessment program and incorporated the findings in academic program reviews, strategic planning, and resource allocation procedures, a number of specific actions have been taken to effect improvements in areas suggested by the various assessment procedures.

As a result of administering the COMP exam to freshmen and seniors and studying patterns of growth in the six areas assessed by the instrument, the general education curriculum – especially in the area of social science – is being strengthened in all colleges as new patterns of courses are developed for the semester system. Within individual colleges the general education core has been shaped by the profile of specific strengths and weaknesses of students in that college as revealed by COMP exam scores.

Sharing department-specific survey results that indicate students' perceptions of the quality of academic programs and related services has prompted faculty in several units to:

- Increase the emphasis on advising;
- Increase opportunities for faculty-student interaction;
- Initiate or expand opportunities for internships that permit students to apply their knowledge and skills in employment settings;
- Improve printed information describing the academic program;
- Initiate or expand student professional organisations;
- Increase faculty involvement in the placement of graduates.

Information from the various assessment activities has influenced the thinking of central administrators and thus shaped the following decisions concerning the allocation of institutional resources:

- Class size has been reduced in selected areas;
- College advising centers have been established or expanded;
- Faculty in certain units have been given released time to participate in advising;
- Improvements in publications for prospective students have been accomplished;
- Stipends of graduate assistants have been increased, and staff have been added to improve services in the area of graduate admissions.

The most extensive set of changes has resulted from the initiatives undertaken by some 40 departments to develop comprehensive exams in the major. As a product of coming to agreement on the content for such a test, faculties have reported the following accomplishments.

- Increased faculty agreement concerning common learning outcomes for all students;
- Development of core objectives or competencies for students;
- Increased direction for converting courses/curricula from quarter to semester format;
- Increased consistency in the teaching of core courses;
- More clearly delineated linkage between lower-division and upper-division courses;
- Limited program review by external consultants on the comprehensive exam;
- Use of external consultants to provide seminars for faculty and students;
- UTK leadership in cooperative efforts of national professional associations to develop competencies and/or comprehensive exams in the discipline.

As a consequence of administering the locally developed comprehensive exams and studying their students' performance, faculties have:

- Acquired baseline data on student achievement that can be used to compare the effectiveness of the quarter and semester curricula;

- Identified program strengths, and weaknesses to be corrected in the semester curriculum;
- Made curriculum changes, including:
  - Stronger core curriculum within the department;
  - Changes in requirement outside the department.
- Initiated instructional improvements that involve increasing each of the following:
  - Structure for courses now that core objectives/competencies are identified;
  - Number of written assignments;
  - Opportunities for students to apply their knowledge and skills through problem-solving, term projects, field trips, internships;
  - Opportunities for demonstrating complex skills on tests, and
  - Used score on the local test to diagnose students' needs for remediation prior to taking the certification exam in the discipline.

November 1986 Vol.10 No. 3

REFERENCES

Banta, T.W. (1985). "Use of Outcomes Information at the University of Tennesse, Knoxville", In P. Ewell (ed.), *Assessing Educational Outcomes. New Directions for Institutional Research*, 47: 19-32. San Francisco : Jossey-Bass.

Banta, T.W. (ed.) (1986). *Performance Funding in Higher Education : A Critical Analysis of Tennessee's Experience*, Boulder, CO: National Center for Higher Education Management Systems (in press).

Banta, T.W. and Fisher, H.S. (1984). "Performance Funding : Tennessee's Experiment", In J. Folger (ed.), *Financial Incentives for Academic Quality. New Directions for Higher Education*, 48: 29-41. San Francisco, Jossey-Bass.

Minkel, C.W. and Richards, M.P. (1981). *Measures of Quality in Graduate Education*. Chattanooga, Tennessee Conference of Graduate Schools.

A Commentary on the Northeast Missouri and Tennessee Evaluation Models

Marianne Bauer
Swedish National Board of Universities and Colleges
Sweden

WANTED: INTERNAL MODELS FOR SELF-EVALUATION

At the IMHE workshop on the role of evaluation the united message sounded that *external* pressure is growing for institutions of higher education to demonstrate their quality and effectiveness.

More and more higher education institutions also seem to accept this external demand for accountability as fair and necessary "with the increasing competition both for tax dollars and for students" as the representatives for the University of Tennessee expressed it.

Opinions differ on how to render such accounts, but one response in meeting the outer pressure that most institutions have in common is to develop *internal* self-evaluation. It appears like an intuitive reaction to safeguard autonomy and to guarantee that the special values and conditions vital to higher education and research will be given due regard. "Self-evaluation at institutional level makes external evaluation lose saliency" (Drenth, J.D. *et al.*), is the hopeful thesis.

This intuitive wisdom, however, does not seem to guarantee that the models and tools for (self-)evaluation are fitted to those conditions and values characteristic of higher education and research. Rather than being congenial to the main missions and tasks of these institutions, models are often borrowed from other fields and sometimes uncritically applied.

A striking example of the application of such a model, totally foreign to higher education's tasks, is the *Value Added Model*, an important ingredient in the evaluation programs at the US universities at Northeast Missouri and Tennessee, described in papers presented to the workshop.

It is frankly stated that the "philosophical underpinnings come from the Value-Added Tax System" saying that "a commercial enterprise should be accountable, for tax purposes, for the value it adds to the finished goods and services". The authors report no impediments to determining "the value added to a person" proceeding through the years of study at the university, other than the degree of complication in implementing this model.

I leave it to the reader to detect the hidden assumptions of the Value-Added Model, while I point at some of the risks of applying it undiscerningly to higher education.

The model demands that you find or develop additive indicators of performance in order to make comparisons between institutions, departments, years or individuals. In the present cases the solution is test results, and the first consequence is that a lot of work and costs must be used for developing and using tests, analysing and registering test data. These laboriously collected data must be made good use of, and indeed they are said to affect all activities in the university.

Since the test results play such an important role in proving the quality of the institution, teachers' (and students') attention is guided towards those aspects that might raise the average test results by some decimal points. Furthermore, there is a risk that the test results with their apparent exactness and comparability get more attention than they deserve, since they catch only specific and sometimes narrow features of what students could learn and experience at the university.

The foundation of the Value Added assessment program is thus a comprehensive student data base which expands with the program. "No university could meet the demands to measure *every* value of *every* individual through *every* period of his or her lifetime", it is conceded, but "it is in striving for the ideal that our assessment program has so dramatically improved". (see McClain, Krueger and Taylor).

It becomes obvious that the ideal mentioned has nothing to do with the academic tasks but with the perfection of an assessment system *per se*. The attention has turned somewhere else from the decisive conditions for teaching and learning.

Furthermore, nobody seems to ask questions about the ethics of keeping such a comprehensive student register (not only concerning achievement in the students' major fields, but also of "effective adult functioning" and "such growth factors as inter-personal skills, self-esteem and functioning in the larger society"), or of the extensive testing of students to prove the quality of the institution and its staff. Goods could be tested in all imaginable aspects; students neither could nor should. But a model can blind you.

The high ambitions of the universities of Northeast Missouri and Tennessee to improve the quality of their activities, and the well organized work to render a detailed account of their achievements are impressive. Even the difficult task of getting the staff committed to an evaluation program has been successful, so that faculty even "led the way in expanding and improving the system of assessment". It seems superfluous to question such astonishing achievement.

However, not least because of the great success, the risks appear considerable for unintended side-effects in the long run of these highly systematic and strong assessment systems. And the external receiver of this information will not question it, since he cannot penetrate the process behind the figures. Only the teachers and researchers themselves can do it.

Evaluation as an integral part of teaching and research at the universities to guarantee quality of performance takes the form of examination, seminars, disputations etc. There has never been an internal urge for summarizing the results of these scrutinizing procedures. The external demand for *accountability* has grown strong within a short period. It is natural that available models and methods have been seized upon from other fields – usually from business/economics (accountability and assessment e.g. are both economic concepts). The uncritical application of such models might be seen as a sign of a half-hearted effort in order to provide the necessary funds in hard times. Or it might be a sign of adaptation to the market and management model which is intruding also upon European universities and colleges.

To provide valid indicators of important features of quality in academic work, I believe we have to start from within, and develop models and tools in agreement with the basic conditions for teaching, learning and research. And then take the trouble to interpret the observations and results into comprehensible and interesting terms for the external public.

Such attempts exist. They appear searching and unsettled. Their strength is not to develop systematic, all embracing evaluation systems. They are cautiously interacting with academic activities, promoting various ways to knowledge and impeding conformity by foreclosed values. They pay more attention to examination than tests and make room also for non-quantifiable qualities.

If such attempts succeed in reflecting essential features of the inner life of the university, we will have something to *add* to the facts and figures of external assessment, something which could correct the threatening misunderstandings of outsiders, and contribute to the understanding of the specific and necessary conditions for academic achievement.

November 1986 Vol. 10 No. 3

Improvement of Quality of Education Through Internal Evaluation (AMOS)

Pieter J. D. Drenth, Willem Van Os and George F. Bernaert
Free University of Amsterdam
The Netherlands

ABSTRACT

AMOS is a model for the analysis of study progress at the level of discipline. The model defines at different moments in the educational process well described signals, enabling analysis of study results in a rather specific way. A flow chart is set up for each field of study with guideline ciphers for study progress at various levels. Agreements and differences between actual success rates and guideline ciphers form the starting point for discussion with the faculties. The use of AMOS within the framework of improvement of the quality of education is discussed. AMOS is an example of the desired compromise between self-motivation and an "administrative" approach.

INTRODUCTION

In the recent Ministerial bill "Hoger Onderwijs: Autonomie en kwaliteit" (Higher Education: Autonomy and Quality) (1985), a distinction is made between internal and external evaluation. The former type of evaluation has to be carried out by the academic institution itself; the latter by independent external bodies. An example of such an independent body is the so called visitation committee which will operate under the auspices of the Inspection Office of the Ministry of Education.

This proposal has generated a lively discussion on the pros and cons of external evaluation (Van Berkel and Bax, 1985). In this paper an exposé will be given of an elaborate system of internal evaluation which exists at the Free University, Amsterdam. It will be maintained that, if such a system is operative at the institutional level, the issue of external evaluation will lose much of its saliency.

MOTIVATIONAL AND ADMINISTRATIVE APPROACH

Almost all attempts to improve the quality of education within the university are based on the utilisation of assessment information on output and qualities of the teaching process. In this respect, a distinction can be made between two strategies for such a utilisation. Firstly, there is the direct feedback of the results to those concerned (teacher, department, faculty). The aim of this feedback is to improve performance, to further development and to bring about change (if necessary). Secondly, one may think of decisions in the context of so called "administrative" measures: allocational decisions with regard to units (personnel, financial means and time), individual decisions regarding rewards, promotion, tenure, advancement, demotion or even retrenchment.

In the strict sense, there can be a question of discrepancy and even conflict between both goals as in personnel assessment in general (Drenth, 1984a). Assessments aimed at change, improvement or adjustment should be geared towards what is lacking, what is at fault in the present behaviour. It should be clear and acceptable to the assessed which faults and shortcomings have given rise to the evaluation. The basis for a remedial strategy could be laid there. The atmosphere should be one of trust and frankness. Feelings of self-justification and self-defence should be minimal or preferably absent.

The situation is different as far as "administrative" decisions are concerned. These should be based on the best possible objective representation of performance or output and the most honest possible process evaluation. The needs for honesty, righteousness and defensibility are then more important than clarity, acceptability and whether it provides a starting point for improvement.

However, other than in personnel assessment in general, with administrative measures on the basis of educational assessment the ultimate goal is always the stimulation of change and improvement. In other words, we are faced with two different means to the same end: improvement of education. The first is the providing of feedback and guidance in order to correctly interpret and implement this feedback. Basically this is the avenue of self-evaluation and improvement through *intrinsic* motivation of the teacher concerned. The second is that of creating optimal conditions, direct and indirect reward and punishment, *extrinsic* motivation through "sticks and carrots". Let us compare these two approaches – they may be called the *motivational* and the *administrative* approach – to the evaluation and improvement of education.

Seen from an educational and psychological point of view, the first (*motivational*) form of guidance is of course the one to be preferred. Self-motivation based on self-evaluation is and remains the best condition for improvement. On the other hand, some of our experiences within the university make us hesitant to give exclusive preference to this avenue. Firstly, the faculties who have called in assistance from our Education Service Office (in Dutch: Onderwijs Research aan de Vrije Universiteit, ORVU) were not always those which we, on the basis of other indications, knew to be the most in need of help. By the same token, those faculties which we knew to need this assistance were not the first in line. The same goes at the meso-level for departments and sections and at the micro-level for individual teachers. Apparently, not everyone strives for improvement in teaching, hindered as one is by ignorance, self-overestimation, stubbornness, self-defence, arrogance or fear, or by an underestimation of the importance of good teaching. Granted, there are examples of excellent study behaviour in spite of bad teaching. There are also examples of unaltered study results even when teaching conditions have improved (Dubin and Taveggia, 1968, Wilbrink and Hofstee, 1984). But it would be a mistake to generalise these incidents into a general rule and to use this as a justifiable alibi for persistent didactic failures.

In summary, the exclusively non-directive, client centered approach leads either insufficiently or not at all to the desired improvement of the quality of teaching and education.

On the other hand, the *administrative* approach to education improvement has perhaps even more limitations. We should not forget that an institute of higher education is a prototype of what Mintzberg (1983) calls a "professional bureaucracy". If we put the primary emphasis on standardisation of output or procedures in such an organisation, then this attempt is doomed to failure. This can only lead to a shift in the nature of the organisation from a professional to a machine bureaucracy – a real bureaucracy in common jargon. Rules and standards with respect to procedures, output and processes prevail in such a bureaucracy. Scientific production and creativity are marginal. Rules and standards exist for their own sake and not for the sake of quality of research and teaching. Often the so called means-ends inversion occurs: the observation of the rules and procedures is considered sufficient; the same inversion – by the way – as is caused by the introduction of the time clock for scientists, leading to an inversion of the means (presence) and goal (scientific production).

The only means available to a professional institution is what Mintzberg calls "standardisation of skills". Formulated in terms relevant for an academic institution: maintaining or raising the recruitment norms, improving selection procedures and providing proper training; i.e., the utmost care with appointments to tenure positions and an extended programme of – if necessary even compulsory – teaching training. The rest must ensue from the professionals and teachers themselves; through motivation and a common ideology, supported by satisfying working conditions and a proper division of tasks. Good management of professional organisations cannot comprise much more than the creation of such optimal conditions.

The message is clear. "Administrative" improvement of education may consist of signalling and explanation, if necessary, objectively recorded in an educational report. Furthermore, conditions could and should be created and optimalised. But real improvement will have to emanate from the faculties themselves. As far as the direct success of "administrative" renewal of education is concerned, scepticism seems to be in place.

AMOS

An example of the desired compromise between the motivational and administrative approaches is to be found in the so-called analysis Model pertaining to the quality of Education within Faculties (in Dutch: Analyse Model voor het Onderwijs op Studierichtingsniveau, AMOS, see Van Os and Bernaert, 1985). This model was developed by the Educational Service Office of the Free University upon the request of the Executive Board of the F.U. In the following we will discuss this model in some more detail.

The model comprises a blueprint of evaluation propositions concerning academic education, including the following components: study progress in the undergraduate (propaedeuse) and graduate (doctoraal) phases specified according to year and discipline; regulations concerning final tests and examinations; control and adaptation of the teaching process, on the basis of information regarding study progress, study requirements, guidance of students and care paid to teaching (at course level). The order here is explicitly from *global* (success rates at the termination of the training period) to *specific* (didactic qualities of the teachers). The faculties are not expected to inform the Executive Board in detail about the above mentioned points of attention, let alone that the Board takes it upon itself to review the performance of individual teachers. The main purpose is for faculties to have at their disposal instruments, concepts and information to strengthen their own education policy.

This gives rise to the question in what circumstances the provision of general information offered by faculties can *no longer* suffice. In other words: the model should consist of well-defined *signals* upon which more detailed analysis should be conducted and/or the faculty should take specific action.

The first important signalling point is the propaedeuse exam after one year of study. The new law of Higher Education of 1981 expects this first year to be both informative (about the choice of study streams to be selected in the second phase) and selective.

An experimental normative flowchart was set up for the first year of students, who enrolled under the new law of 1981, the cohort 1982 (see fig. 1).This normative flowchart comprised the following elements (see Van Os, 1985):

a) The starting point is 100 per cent of students who registered for the first time on the 1st October 1982 in the faculty in question;

b) It is assumed that at the end of the first course year, 50 per cent pass the propaedeuse examination – 50 per cent forms the first guideline cipher;

c) It is expected that the 50 per cent who completed the propaedeuse phase are also able to continue and complete the doctoral programme without substantial delays. This expectation is quantified in the table by assuming per doctoral year a maximum delay of 7½ per cent, so that ultimately 27½ per cent (the majority of the 50 per cent) will complete the doctoral phase within the specified course time;

d) Officially the maximum time allowed for the propaedeuse phase is two years. A guideline ratio of 75 per cent is set: 50 per cent passing at first attempt (see point 2), 25 per cent who need an extra year. In the doctoral phase, it is assumed that this 25 per cent (who started after one year of delay) plus the 3 x7.5 per cent who have a delayed doctoral study (see point 3), almost all succeed in getting their doctorandus degree within the maximally allowed study time (which is 6 years). It is assumed that only 5 per cent will not succeed, which results in 42.5 per cent success, be it delayed;

Figure 1
FLOWCHART OF STUDY PROGRESS, COHORT 1982

	ENROLMENT	COURSE YEARS COMPLETED				DROPOUT
		1. Prop.	2	3	4 Doct.	
1.10. 1982	100					
31.08.1983		50				20
31.08.1984		25	42.5			5
31.08.1985				35		
31.08.1986					27.5	
31.08.1987			25+(3 ×7.5)			5
31.08.1988					42.5	
Total		**75**			**70**	**30**

The percentages in the diagonal (42.5%, 35% and 27.5%) form the *guidelines ciphers* for the study progress in the three-year doctoral course.

e) The total success rate will therefore be 70 per cent: 27.5 per cent succeeds within
the 4-year period. An additional 42.5 per cent succeeds in the following two
years.

FURTHER ACTION

In case where the actual study progress deviates from the guideline ciphers given in the
scheme, further analysis should be carried out. This research should be conducted by the
faculty with the implicit assumption that if study progress leaves something to be desired, then
the responsibility lies with the faculty.

It is feasible that an acceptable explanation can be presented by the faculty for possible
negative results. Study output and success rates are multicausal phenomena and many
interacting, compensating or additive factors may play a role (Drenth, 1984).

It is the task of the faculty to demonstrate that students (and not the teaching) are
responsible for a negatively deviating study progress, if such a claim is being put forward. A
few possibilities can be mentioned (see Van Os, Bernaert and Kok, 1984): the faculty in
question could be characterised by a large number of first year students with a less than
adequate pre-university training; by unsuitable students in a cognitive sense; by students who
insufficiently participate in the training. The study could be more difficult or more requiring
than an average study or act as a parking-place study for students who have to wait for
enrollment in the study of their first choice (often medicine), or students may be less intent on
completing the course (study as a hobby), etc.

The inclusion of such factors in the model is important for two reasons. In the first place
because of the substantial influence that they may have in various instances. Secondly, in
doing so, it becomes apparent that the analysis model does not intend to use only the net
success rate of a faculty as standard for the performance of education.

Anyway, the discussion has left the level of global statements and stereotypes. The
faculties are expected to produce facts and figures to support explanations. Primary, but not
sole, attention is paid to salient deviations of the guideline ciphers. Even success rates close to
the guideline ciphers cannot always be reassuring. To give an example: poor training,
unmotivated students or a bad curriculum organisation can be well compensated by too light a
programme or too low examination norms.

The faculties are urged to establish a committee which is responsible for the evaluation of
the AMOS-results. This committee should be given freedom to operate in a way which is felt
necessary to carry this reponsibility.

This means, for example, that those providing the teaching should inform the committee
to the best of their ability, and that access should be given to registration of student progress.
Also, the committee should have the means at its disposal to, for example, conduct a survey
amongst students, if considered necessary. Herewith this committee can make use of or ask to
apply questionnaires to be filled in by students, which are available at the Free University.
Since 1979, *standard questionnaires* have been used in various evaluation procedures (one for
lectures, one for laboratory practicals) in the Medical Faculty, Psychology, Economy and
Dentistry.

These standard questionnaires have several advantages: in the first place, interpretation
of the survey results is simplified. The questionnaires have been used with a large number of
university lectures in various faculties over a period of several years. Not only is an *average
score* calculated on each question (over all teachers), but also the standard deviation. The
latter is used to demarcate the ranges near the average, whereby the average plus and minus

one standard deviation defines the area in which roughly ⅔ of the teachers "score": the 67 per cent interval. Should a teacher on any question get a score which is less than the average *minus* one standard deviation, then this implies that on that question, one scores *lower* than 5 out of 6 teachers. If a teacher scores higher than the average *plus* one standard deviation, then he or she leaves 5 out of 6 teachers "behind" on this question (see also van Os, 1984a).

Of course, with the scores on the questionnaire the last word on the teacher has not necessarily been said: students may judge the (un-) popularity of a subject, the ease or difficulty of a subject, the severity of the examinations; the students can make "mistakes", too many may have grievances or let themselves be influenced by "circumstances", etc. This can be brought forward and discussed with the students. The "negative deviation" should act as a *signal*. Apparently there is something wrong with the particular aspect of the teaching and it should be discussed.

A second advantage of the use of such a standard instrument is that "improvements" over a number of years for a teacher teaching the same course can be demonstrated.

A third advantage refers to the fact that the results of the analysis are more easily *accepted* by the teachers since the data concerned are objective and can be interpreted unambiguously and since all teachers are "assessed" in a similar way; no exceptions are made.

Important in this AMOS procedure is the fact that the results are used primarily for feedback to and as a starting point for discussions with the faculties. They have to work with it and develop a strategy to deal with the results adequately. As such, it is an example of the *motivational* approach. but at the same time, it is clear that also elements of the *administrative* approach are present. The model is initiated by the Central Administration and is carried out by the (Central) Education Service Office (ORVU) at the Free University. Furthermore, the results of AMOS are also centrally registered and evaluated. Finally, a small steering committee is set up at central level (one member of the Executive Board, one member of ORVU and one member of the University Planning Bureau) to direct further surveillance and improvement of educational processes and outcomes.

As has been said, we see in AMOS an example of a combination of the motivational and administration approaches to the improvement of the quality of education. Moreover, AMOS satisfies, I believe, the criteria for such instruments (see Drenth, 1986). The indications of study progress are *relevant* and *valid* and set up in a *reliable* manner. They are also *transparent* in the sense that the system has been fully discussed with and explained to the faculty. In fact, the system is improved and given shape in an iterative interaction with the faculties. Finally, preceding the introduction of the system, in a number of informative sessions and discussions, concensus is obtained from the faculty to commence work with these instruments. This careful preparation has guaranteed maximum *acceptabiliby* on the part of the faculties.

EXTERNAL EVALUATION?

The issue of the usefulness and sense of external evaluation for the improvement of education can be briefly noted. What is said about the administrative approach to improvement in education and particularly about its limitations if carried out by the university administration, is even more true for the national administration. Without it is complemented by the motivational approach within the institution itself, a complement upon which great emphasis should be placed, since it is the only real basis for educational improvement, it will come to nothing. The national government is in even less of a position than the central institutional management to improve the quality of training through intrinsic motivation.

Therefore, the government should limit itself to the creation of proper conditions even more than the university management.

Nevertheless, the central government, as much as the institutional management, may attempt to obtain guarantees for a responsible utilisation of (central) funds through registration and process control. The government has the right to examine to what extent the academic institutions take their responsibility for the quality of education seriously.

Universities do not need to resist governmental visiting committees. It is important that one keeps one's own house in order. Of course, not all need to adopt the AMOS system. Other comparable systems are available or can be developed. Moreover, the AMOS registration system is only a beginning. At a later stage, more specific problems present themselves and the need arises for further analysis of particular facets of educational organisation and the teaching process. In the previous paragraphs, we have referred to the more specific instruments that may be useful in this analysis. If a university has "order at home" through a profound system of diagnosis and analysis, this can, on the one hand, offer propitious information to the visiting committees and will, on the other hand, reduce the probability of unexpected, undesirable assessment by such a committee.

November 1986 Vol. 10 No. 3

REFERENCES

Berkel, H.J.M. van, and Bax, A.E. (1985). *Inspectie of Interne Evaluatie: Waarborgen voor de Kwalliteit van het Hoger Onderwijs*? Amsterdam: Versluijs.

Drenth, P.J.D. (1984). *Slaagpercentages in de propedeuse: relevant voor beleid?* Amsterdam: Vrije Universiteit (opening speech).

Drenth, P.J.D. (1984a)."Personnel Appraisal". In: P.J.D. Drenth, Hk. Thierry, P.J. Willems and Ch.J. de Wolff (Eds). *Handbook of Work and Organisational Psychology*. London: Wiley.

Drenth, P.J.D. (1986). *Quality in Higher Education: Evaluation and Promotion*. Paper for CRE conference, Copenhagen, April.

Dubin, R. and Taveggia, T.C. (1968). *The Teaching-Learning Paradox: a Comparative Analysis of College Teaching Methods*. Eugene: University of Oregon.

Ministerie van Onderwijs en Wetenschappen (1985). *Concept Beleidsnota Hoger Onderwijs: Autonomie en Kwaliteit*. Den Haag: Staatsdrukkerij.

Mintzberg, H. (1983). *Structure in Fives: Designing Effective Organizations*. New York: Prentice Hall.

Os, W. van (1984). "Evaluatie van een nieuw propedeuseprogramme". *Nederlands Tijdschrift voor Tandheelkunde*, 91, 356-362.

Os, W. van (1984a). Meten en interpreteren van meningen over het onderwijs. In *Compact Jaarverslag 1983, Vrije Universiteit*. Amsterdam: Vrije Universiteit.

Os, W. van (1985). *Evaluatie van een nieuw studieprogramma - grenswaarden, richtgetallen en kwaliteitsoordelen*. Amsterdam: Vrije Universiteit.

Os, W. van, Bernaert, G.F. and Kok, E.J. (1984). *Analyse Model voor het Onderwijs in Studierichtingen*. Amsterdam: Vrije Universiteit, Afdeling Onderwijsresearch.

Os, W. van, and Bernaert, G.F. (1985). "Kwaliteit moet blijken; het evaluatiesysteem AMOS". In: H.J.M. van Berkel, A.E. Bax en J.W. Holleman (Eds.), *Kwaliteit van het Hoger Onderwijs; Bewaking en Verbetering*. Amsterdam: Versluijs.

Wilbrink, W., and Hofstee, W.K.B. (1984). "Docentbeoordeling". *Onderzoek van Onderwijs*. 13, 52-55.

A Preliminary Assessment of a
New Method of Course Evaluation Based on
Directed Small Group Discussions

Robert W. Talbot and Georges Bordage
University Laval
Canada

ABSTRACT

*The purpose of the study is to obtain a first estimation of the
reliability and validity of a new method for course evaluation
based on directed small group discussions. The new method is
student-centred, that is, the evaluations concerning the courses
are generated directly by the students, as opposed to a
questionnaire prepared by the professor and administered to the
students. For this preliminary study, only three undergraduate
courses were reviewed from three different departments:
medicine, physical education and law. Overall, the results from
this initial study are encouraging: the method is reliable, the
students are satisfied, and a number of suggestions were made by
the students to improve the courses. However there are important
discrepancies between the students and the professors in the
objects of evaluation. Furthermore, the professors were not all
equally satisfied with the evaluation reports from the new method.
These later findings suggest that further research is warranted to
clarify the disparities between the students and the professors.*

INTRODUCTION

In the fall of 1982 the Programme Committee of the Faculty of Medicine of Laval
University was looking for a method of course evaluation based directly on the students'
perception of the courses. According to the literature, this kind of evaluation is more effective
and stimulating (Rotem and Glassman, 1979) and enables students to make reliable and
relevant comments (Constin *et al.*, 1971; Gage, 1974; Gillmore, Kanz and Narracato, 1978;
Clark and Redmond, 1982). Therefore, the object is to obtain information directly from the
students themselves rather than through a written questionnaire prepared by the professor.

The nominal group process (Dolbecq *et al.*, 1975; Aubin, 1979) was chosen as it met
these conditions. However, the application of this technique was a trying experience. It took no

less than four hours to evaluate a single course. Lomax and McLeman (1984) arrived at the same conclusion after using this technique in circumstances similar to our own. The technique was consequently dropped in favour of a new method of evaluation developed out in the field. This method of course evaluation is based on directed small group discussions, derived from the nominal group technique but made much more simple. It takes less time to apply and meets all the requirements of the Programme Committee.

A detailed description of the method is given below. The essential point to bear in mind is that it takes place in three steps and involves the participation of small groups of students chosen at random from each course.

As this was a new method being developed, it was important to test its reliability and validity. Once the method had been tried out on three courses in the Faculty of Medicine, a certain number of questions were raised concerning the reliability and validity of the new method:

1. Do the students in a given group agree among themselves as to the assessment of the given course?
2. Do the observations collected from one group of students chosen at random differ from those taken from another group of students also chosen at random from the same course?
3. Do the observations made by the students correspond to the information which the teacher wishes to obtain about his course?
4. Do the students contribute elements of solutions to the problems noted in a course?
5. To what extent are students and teachers interested in this new form of course evaluation?

In order to obtain answers to these five questions, an evaluation procedure was established and applied to three courses for which an evaluation had been requested. In each of these courses two groups of students were chosen at random and the teacher responsible for the course was invited to prepare a written evaluation questionnaire relating to those subjects in his course that he personally wished to evaluate. This questionnaire was circulated to the students who were not selected for the small groups.

Methods of evaluation

Two methods were used to answer to the preceding five questions: the method of course evaluation based on directed small group discussions and the questionnaire prepared by the teacher responsible for the course. The first method is based on the students' own perception of the strengths and weaknesses of the course. The second method is based on the students' perceptions, as expressed on a Likert scale, of the aspects of the course defined by the teacher. Using Dufresne's item bank for course evaluation (1981) seven aspects of the course were targeted as the aspects of evaluation: objectives; content, texts, required reading and course notes; teaching methods and self-learning materials; methods of formative and summative evaluation; and miscellaneous aspects and recommendations. These different aspects of a course served as a reference both for the preparation of the questionnaires and for the classification of the observations obtained from the students in the small groups.

Method of evaluation based on directed small group discussions

The evaluation of a course by "directed small group discussions" proceeds in three steps:

1. The formulation of the assessments by each student;
2. The pooling of the assessments; and
3. The establishment by the group of a level for agreement for each assessment.

First step: Each student writes his impressions of the course on cards (8 cm × 13 cm). Each card contains only one observation or assessment corresponding to a single object of evaluation. The observations can be of a negative or a positive nature. The student can use as many cards as he wishes. Each observation must be expressed clearly, concisely and as specifically as possible. This step ends when every student has finished writing his observations (see Figure 1).

Figure 1

EXAMPLES OF COMMENTS MADE BY THE STUDENTS CONCERNING A COURSE

"The first examination contained questions which we had not covered during the course."
"The laboratory reports are short, clear, and precise; no unnecessary padding."
"The teacher should give more comments on his evaluations of the laboratory report."

Second step: The group leader first asks the students to classify their observations according to the seven categories mentioned earlier. A student then states one observation as noted on the first card. This procedure is repeated until all the cards have been read; however, once an observation has already been made, it is not repeated by subsequent students. Each observation is given an order number which the student must note on his card. No discussion or comments are allowed during the second stage. The students are also asked to note on a separate sheet of paper the number of the observations with which they are not entirely in agreement, on the understanding that it will be possible to discuss and vote on all the numbers so noted. If a number is not noted by any students, it is then concluded that the group has a unanimous opinion with regard to this observation. The process continues in a round table fashion until all the observations have been collected for each category.

Third step: The third step is in two parts: making revisions of or additions to the observations already noted, and voting by the group on all these revisions or litigations. The revision process is conducted by the group leader, who reads out the numbers. Whenever a student hears a number relating to an observation which he thinks should be explained or revised, he asks for the floor. The leader then asks the student to read the observation. Immediately after reading the observation, and even before there has been a preliminary discussion, the leader asks the group to vote on the observation in order to establish a first level of agreement. After this vote there is an open discussion and students can exchange views on the observation with the object of finding a new formulation or adding further information which would enable the group to achieve a consensus, or at least to come closer to it. Once the leader notes that the requested additional information is complete, he asks the student who provided it orally to note it on his card. The student reads aloud what he has written as a revised observation, after which the leader calls for a vote; the student then enters the result of the vote on the card. Thus, there can be a main observation, together with several revisions, each of which is noted on separate cards.

At the end of the third step the discussion group leader collects the cards according to category names and order numbers. These observations are then typed and transmitted in full to the person responsible for the course, except that the names of the teachers are given in a code which is known only to the person responsible for the course and, where appropriate, the teacher in question (see Annex).

The method of evaluation by written questionnaire

In order to determine just how much each teacher expected from the evaluation of his course, each teacher drafted his own questionnaire. To prepare their questionnaire, teachers used an item bank for course evaluation containing about 1 000 items relating to various aspects of a course (Dufresne, 1981). (See Figure 2.) Each student receives the questionnaire accompanied by a computerized answer sheet. At the end of the written questionnaire there is a separate sheet on which students can make suggestions or recommendations for improving the course.

Figure 2

EXAMPLES OF ITEMS TAKEN FROM A QUESTIONNAIRE

	Completely disagree	Partially disagree	Partially agree	Completely agree
The course notes are well presented.	1	2	3	4
The course notes are complete.	1	2	3	4
The evaluation of my performance is in reaction to the course objectives.	1	2	3	4
The examination questions measure well what was taught.	1	2	3	4

Courses

The students involved in this study were selected from three courses given at Université Laval during the fall term of 1983, in three different schools:

1. Course A is a course in the basic sciences in medicine; the teacher had no written questionnaire and consequently had to prepare one (74 questions) without knowing that it would be used for the present study;
2. Course B is a course in basic sciences in physical education; the teacher was already using a written questionnaire with 33 questions;
3. Course C is an introductory course in law; an existing questionnaire containing 56 questions was used without any changes.

Students

The size of the groups for the new method of evaluation is the same as the one for the nominal group process (Dolbecq *et al.*, 1975). For each course, two groups of 10 to 15 students were formed with the help of a table of random numbers. Humphreys, Bondini Salas and Messer (1984) also suggest the same number of participants per group. The new method of evaluation was applied almost simultaneously to each of these groups. For each course, a third group was formed, consisting of the remainder of the students in the course who had not been assigned to the two previous groups. This latter group completed the questionnaire (see Table 1).

Table 1

NUMBER OF STUDENTS IN EACH SUBGROUP FOR EACH COURSE

| Course | Method of evaluation by directed small group discussion: | | Questionnaire |
	First group	Second group	
A Medicine	A_1: 14	A_2: 14	77
B Physic. Educ.	B_1: 10	B_2: 10	91
C Law	C_1: 14	C_2: 14	75
Total	38	38	243

Procedures

The new method was applied four to five weeks after the end of the courses. Such an interval is considered acceptable (Daw and Gage, 1967) and makes it possible to obtain feedback on the course as a whole, including the final examination. Then the students are more amenable to participating in an evaluation exercise, since they are no longer preoccupied with the preparation of their final examinations. At the students' own suggestion, meetings took place during lunch hours. Each small group evaluation occurred within one day of each other in order to reduce possible contamination from group to group, although the students were warned not to discuss the evaluation with their colleagues. The meetings lasted an average 87 minutes (1 hr. 27 min.; s = 14 minutes), from a minimum of 70 minutes to a maximum of 105 minutes.

The written questionnaire was administered to students who did not participate in the small groups. The evaluation was given in a classroom with the whole group present.

The overall participation rate was 89 per cent. According to a univariate analysis of variance between the three groups of students for each course (two small groups and one large group), there are no significant differences in their grade point average ($p \geqslant 0.64$).

Data tabulation

All the observations by the students in the small groups were tabulated according to three rules:

1. Observations are considered equivalent when they contain similar facts and when the basic ideas are the same. Here is an example of two observations which were judged equivalent:

   A_1-31+:   Audiovisual methods generally used judiciously.
   A_2-38+:   The many visual illustrations at the lectures were used well.

2. Whenever an observation is revised during the second step of the method, the revised observation is added to the original observation and identified by the letter R (revised), inserted before the number assigned to the principal observation. The principal observation and the revised observation are then considered as a single observation for subsequent data processing purposes.

3. An observation is considered to be an "element of a solution" when it is expressed in the form of a "suggestion" or "recommendation" to the teacher to correct or improve his course. A single statement of facts is not regarded as an "element of a solution", even though, implicitly, it may suggest an improvement (see Figure 3).

Figure 3

EXAMPLES OF SOLUTIONS AS OPPOSED TO STATEMENTS OF FACTS

		Solutions
W:	"Teacher A skips too often from one subject to another. Use a pre-established order according to the objectives."	Yes
X:	"Students should receive photocopied notes."	Yes
Y:	"The content is not excessive but time is too short."	No
Z:	"Specify the objectives of the course more clearly; i.e., they should be distinguished from the content."	Yes

To test the reliability of the tabulation rules, a third person independently tabulated according to the same rules, 10 per cent of the observations (15 observations) taken at random from one of the small groups, group A1. Comparison of these 15 observations between groups A1 and B, and between A1 and the questionnaire showed a 93 per cent agreement rate between the two raters. There is 85 per cent agreement between the two compilers for the identification of "elements of a solution". The accepted degree of agreement between two independent judges in such circumstances is estimated to be 80 per cent (Côté and Plante, 1979). The tabulation was therefore satisfactory.

RESULTS

The results are presented in the same order as the initial research questions.

Intra-group concordance

The number of observations generated in each small group varied between 74 and 107, with an average of 86. 77 per cent of these observations were accepted unanimously without discussion. 84 per cent of observations were accepted unanimously after discussion and revisions. For the remaining 16 per cent, 7 per cent were accepted by a majority vote and 9 per cent represent the opinion of one or two students.

Inter-group concordance

On the average, a little over half (55 per cent) of the observations made by groups A1, B1 and C1 were similar to those of the parallel groups A2, B2 and C2. The respective percentages of similar observations in the three pairs of groups are 40 per cent (32/80), 62 per cent (46/76) and 63 per cent (55/88).

In order to judge more accurately the nature of the observations classified as different, these were reclassified in two subcategories: that is, "entirely different", where the object of the evaluation was not discussed by the other group, and "nuances", where the object of evaluation was common to both groups but involved different observations. (See Figure 4.)

Out of the 248 observations judged different, one-third were nuances. Thus, 70 per cent of the observations produced by two randomly selected groups for the same course relate to the same object of evaluation, that is, 55 per cent of equivalent observations, plus 15 per cent of nuances (i.e. one-third of 45 per cent).

Figure 4

EXAMPLE OF OBSERVATIONS REGARDED AS NUANCES

A1   Too much required reading for the course (as we had not been told where to stop we often read more than necessary).

A2   Content interesting but do not know where to stop when reading references to supplement the course notes (which are often incomplete).

Student/teacher perceptions

One-third of the information stemming from the new method corresponds to the content of the questionnaire prepared by the teacher. This information common to the two methods was compared by using the ratings stated on the questionnaire (1, very negative ... and 4, very positive); the object of this comparison is to determine whether the common information across the students and the teachers received particularly unfavourable or favourable ratings from students on the questionnaire. For course C, 92 per cent of the common information was rated negatively on the questionnaire. For courses A and B, the proportion was 50 per cent and 69 per cent respectively.

The average quantity of information obtained through the new method (i.e. 86 observations per group) was greater than the average number of items contained in the questionnaire, that is 54.

Elements of solutions

The number of solutions proposed by the students participating in the new method varied from 19 to 29 solutions per group, for an average of 22. The students using the questionnaire proposed no solutions, despite the fact that a page was provided for this purpose at the end of each questionnaire.

Student and teacher satisfaction

All the students who participated in the study had already had the experience of evaluating a course by the use of a questionnaire similar to the one used for the three courses. In order to measure the degree of student satisfaction with the new method, participants in the six small groups were asked to indicate their level of satisfaction on a scale from 1 to 4 (very dissatisfied to very satisfied) . Except for two "dissatisfied" students, all stated that they were "very satisfied" or "satisfied" with the new method.

Almost all the students (96 per cent) stated that they would be willing to use this method to evaluate future courses. Those who objected explained that it was because this method did not offer any more guarantees than other methods that the course evaluations could actually lead to real improvements. All the students in the small groups preferred the new method to the questionnaire.

The teachers' response to the results of the small group evaluations varied. The course A teacher was "dissatisfied" with the results: in his opinion "this method gives the students the opportunity to let off steam and the results obtained are neither objective nor constructive". The course B teacher said he was very satisfied and intended to evaluate his course solely by using the directed small group discussions. He added that he had corrected about 70 per cent of the deficiencies noted by the students concerning his course. The course C teacher said that she was "satisfied"; however, she felt she could have predicted most of the dissatisfactions noted by the students in the small groups.

Evaluating Higher Education

DISCUSSION

The main purpose of this preliminary study was to test the reliability and validity of the assessments made by students when evaluating courses by a new method based on small group directed discussions. Certain conclusions do emerge from the evaluation of the three courses.

The fact that 84 per cent of the observations were unanimously agreed on by the students and that only 9 per cent represent isolated opinions lead us to conclude that students' perceptions are uniform and the information given is reliable.

There is no standard reference to guide us in judging whether the level of concordance between the two small groups in a given course, i.e. 70 per cent of common objects of evaluation, is a satisfactory level of reliability. The order of magnitude achieved appears to us satisfactory.

Are two small groups necessary to evaluate a course? The teacher who has his course evaluated by only one small group chosen at random is able to work on about 70 per cent of the students' demands if two groups had been used. It is suggested that it is preferable to gather evaluations from a single small group of students and to follow-up on their evaluations than to collect the opinions of two groups. This suggestion is based on the thesis that a second evaluation will provide little new information and that the introduction of changes relating to the students' demands is an indication of the teacher's concern for his students.

Other studies (Rotem and Glasman, 1979; Mellon, 1984; Clark and Redmond, 1982) have already shown that students are very interested in participating in this type of small group course evaluation. While almost all the students were ready to repeat the experiment with the new method, the three teachers had divergent views. The first was unsatisfied, the second very satisfied and the third satisfied. It is difficult to reach a conclusion about teacher satisfaction given the limited number of teachers involved. However, the different levels of satisfaction on the part of the teachers and the fact that only one-third of the observations concerning the objects of evaluation are common to the two methods point to the need for further research on teacher-student disparities.

The solutions proposed by the students constitute a net advantage for the new method. Rotem and Glasman (1971) believe that this kind of feedback is more likely to lead to changes later.

CONCLUSION

The results of this preliminary study of a new method of course evaluation based on directed small group discussions indicate that the information collected from the new method is reliable. There are however considerable discrepancies between students' and teachers' perceptions of the objects of evaluation. Moreover, the three teachers' perceptions of the evaluation results differ substantially. Further research is clearly needed to clarify the nature of the disparities and the perceptions. At the same time the collection of solutions obtained by using the new method represents a clear advantage of the directed small group discussion method over the questionnaire.

REFERENCES

Aubin, G. (1979). *La technique du groupe nominal appliquée à l'analyse locale des programmes de formation.* Montréal, Canada: 38 p.

Callahan, M.P. et Manson, A. (1974). Course content and program evaluation model, final report. Madison, Wisconsin, Wisconsin State Board of vocational technical and adult education: 426 p.

Clark, J.D. et Redmond, M.V. (1982). *Small group instructional diagnosis: final report.* Washington University, Seattle, Dept. of Biology Education.

Costin, F., Greenough, W.T. et Menges, R.J. (1971). Students rating of college teaching. *American Educational Research Journal, II*:259-274.

Côté, R., et Plante, J. (1979). *Analyse des modifications de comportement,* Beauchemin: 255 p.

Daw, R.W. et Gage, N.L. (1967). Effect of feedback from teachers to principals, *Journal of Educational Psychology,* 1967, *58:*181-188.

Dolbecq, A.L., Van de Ven, A. et collaborateurs (1974). The effectiveness of nominal, delphi and interacting group decision-making processes. *Academy of Management Journal, XVII(4)*:605-621.

Dufresne, R. (1981a). Système d'évaluation des cours: la banque d'item. Service de pédagogie universitaire, Université Laval, 128 p.

Dufresne, R. (1981b). Guide d'utilisation de la banque d'item. Service de pédagogie universitaire, Université Laval, 34 p.

Gage, N.L. (1974). Students' ratings of college teaching: their justification and proper use. In N.S. Glasman and B.R. Killait (ed.), *Second U.C.S.B. Conference on Effective Teaching,* Santa Barbara, California: University of California.

Gillmore, G.M., Kanz, M.R. et Narracato, R.W. (1978). The generalizability of student ratings of instruction: estimation of the teacher and course components. *Journal of Educational Measurement, XV(1)*:1-13.

Humphreys, W.L., Bondini Salas, S. et Messer, P. (1984). The evaluation of instructors and related personnel decisions. *Teaching-Learning Issues, 54*:3-13.

Lomax, P. et McLeman, P. (1984). The uses and abuses of nominal group technique in polytechnic course evaluation. *Studies in Higher Education, IX(2)*:183:190.

Mellon, C.A. (1984). Group Consensus Evaluation; a procedure for gathering qualitative data. *Journal of Instructional Development, VII(1)*:18-22.

Rotem, A. and Glasman, M.S. (1979). On the effectiveness of students'evaluative feedback to university instructors. *Review of Educational Research, 49(3)*:497-511.

Walker, G.F. (December 1984). Structured group discussion as a means for obtaining feedback. Actes de la "Annual SHRE Conference on Education for the Professions", Imperial College of Science and Technology, London.

EXCERPTS FROM AN EVALUATION REPORT FROM GROUP B-1[1]

A.   Section on objectives

Evaluation
Number
(of step 2)

1	+[2]		I think that the objectives of the course met my expectations fully in that the course was very practical and I think we have seen things which are essential for a physical educator to know.
2			The laboratories fit well in the course.
R[3]	−2.1	−	Adiposity was not studied sufficiently in class to justify a laboratory on the topic (we had one laboratory for one course). 2/10[4]
R	−2.2		Not enough laboratories. 7/10
R	−2.3		Concerning comment No. 2, I was referring to the content, not the number of laboratories. 9/10
R	−2.4		There is no real need to elaborate on the theory of fatty tissue (laboratory) as we have a biochemistry course and the teacher refers to it. 7/10
R	−2.5		A course should be complete in itself. 10/10
3		−	Teacher A skips too often from one subject to another. Use a pre-established order according to the objectives.
4		+	The objectives of the course are well defined at the beginning and followed closely throughout.
5		+	Satisfactory objectives.
6		−	Objectives difficult to achieve (time). 8/10
7		+	The course objectives are clear.

B.   Section on Texts and Readings

8		+	The quantity of reading was adequate. 8/10

R	8.1	−	Too much reading for the first part of the course. 8/10
9		+	The texts and readings corresponded to a reasonable number of hours for the student. 7/10
R	9.1	−	Too much reading before the first examination. 10/10
10	9.1	−	The proposed texts and reading summarize the courses fairly well.
11		+	No need to read the book in order to get an "A" in the course, as the course notes are sufficient. 1/10
12		−	The course notes should be better structured by teacher A.
13		−	There are chapters in the book that were fairly complicated and, moreover, were in English.
14		−	Not enough specific references to McArdle's book. 6/10
15		−	Students should have photocopied course notes for each teacher.
16		−	We cannot understand the explanations given in certain courses, as we take a lot of notes.
17		−	Note taking is to rapid.
18		−	There is much too much reading at the beginning of the course.

1. Students in Group B-1 made a total of 76 observations.
2. Opinion of students as to the positive (i.e. +) or negative (i.e. −) character of the assessment.
3. Revisions during the third step.
4. Result of the vote when observations are not unanimous.

Institutional Self-Evaluation in Sweden[1]

Ann-Marie Furumark
National Board of Universities and Colleges
Stockholm
Sweden

ABSTRACT

This paper describes the background and developments of a project on institutional self-evaluation, carried out by the National Board of Universities and Colleges in Sweden. The 1977 reform of the Swedish higher education system implied i.a. a transition to a more decentralized system of decision-making. Due to economic restrictions institutions of higher education are pressed to implement change with little or no increase in financial resources. In order to preserve their autonomy institutions will have to improve their capacity for self-renewal and reappraisal of existing programmes. The purpose of a centrally sponsored project is to foster institutional self-study and self-evaluation. Methods used are conferences, seminars etc. (to sell the idea), pilot experiments (to establish models and methods for further dissemination) and special studies (to facilitate the process of self-evaluation). In conclusion, the paper lists some critical issues in self-evaluation.

INTRODUCTION

The 1977 Reform of Swedish Higher Education

The most important element of the 1977 reform of Swedish higher education was that it created a unified system, combining institutions and study programmes that were previously administered separately. The higher education system (Swedish *högskola*) now includes practically all post-secondary education.

Another feature of the reform is broadened recruitment, to be achieved i.a. by new, more liberal admission rules. Essentially the same rules apply to the entire system. To reach new categories of students, educational facilities have been diffused through the establishment of higher education institutions in several new locations, which prior to

---

1. This paper was presented at the Fifth IMHE General Conference held in Paris on 8th-10th September, 1980.

the reform had only a limited programme of "non-academic" postsecondary education (e.g. a teacher training college or a school for social workers). At present there are 31 central-government operated institutions at 21 locations in Sweden. Research facilities, however, are still concentrated in the universities and some professional colleges.

A significant feature of the reformed system is the decentralization of decision-making powers from national to regional and local levels. In this respect the new budgetary system is seen as central to the reform as a whole. Before the reform, higher education grants were essentially a system of line-item appropriations, and monies were distributed in great detail according to spending categories without virement. In the new system, funds are allocated for broad "output" functions in two dominating categories: undergraduate education and postgraduate training and research. These block grants are also meant to cover costs for administration and central services. Thus, institutions now have the freedom – *and* responsibility – to decide on priorities between different institutional activities.

To cope with this new budgetary system and to be able to use the degrees of freedom that it offers, it is necessary for all concerned to be informed of existing resources and alternative ways in which resources can be used.

In accordance with the decentralization principle, governance and management structures have undergone considerable change. Representatives of public interests are included on the governing boards of institutions, securing the democratic/political influence at local level. The local programme committee, which are responsible for planning the organisation and content of undergraduate training programmes, include outside representatives of the appropriate occupational areas.

The 1977 reform of higher education was conceived and first decided upon at a time when economic restrictions had not yet made themselves felt to a very great extent. But today Sweden, as many other countries, has to live with fiscal austerity, and higher education institutions are pressed to implement change and innovation with little or no increase in financial resources.

In particular the small, new institutions face difficult times. Although they have not been able to expand at the pace foreseen they have emphasized goals and tasks other than the established universities, taking up a role in regional development and community service, catering in new ways for mature and part-time students etc. At the same time, with the growing financial stringency, the emphasis is shifting within the framework of overall goals for the entire higher education system, more weight being given to research and technical development than to social goals like the equal distribution of higher education opportunities.

These circumstances, of course, make it all the more important that individual institutions know what they are doing, what role they play in the system, and where they are going.

The Follow-Up of the Reform

The central government agency supervising the higher education system is the National Board of Universities and Colleges, which is directly responsible to the cabinet. The Board is commissioned by the government to evaluate the reform of higher education with the main purpose of providing information for central decision-making. But results are published as they emerge, so that they may also be used as a basis for local decisions on desirable changes.

There is in fact a growing awareness that to have any significant impact most changes and adjustments should be made by the higher education institutions themselves. Generally there seems to have begun a swing away from the centre-periphery, "social engineering" reform strategy towards a more dynamic, process-oriented perspective, where self-evaluation and the capacity for self-renewal are key concepts.

Considering these developments it is only natural that a project on institutional self-evaluation is also part of the follow-up programme.

THE SELF-EVALUATION PROJECT

The Concept of Institutional Self-Evaluation

The Swedish term (*verksamhetsvärdering*) used in the project does not correspond exactly to "institutional self-evaluation". Literally translated it would rather be "activity evaluation" which signifies that the evaluation process may have as its object any kind of institutional activity and take place at any level or working unit within an institution. In the project, however, efforts are concentrated on departmental and institutional levels. The term evaluation, in this connection, must also be allowed to cover less pretentious, "unscientific" methods of assessment. Where such methods are used, "self-study" may be a more suitable term. In this paper "self-evaluation" and "self-study" are used synonymously.

In recent years, decentralization has been a guiding principle in higher education as in most areas of Swedish state administration. There is the firm conviction that decentralization will first and foremost promote democracy but also lead to more enthusiastic local commitment and greater efficiency. When central authorities decide to loosen their grip and refrain from governing through detailed prescriptions, it must be assumed that they will also have confidence in the capacity and responsibility of local authorities under their jurisdiction. To justify this confidence, higher education institutions must transform themselves into self-evaluating and self-renewing organisations, limiting the need for central control and major central reforms.

In Sweden there is no formalized outside control of the quality and performance of individual higher education institutions. Central decisions on resource allocations are not based on formal assessment of the educational outcomes of various institutions. The implication is that institutions themselves bear the full responsibility to control and improve their own performance. But if the current economic difficulties continue to prevail or even get worse, it is not to be excluded that there might be pressure on higher education institutions to account for their performance in a more articulate manner. Thus, the future autonomy of institutions, and not least the newly-established ones, depend on their capacity for self-renewal and readiness to deal with efficiency problems.

However, in our opinion institutional self-evaluation should not be primarily intended to provide information for superior authorities as a basis for their decision-making. Neither is it a process by which institutions account for their efficiency, quality and performance to outside interested parties. These functions must be filled in other, more formal ways, in connection with budgetary estimates and annual reports. Instead, *self-evaluation should be regarded as a strictly internal affair meant to provide a better basis for decisions that are taken by and within the institutions themselves.* This of course does not exclude that outside expertise is invited to take part in the assessment, or that the results of self-evaluation are used for external purposes as well.

It follows that self-evaluation should not be ordered or prescribed from above. It should be an enterprise initiated and shaped by the institutions or departments themselves, in order to serve their own internal needs for knowledge, insight and awareness concerning what they are doing, how well they do it and at what costs, so that they may raise their capacity for reappraisal of priorities and redirection of resources for renewal.

The Purpose of the Project

The purpose of the project is to stimulate and foster critical self-study at all levels of the higher education system with the ultimate aim to improve effectiveness and efficiency. Being launched at a time when financial difficulties were just commencing, the concept of institutional self-evaluation is often associated with stagnation, retrenchment and bad times in general. There is the obvious danger that this may reduce the motivation to critically analyse established activities in order to make room for new ones. Where this occurs, the incentives for self-study are at best negative – punishments may fail to be inflicted, and things may turn out better than expected.

There are however reasons for taking a more optimistic view of the readiness of individuals and institutions to take part in self-evaluation. The idea of institutional self-study, as defined in our national project, has of course not appeared out of thin air. It should be seen in relation with the democratization of society in general and the increased participation of citizens in decisions that affect their own lives and jobs. Recent legislation on co-determination in working life also applies to universities and colleges, and formal arrangements for student participation in academic matters are of a still older date.

All this has generated growing needs for common discussions on goals, values and performance in relation to the use of existing resources, as well as for a better understanding of the ways and means to achieve desired change. These needs may prove to be as strong an incitement to institutional self-study as outside pressures and a general uncertainty about the future. Self-evaluation, if exclusively associated with financial restrictions, may be only a strategy for survival. If viewed in the wider context of participation and the joining of forces for common goals, self-evaluation is part of a strategy for renewal and development.

The Initial Phase

The first stage of the project, which started in 1977, was mainly devoted to collecting theoretical knowledge and information on practical experiences of institutional self-evaluation and similar activities, mainly from the USA. It was found that the numerous US experiments with institutional self-evaluation, costly, large-scale and highly systematized as they often are, do not easily lend themselves to transfer and adaptation to the Swedish setting. But very much can be learned from them on models and methods and most of all on the general nature and conditions of self-evaluation.

At the same time efforts were made to sell the idea of institutional self-evaluation in different, mostly "soft" ways. The project management at the National Board introduced the project at many staff development courses and at various courses and conferences arranged for other purposes. At specially arranged workshops, participants were engaged in a simulation exercise, the aim of which was to trim the university budget by a given percentage, using actual quantitative data, expert knowledge and value judgements. Although quite successful these workshops highlighted the difficulties involved in coping with goal conflicts and in finding criteria and measures of quality and relating them to economic realities.

Through the activities of the first stage of the project, the idea of institutional self-evaluation has been fairly well established in the Swedish higher education system. Thus the term is widely used by departments and institutions in budgetary estimates, planning documents, policy statements etc. It is however not always easy to know whether this implies that self-study in the proper sense actually takes place within institutions to a very great extent, or if the results of self-evaluation are integrated in the academic planning. Until there are many more visible examples of self-evaluation, we can't truly claim that it is a normal practice in Swedish higher education institutions.

Current Developments

In the current phase of the project, running from mid-1979, we are thus faced by the problem of how to firmly establish institutional self-evaluation. We have to find working methods within the project itself that make it clear that we are not adherents of the centre-periphery innovation strategy, which is indeed the very opposite of self-renewal, contrary to all our thoughts on the aims and nature of self-study. So there is no intention to prescribe centrally a certain system or specific methods by which institutions should evaluate themselves. Besides, we are convinced that no one model can be developed to suit all the varying needs for self-study within the unified but still highly diversified system of higher education.

There are in fact two very different ways of looking at the role and function of institutional self-evaluation. By some people, mostly administrators, self-evaluation is seen as part of the formalized planning and budgetary procedure of an institution. Consequently, it should be a rational, regular, recurrent activity with set routines, aided by information systems, goal charts, questionnaire forms etc. This would be a way, they think, to make sure that self-evaluation takes place in all units and that results are integrated in decision-making.

Others take a less rationalistic, more dynamic view of self-evaluation, much in accordance with the definition adopted by the project. This view is best expressed in the words of a Swedish professor of the History of Literature:

"Change is necessary in higher education, but it must be allowed to take place at a pace that permits us to preserve the viable parts of tradition. If innovations are to be really vital they can't be achieved by prescription or organisational measures – one must provide time and incentives for spontaneous creativity and critical appraisal within the institutions themselves. That is why I definitely do not believe in regulations or scheduling, an annual evaluation cycle in the manner of the timetable for the budgetary procedure, but very much more in having confidence in people without reservations, silent or explicit."

In the following we shall give a brief survey of different types of activities that are going on within the field of institutional self-evaluation. It must be pointed out that from our central observation point we have of course no possibility of knowing all that is going on at the universities and colleges. Furthermore it is in the nature of self-study to be an internal and sometimes quite intimate process, the results of which are not always reported in an open manner. Some local self-study experiments have a direct connection with the national project. In other instances initiatives were taken independently, but we have reasons to believe that they have been inspired by the project.

At one university the Council and the central administration have endeavoured to introduce universal self-evaluation at all levels within the institution. In the directives for the budgetary procedure in 1979/80, departments, programme committees, faculty boards and service units were told to submit self-evaluation reports of all activities carried out during the academic year of 1978/79, to be used as a basis for local decisions on resource allocations for 1980/81 and for the budgetary estimates for 1981/82. At this institution there had been previous self-evaluation experiments which according to the Council had been lacking in structure and uniformity. This time it was intended to try a more systematic procedure: all institutional activities should be comprised in the evaluation and planning process, all available statistical information should be used as far as possible, reports should be structured in a similar manner so as to facilitate analysis and comparison, and focus on essential problem areas so as to provide a basis for decisions on desirable changes. The overall aims of the self-study were to achieve an optimal use of resources, to improve communication within the institution as well as with regional and central authorities, and to provide a basis for decisions on the redirection of resources for new or strengthened programmes by means of reductions or withdrawals in other areas.

It is the Council's opinion that this new procedure has many advantages. Aided by statistical data prepared by the central administration, departments have for the most part delivered surprisingly rich reports of their activities. This has to a great extent facilitated priority decisions taken by the programme committees and the Council. Furthermore the Council feels that it is now getting a more comprehensive picture of conditions and circumstances in different parts of this large institution. On the negative side there have been complaints of increased work loads and fears of growing bureaucratization. To counter such developments there are plans for a changed procedure in 1980/81.

At another big university a similar procedure was followed. In the directives issued for the internal planning and budgetary work the University Council stressed the need for self-evaluation as a basis for realistic, long-term planning. All departments and programme committees were asked to propose and specify measures for developing programme quality within their range of operation. It was assumed that these proposals would be based on analyses of existing programmes, under the aspects of subject content and research orientation, vocational/professional orientation, and effectiveness of the teaching/learning process. Proposals could concern new study courses, arrangements to support student learning, various pedagogic development projects, staff development etc., and were listed in priority order on special forms. These were used as a basis for the final decisions by the University Council.

Although this procedure no doubt produced more involvement and more careful consideration at all levels in the planning process, it can hardly be termed as an example of institutional self-evaluation in the proper sense. The self-evaluation part of the budgetary planning was confined to a small part of the total budget, i.e. resources available for local development work. The emphasis was on new proposals, and in this context there was no pressure for reordering of priorities, let alone for discontinuation of established activities. Furthermore the work was carried out during a very short period of time, to fit in the timetable of the planning cycle, allowing little time for a dialogue between different levels in the organisation. This is not surprising, bearing in mind that this university has 157 departments, 30 programme committees and some 23 000 students.

What we have just described are of course two examples of the rationalist approach to institutional self-evaluation. Both represent interesting first efforts to establish self-study as an integrated part in the planning procedure. Characteristic of this approach is the tendency to look more to the palpable *products* of self-study, as progress reports and planning documents, than to the *process* itself. From the point of view of the participants the initiative comes from superior decision-making bodies, the forms and the timetable are more or less fixed and prescribed, and the products are to be used primarily outside the self-studying unit.

As far as we can judge there has been little motivation or room for a real critical appraisal of established programmes, with broad participation by all concerned within the units. On the other hand we feel that through these procedures the foundation has been laid for more radical self-evaluation experiments, not least with respect to the careful description in quantitative terms that must be the first step in any self-study undertaking.

We now proceed to describe briefly some self-evaluation activities that mostly represent the other, non-bureaucratic view of self-evaluation.

At Sweden's northernmost university experiments with self-evaluation started in some departments as early as 1977, mainly as part of the work on annual reports. Now self-evaluation is a continuous systematic activity in the departments of biology, physics and mathematics. Evaluation is based on organised staff and student discussions with broad participation, course ratings and student interviews as well as on economic and other statistical data. Care is taken to avoid monotony and routinization by shifting the focus of inquiry from one year to another. Results are used chiefly for internal planning and development purposes but also serve as arguments in the budgetary procedure.

A somewhat different self-evaluation project was launched at the same university by the Division for Education and Research of the central administration. This division includes units for budget and educational planning, study counselling, study administration and local admissions, and the teaching media centre. It has a staff of 50. It was decided to evaluate the function and organisation of the division as a whole, for the purpose of getting a better basis for the planning of future activities. We think that this project is of special interest from several points of view. Although it is an example of self-evaluation focussed on a service function, it has a simple design that could easily be transferred and adapted for other self-study purposes. Here are the main points of the design.

- Establish, at a general staff meeting, the idea and purpose of the self-evaluation and secure consensus on the design and organisation of the project (commitment, involvement)
- Identify strong and weak sides of the activities and organisation of all units (description, stock taking, problem definition). This was done through questionnaires, internally and externally.
- Formulate tentative goals for possible changes and circulate to all units for opinions (interpretation)
- Propose and adopt an action programme in the short and medium term (operationalization).

At a medium-sized university of Central Sweden the planning committee for the humanities and the natural sciences has taken steps to introduce institutional self-evaluation into its area of responsibility. Two multidisciplinary departments have volunteered to design and test models for self-study. The first phase of these experiments has just been completed, and the reports are studied within the departments, as a basis for decisions on the continuation of the project.

The programme committee in charge of planning the undergraduate study programmes within the field of social sciences at another university has initiated a project for developing methods and techniques for evaluation at department and committee levels. It is intended to combine two perspectives: one internal in the manner of self-evaluation, seen mainly as organisation development, the other external where outsider judgements will be sought on the quality and market value of the programmes concerned.

In the national project special attention is given to the small newly-established colleges, on the assumption that at these institutions self-study has a significant role to play, struggling as they are for consolidation and development in no easy conditions. At some of these colleges plans are far advanced for self-evaluation projects,while others are still considering the possibilities.

In conclusion, we feel sure that from all these various experiments models, methods and experiences will emerge that will make more institutions and departments think it worthwile to embark on experiments of their own. To that end, we intend to monitor continuously as far as possible what is going on in the field of institutional self-study, gathering information and making it available in suitable forms.

Plans and Needs for the Future

In the national project we plan to go on working through conferences, courses and workshops and through personal contacts with people in key positions at universities and colleges. When activities are initiated locally we support and encourage them, financially or otherwise. Where nothing happens of itself, we try to get things going in various ways: asking questions, paying visits, arranging conferences, referring to other persons or institutions with some experience of their own etc.

Furthermore it is intended to carry out special studies in order to develop aids, methods and routines that will facilitate the self-evaluation process. One important field for development work is financial management. Whatever view is taken of self-study it will hardly be worth the time and effort if financial aspects are not part of it. At present, financial planning and accounting in Swedish higher education institutions are not sufficiently, if at all, integrated with operational planning and assessment of educational outcomes. To planners, teachers and students, who are all partners in the self-evaluation process, financial information is not often readily available, at least not in terms relevant to what actually takes place in education and research, be it unit costs or other similar devices.

A special development effort in this area will concern the small colleges of higher education. Later this month a workshop will be arranged for administrators and planners from most of the small colleges. The participants will engage in reviewing theory, practice and problems related to the financial management of the small institution and plan jointly a development project with the purpose of improving the quality of financial administration. On this basis it is intended to start development work at two or three colleges, geared to the special needs of the individual institutions. Considering that small colleges have many things in common, the outcomes of the project will hopefully prove to be generally useful.

From our experience so far we know that there is a great need for information material on institutional self-evaluation and separate issues involved, to be used as support and reference at courses and conferences and in local experiments, a book-shelf as it were full of useful reading. Some of it exists and has only to be brought to attention, other books are no doubt there but have yet to be discovered. Subject areas concerned are evaluation, organisation development, planning, management, staff development etc. But we also need to publish books and reports for our own national purposes. At present we are compiling a debate publication, containing contributions on different aspects of the theory and practice of institutional self-evaluation. What we have in mind is not a manual, but a book that may promote the idea and be conducive to critical discussion and debate on self-study. As we have mentioned above there is also a great need for reports of practical examples, domestic and from other countries.

The national project on self-evaluation can't go on for ever. In fact its first task should be to make itself superfluous. One effective way of achieving this, according to our opinion, is building up a network of resource persons and institutions, prepared to share their knowledge and experience with others who are starting experiments of their own.

In this context we attach great importance to international contacts. During the initial phase of the project the project manager at that time paid several visits to US universities, collecting a wealth of experiences and material of great value to the Swedish project. Recently links have been established with higher education institutions of the UK. One interesting part is played by the Staff Development Programme of the National Board of Universities and Colleges. In co-operation with the British Co-ordinating Committee for the Training of University Teachers it sponsored a bi-national workshop at the University of Durham in April, 1980, on the theme of Evaluating the Academic Department. Apart from increasing the appetite for international co-operation, the workshop generated ideas and plans that are now taking form at several Swedish institutions, encouraged by the national self-study project. Two more bi-national workshops on the same theme are scheduled for 1980/81, in the Netherlands and the Federal Republic of Germany respectively.

SOME CRITICAL ISSUES IN SELF-EVALUATION

This paper has described the national Swedish project on institutional self-evaluation, current developments and plans for the future. Little has been said about the process of self-study. The reason for this we shall state with the words of an astute educational planner and Doctor of Physics at a Swedish university. She says:

"There are a thousand ways to conduct self-evaluation. The important thing is to choose one and get going."

However, in conclusion, we shall list briefly some critical issues related to the self-evaluation process which have come up for discussion on numerous occasions.

Problem Awareness and Definition

To be useful, self-evaluation must focus not only on problems but on "good" problems, the solutions to which will contribute to innovation and growth within the institution. Many self-study efforts are thought to fail because the process of problem definition is overlooked or summarily dealt with. In the rationalist approach to self-evaluation, problems are defined in the top-down manner, often without previous scanning of problems as perceived by those who are to conduct the self-study and who will be most affected by its results. Where there is no shared ownership of problems, there will be little enthusiasm for analysing them and even less for finding ways to solve them.

What constitutes a good problem? Who decides what the problems are? When there is silence and no commotion, are there no problems? Is problem scanning the first step in self-evaluation?

Mobilization, Involvement and Support

Broad involvement of all concerned, general commitment or at least consent, at an early stage of the process is thought to be an indispensable condition for the success of self-study. In the same way as problems ought to be everybody's problems, some consensus is needed that they ought to be solved. Among the members of an academic department there will always be the indifferent, those whose main interests are focussed somewhere outside their professional lives. To others, impending scrutiny and analysis may be a threat. It is possible to cope with indifferences. But active resistance must be reduced early on.

What will mobilize people for self-evaluation? Who benefits by it? What rewards can be promised? Must special incentives be developed?

Using the Results

Complaints are often heard that knowledge obtained through professional evaluation programmes, however costly and scientifically sound, has little impact on planning and decision-making. If this is true for higher education, one reason may be that evaluation external to an institution will not be heeded by those responsible for implementing recommended changes. At the other extreme, continuous every-day assessment may be too integrated, too "reformist" in character, for any significant changes to take place as a result. Self-evaluation, being an internal affair but a planned and organised activity with set goals, is assumed to have more forceful effects with regard to change and innovation.

What will ensure that the results of self-evaluation are really used and integrated in decision-making?

Degree of Institutionalization

As has been mentioned above, one view of self-evaluation maintains that it should be a process firmly integrated in the planning and budgetary cycle of the institution. Others think that self-study should be a dynamic, loosely controlled process, giving scope for spontaneous creativity and truly critical appraisal.

Is self-evaluation chiefly a management function? Are permanent arrangements needed to make sure that self-study takes place? Are regulations and routines detrimental to the creative quality of self-appraisal?

Evaluation Methods

Evaluation is often looked upon as a matter that could be left to a limited number of professionals and to a few departments curious about their own performance. The idea of self-evaluation is based on the conviction that each institution, each department, has to study its own activities as well as it can within the limits of its resources and expertise. So, self-evaluation requires that methods are available to all and that techniques can be developed that are manageable with little or no outside assistance.

Can evaluation be demystified? What are the minimum methodical requirements for self-evaluation to be scientifically respectable?

The Credibility of Self-Evaluation

It is assumed that the best conditions for renewal and development within institutions are created by thorough critical self-appraisal with broad internal participation. By definition, self-evaluation thus emphasizes the professional and intra-institutional perspective. Even if efforts are made to take into account opinions of external interested – or neutral – parties, the final judgements will always be based on the values of those performing the self-study. But major decisions on the future of higher education institutions will still have to be taken by superior authorities, relying on criteria that are not always the same as those of the institutions. The economic slowdown may well sharpen divergences of views.

Will central decision-makers have confidence in the ability of institutions to control and improve their own performance? To be credible, must self-evaluation be supplemented by external assessment?

November 1981 Vol. 5 No. 3

Assessing Institutional Performance:
The Importance of Being Careful

Leonard C. Romney,
University Corporation for Atmospheric Research,
Boulder, Colorado,

Gerald Bogen,
University of Oregon
Eugene, Oregon,

and
Sidney S. Micek,
National Centre for Higher Education Management Systems,
Boulder, Colorado,
United States

ABSTRACT

For many, assessing institutional performance evokes positive sensations regarding rational management and effective responses to accountability demands. Yet, the process of institutional performance assessment carries with it potential liabilities and warrants careful consideration. This article describes the political, methodological, economic, and philosophical cautions that should be considered and suggests the procedures for effectively dealing with these issues.

INTRODUCTION

"If it were not so painful, we might examine with considerable intellectual interest the experience of public and private (higher educational) institutions beset with diminishing demands for services and rising costs, increasing institutional rigidities and not productivity increases. Unpleasant as it may be, educational administrators are having to ask the tough questions: What are our objectives? How would we know if we achieved them?" (Wagner and Weathersby, 1971 : 2-3).

Knowing one's objectives and assessing the degree of their achievement, constitute the essence of institutional performance assessment. We shall argue in the following pages that although there may appear to be compelling reasons for initiating efforts to assess institutional performance, unexamined and ill-considered performance assessment efforts may cause one to proceed slowly and with great difficulty.

Clearly the internal and external pressures for higher education institutions to periodically assess their achievements are mounting. Talk of institutional performance assessment in most higher education sectors stimulates a variety of responses, ranging from fear to guarded optimism, from anger to apathy, from puzzlement to aggression. Performance assessment is repugnant to many simply because on the surface it offers little promise for acknowledging truly productive situations, i. e. , those pertaining to quality and long-range impacts. Others see "performance assessment" as a basically needed and productive exercise, conducted to answer institutional critics and substantiate needs for financial support and to aid in the myriad program planning and resource allocation decisions.

The increasing concern about performance in higher education stems from pressures that do not affect higher education alone but are expressed in virtually all facets of society in the United States, if not the entire world community. Possibly the most universal pressure today is the continuing and apparently increasing rate of inflation that affects each of us. Other issues of almost equal influence include expanding commitments to the principles of consumerism, slowly but steadily aging populations, demands by innumerable special-interest groups for equitable (and immediate) satisfaction of their wishes and needs, and the finite pool of public funds, constrained and controlled by an ever more forcefully expressed public will regarding the funding of public needs and services.

In addition to these generally pervasive forces, pressures endemic to American higher education are generating concern about institutional performance. They include deteriorating levels of public confidence in the commitment and ability of higher education to fulfill the public's expectations; imagined though likely false suspicion that higher education deliberately avoids responding accurately or completely to its inquisitors and critics; an aging professoriate accused of being lulled into stagnation by tenure guarantees; and a growing reliance on the bargaining table for resolving academic issues.

Taken singly, each of the pressures could probably be responded to in a practical, innovative fashion without undue disruption of institutional operations. However, in concert these pressures create a relentless force, requiring us to examine our levels of performance and improve them in every feasible way so that they are consistent with the missions higher education institutions in the United States are chartered to pursue. Although academe is not alone in its need to

substantiate and improve its levels of performance, it would be cynical
to claim exemption from such responsibilities on the ground that we are
no worse than some others. Avoidance, neglect, or apathy with regard
to institutional performance assessment is not what we owe our
constituencies and not what they are likely to tolerate.

INSTITUTIONAL PERFORMANCE ASSESSMENT -
A DEFINITION

Just how institutional performance assessment ought to be
conducted and to what depths one ought to go are hardly clear-cut issues.
In general, we shall regard institutional performance assessment to be
the measurement or observation of the effective and efficient accomplishment of the expectations of the institution's constituencies. Romney,
Gray, and Weldon (1978) present a definition of productivity that not only
closely matches our general view of institutional performance assessment, but also offers a simple model that provides more detail on the
definition. They argue that "productivity", which when examined at the
institutional level becomes "institutional performance assessment", is
an examination of the goal achievement process. That process,
displayed in Figure 1, consists in its simplest form "of at least four
distinct stages in which:

1. goals are set,
2. resources are committed for the support of these goals,
3. committed resources are expended in an effort to achieve the
   goals, and
4. outcomes result". (Romney, Gray and Weldon, 1978: 7).

None of these stages of the goal achievement process can be
omitted when one is concerned with institutional performance
assessment.

Figure 1. THE GOAL ACHIEVEMENT PROCESS
IN HIGHER EDUCATION

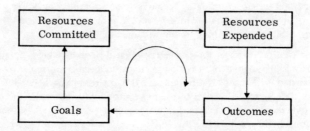

In this view, then, institutional performance assessment consists of contrasting the end and beginning points of each stage of the goal achievement process. It is not the purpose of this document to describe how that may be done. Rather, we propose now to array before the reader, our views, based on experience and thought, as to what liabilities potentially await this institutional performance assessment process.

INSTITUTIONAL PERFORMANCE ASSESSMENT – POTENTIAL LIABILITIES AND DISADVANTAGES

The liabilities and disadvantages that we associate with the process and outcomes of institutional performance assessment can be categorized conveniently in four distinct groupings:

1. Political Liabilities:
    These cautions relate to the negative effects institutional performance may have on formal and informal coalitions within the institution, on the existing balance of power, on current mechanisms for achieving consensus and effecting compromise, and on relationships with authoritative agencies outside institutional boundaries.

2. Methodological Cautions:
    This set of warnings stems primarily from our understanding of the state-of-the-art of performance assessment and evaluation, its limitations, and the possibilities for either ignorant or blatant misuse.

3. Economic Concerns:
    These cautions pertain to the potential costs of the assessment effort, especially as they are contrasted with the potential benefits.

4. Philosophical Caveats:
    This set of limitations relates primarily to the implications of institutional performance assessment for individual and organisational behavior patterns, for missions and purposes, and for the principles and practices of institutional control and operation.

It is important to note that rarely if ever will all or even a majority of these cautions apply to any given set of institutional circumstances. In fact some of the individual, specific concerns we outline are mutually exclusive. It is also important to note however, that even though regarded singly or in isolation from other cautions some concerns may appear rather innocuous. Nevertheless, when they occur with others, the combination can be catalytic and devastating to

say the least. Familiarity with institutional behavior and an ability
to anticipate the reaction of affected parties are the only preventative
or curative agents in such instances. Now to the cautions themselves.

Political Cautions

When considering institutional performance assessment, we
believe the most potentially rending implications for the warp and woof
of the institution's political fabric are the following:

Morale Problems. The administrative maxim, "if something
appears to be going well, leave it at rest," may well apply in the case
of institutional performance assessment. Obsession with assessment,
especially when institutional constituencies appear satisfied and when
funding is adequate and stable, may foster dissonance among internal
interest groups and shatter the tenuous balance of institutional
productivity, personal satisfaction, and positive tension in the organisation.

Disruptions of Incentive Patterns. Every institution has its own
set of established incentives, patterns developed by explicit policy,
tradition, and evolving expectations. Typically, these incentive
patterns are closely related and virtually intermixed. Performance
assessment has the potential for blindly disrupting this pattern and
scrambling the institution's incentive structure in unpredictable and
possibly destructive ways.

Increased Bureaucracy, Rigidity and Inflexibility. A third potential
political liability that may be associated with an institutional performance assessment effort pertains to the proverbial tail wagging the
proverbial dog. That is, one of the disadvantageous consequences could
well be unwanted institutional rigidities. Eyes fixed only upon the
accomplishment of a given set of measurable institutional goals may
become obdurate to change, to options, or to alternate courses of
action. Such tunnel vision often develops a myopic perspective of
institutional purpose and activity. To carry the analogy one step further,
an associated consequence is the loss of peripheral vision or the loss of
the ability to sense and grasp appropriate opportunities.

Exposé of Cherished Activities and Practices. Over the years
every organisation develops what best can be called cherished activities
and pursuits, efforts that are entirely ethical and appropriate. If lost
in the harsh glare of a public performance review, the stature and
impact of the institution would be disproportionately diminished.

Commitment to Results. A major political issue related to institutional performance assessment has to do with the nature and degree of institutional commitment to accept and abide by the results of the effort. Should that commitment be lacking or conditioned, in the first place, the assessment process itself is emasculated and, in the second place, the results are just so much dust in the wind. Less than full commitment is indeed a serious liability.

Unrealistic Expectations. Conceivably, there is the potential for an effect associated with institutional performance assessment efforts whereby expectations for better performance are raised regardless of the actual outcomes of the study or the potential for growth, change, or innovation. Some members of the campus and external community could perceive a performance assessment project as an assurance that change will result when in fact it may not or even should not, or indeed cannot occur.

Reduced Prerogatives. This type of assessment project, if conducted well, warrants openness and will likely result in the sharing of data about relative levels of achievement. At the same time, however, such a process may result in the community's desire and assumed ability to "second guess" decisions, and may in fact force the management team to make some decisions that it might otherwise choose not to make.

External Intervention. If openness results from the goal assessment process and the external community does not share in the values and directions desired, intrusion might result, to the current and future detriment of the institution. Educational consumerism is, at best, a risk. Thus, the administrative maxim, "don't ask a question if you aren't prepared to live with the answer", has especial significance in the case of institutional goal assessment. Constituency disaffection with current achievements can lead to directions being forced upon the organisation.

Methodological Cautions

When the question of institutional performance assessment is raised, a proper and complete answer must account for the procedural or methodological considerations in which such efforts are so thoroughly embedded. The state-of-the-art of evaluation, though remarkably advanced in recent years, signals "caution" and "proceed circumspectly" to the informed user. Among the most telling, perhaps disturbing, warnings emanating from evaluation efforts as they pertain to institutional performance assessment are the following:

<u>Misapplication</u>. Frequently, evaluation tools e. g. , achievement
tests or survey questionnaires, are situation-specific; that is, they
are developed to meet the needs of a particular set of evaluation
circumstances. And, indeed, in those situations they yield the kind
of evaluative information sought. It is frequently tempting, however,
to use such tools in other, perhaps unrelated situations for which they
are neither intended nor appropriate. Moreover, a related disadvantage
stems from the all-too-frequent practice of putting one's entire
analytical emphasis in one place. Institutional performance assessment is not the only important nor perhaps even the most important
research topic. One must be equally concerned for example, with
analysis of institutional markets, of population trends and expectations.
To consider performance assessment as the sole form of organisational
research would be unfortunate and silly if not downright dangerous.

<u>Measurement Limitations</u>. Some aspects of institutional mission
and goals may not lend themselves to quantification, i. e. , to measurement or to observation. Kenneth Boulding (1966) has claimed that the
more important a particular goal is, the less amenable the goal is to
quantitative measurement. Efforts to measure institutional goal
achievement in a comprehensive fashion may from the outset be an
impossibility. Moreover, it is difficult to argue that the measures of
performance we have are comprehensive, valid or reliable. Boulding's
comments about goals may be paraphrased to reflect the state-of-the-
art regarding the indicators of performance themselves. That is, the
indicators we have may be secondary in comparison to those we should
have or would like to have. For example, we have only the most
rudimentary indications of program quality; we know little of the
long range impact of higher education, much less whether or not this
impact relates to specifically identified circumstances or the general
environment of our institutions. This simply and clearly means that
the current effectiveness of institutional performance assessment may
limit our ability to obtain an adequate and accurate measure of performance. Indeed, current capabilities, though attractive and in some
cases sophisticated, may beguile us into believing that we have the
answer when, in fact, the information we have obtained may be
deceptively oversimplified.

<u>Joint Outcome Cautions</u>. A traditional and honored concept in
higher education pertains to the achievement of multiple objectives with
a single activity. For example, the workings of faculty and graduate
students together on a particular study often will provide both learning
as well as new knowledge outcomes. We have not yet discovered the
keys needed to decipher this jointness puzzle nor have acceptable
means been adopted for accounting for it in assessment procedures.
Not to reflect jointness or joint outcomes in assessment is inaccurate
while to reflect it is currently beyond our grasp.

Unit of Analysis Concerns. Recent research suggests that performance assessment conducted at the institutional level may be focused
on the wrong level in higher education. The findings of researchers,
such as Biglan (1973), Smart and Elton (1975), and Hartnett and
Centra (1977), suggest that the most relevant focus for assessing
performance may be at the discipline or department level, above which
varying levels of achievement become considerably diffused through
aggregation.

Timeliness Concerns. We also implore the reader to consider
issues related to timeliness prior to initiating an institutional performance assessment effort. First, there is the question of whether the
organisation is in a phase of its development which on the one hand
can tolerate and survive an intensive performance assessment effort
and which on the other, actually matches the assumption of the assessment to be performed. Lack of synchronization between institutional
life stages and style of performance assessment could result in an
exercise of shadow chasing.

Staff Capabilities. A final consideration with regard to methodological limitations has to do with the capabilities of staff to accomplish
the ends associated with institutional performance assessment. One
must rationally, objectively and seriously consider whether or not the
analytical skills as well as the sensitivity to institutional circumstances
are sufficiently represented in current staff to warrant one's launching
an institutional performance assessment effort.

Economic Limitations

We suspect, though our span of familiarity is restricted to higher
education in the United States, that concern about costs, financial
exigencies, and economic tightness are virtually worldwide. In an
attempt to reflect this rather limiting economic outlook, we suggest
the following constraints and limitations on institutional performance
assessment.

Marginal Returns. The process of assessing performance as
represented by the achievement of institutional goals might in fact
realize only marginal returns because of insufficient institutional
flexibility. The collective faculty, as an institutional resource, are
largely fixed; they represent a continuous, rather well-defined
economic commitment for as long as one dares to look into the future.
Institutional personnel policies and practices such as tenure or
collective bargaining may further reduce administrative options and
institutional flexibility beyond the point of useful effort to adjust or
adapt. In such cases, performance assessment may not be worth the

effort, especially if one expects returns related to redirection or redesign of programs. Simply stated, the costs may not be justified by the potential returns.

Resource Consumption. Depending on how efficiently the institutional performance assessment effort is conducted, one could incur sizable personnel and monetary costs, an especially sobering possibility when precious resources are in high demand to address other issues deemed more pressing. Gains of an assessment project may be more than offset by losses in assets and opportunities. The issue of costs relates directly to that of values in that it will be the prevalence of value preferences that will determine to which end monies are devoted.

Relative Resource Questions. Given the overriding prevalence of financial exigencies and pressures, institutional authorities must ensure that currently available resources be put to the best uses possible. The difficult question, of course, is whether or not institutional performance assessment is the best use of tight money. Clearly the alternative demands are legion. The answer clearly lies in an adept balancing of potential resource consumption, likely constituent satisfaction, and gains in political advantage. That balancing is clearly both an institutional prerogative and dilemma.

Philosophical Cautions

Finally, we list several items pertaining to what we have, for lack of more suitable terminology, labeled philosophical cautions, i. e., those cautions and limitations attendant to institutional performance assessment which emanate from ethical and moral codes and from philosophical principles underlying higher educational institutions. Briefly, these are as follows:

Organisational and Institutional Autonomy and Flexibility. Once the door to institutional performance assessment is ajar, it is likely that it will never be closed again. The end result may be the eventual toppling of some of higher education's most celebrated icons, autonomy and flexibility. Because an organisation has embarked on a self-study of its performance, expectations for subsequent action are often heightened. These expectations are especially difficult to defuse and may prove embarrassing at the very least when the study results in conclusions that no action, no new programs, or no new emphases or efforts are required. Unfulfilled expectations will most likely soon lead to external action, interventions, or at the very least public relations headaches. This kind of pressure and state of unrest usually lead to permanent loss of flexibility or options because they are taken away by the imposition of external demands or requirements.

Span of Control. One must also be concerned to ask whether or not the results of the institutional performance assessment will be associated with the matters over which the organisation has a modicum of control. The most obvious example pertains to teaching and learning. Most performance assessment exercises are written to assess student learning, student achievement, etc. Yet, learning is an individual response to opportunities created and offered by the institution. Learning depends largely on what the student is willing or able to devote to the effort.

Accordingly, to evaluate or assess institutional performance only on the basis of student learning is not only inappropriate, it is unfair.

SUMMARY

For any given institution it may be impossible to divine any pervasive mandate as to whether or not to proceed with a program for assessing institutional performance. We have focused on a rather lengthy list of cautions, limitations, and disadvantages. These clearly accentuate the negative at the expense of the positive, which factors are delineated elsewhere. We suggest that the limitations are important enough to weigh and balance along with the assets. We believe also that sometimes the balance will indicate cessation or avoidance. But it is also clear that healthy institutions can survive, indeed prosper, under conditions wrought by institutional performance assessment. By merely being involved, valuable benefits such as reality checks, increased organisational unity, and stimulated pan-institutional communications may result. These benefits in and of themselves may not warrant complete involvement or commitment to the process. The balancing of assets and liabilities must be performed. In the final analysis, we say emphatically, "proceed with caution!".

May 1979 Vol. 3 No. 1

REFERENCES

Biglan, A. (1973). "Relationships between Subject Matter Characteristics and the Structure and Output of University Departments." Applied Psychology, 27. 3 : 204-213.

Boulding, K. (1966). "The Ethics of Rational Decision." Management Science, 12. 6 : B161-B169.

Harnett, R. and Centra, J. (1977). "The Effects of Academic Departments on Student Learning." Journal of Higher Education, XLVIII. 5: 491-507.

Romney, L. C. , Gray, R. G. and Weldon, H. K. (1978). Departmental Productivity: A Conceptual Framework. Boulder, Colorado: National Center for Higher Education Management Systems.

Smart, J. C. and Elton, C. F. (1975). "Goal Orientations of Academic Departments: A Test of Biglan's Model. " Journal of Applied Psychology, 60. 5 : 580-588.

Wagner, W. and Weathersby, G. (October 1971). Optimality in College Planning: A Control Theoretical Approach. Berkeley, California: Office of the President, University of California.

The Second Irony:
The System of Institutional Evaluation of Higher Education in the United States

H. R. Kells
Rutgers University
New Brunswick, New Jersey
United States

ABSTRACT

The system of institutional evaluation of higher education in the United States is described, including the aspects performed by the state governments, by the voluntary peer institutional accreditation system, and by the institutions themselves. Trends are discussed as are some theoretical and policy considerations. The possible application of the U.S. scheme in other settings is considered, and the author cautions those who would apply it in more centrally planned systems without a history of local self-evaluation and an adequate administrative capacity at the institutional level.

Two ironies characterize the contemporary reactions of international educational leaders to the American higher education system. The first is that the U.S. scheme, long maligned as a non-systematic melange without any standards, has come to command considerable interest, if not respect, both within the community of American organizational analysts and among their counterparts in a wide range of other systems.

Burton Clark (1976) provided the first coherent and most insightful analysis of the somewhat unexpected virtues of the system which evolved in the U.S., when he presented the thoughtful apology entitled "The Benefits of Disorder". In short, what Clark depicted and what many observers from both developing and post-industrial societies are now viewing more favorably is a large, complex system of egalitarian, competitive, flexible, responsible, autonomous, and diverse institutions. He argued that compared to most other systems, U.S. institutions can be relatively flexible, competitive and unpoliticized because most of the power in the "system" is held at the top of each institution and not by the government on one end of the spectrum or by the faculty and students at the other. As Clark pointed out, the power is in the middle of the U.S. system and this makes the aforementioned characteristics either possible or necessary. As one might expect, over time the U.S. got the educational system most appropriate and best matched to or reflective of its basic cultural tenets – individualism and competition tempered by what Alexis de Toqueville recognized in the 19th century as a vital ingredient in the American scheme. He and, more recently, Fred Harcleroad (1983) have noted the large incidence of voluntary cooperative efforts by individuals and groups at every level of society, particularly at the local level and especially motivated to prevent what is seen as unnecessary intrusion of government into education and certain other societal arenas. The problems and abuses of this young and evolving system notwithstanding, it is quite a turnabout to find the levels of interest in, and high incidence of international exchange to experience, the U.S. "non-system".

The second irony perceived by this observer and that which will be the major subject of this written exploration is far more dramatic and unexpected than the first. It is the notion that the American scheme of institutional evaluation which is largely self- (as opposed to governmental) regulatory in nature is of increasing interest to systems which for several decades have derided it and claimed for themselves unequalled levels of control and quality through centralized ministerial or other government mechanisms for planning, program content, and financial matters. Some of us have argued for years that for purposes of enhancing institutional effectiveness and management capabilities, the self-regulatory scheme at its best is far more effective over time than an external inspectorial control or planning scheme. What's more, it is increasingly clear to this writer that on the average far more and more useful institutional and programmatic evaluation goes on in the U.S. market-oriented system than in the more centrally planned ministerial systems. While the U.S. system may appear chaotic to the outsider or newcomer, and while there are surely not national controls on the meaning and quality of the degree, a matter of serious concern in the U.S. of late, the elements of the U.S. evaluation system at the institutional and programmatic level described below involve a very wide range of faculty members and administrators in serious, critical, and often improvement-related assessment on a cyclical basis which promotes long-term adjustments and increasingly solid strategic choices (Keller, 1982). Many Americans have criticized the effectiveness of the average U.S. university management team and the functioning of accreditation related self-study and planning processes (Kells, 1976, 1981). Nonetheless, it must be admitted that with the exception of a very hopeful integrated effort recently formulated but largely untried in British Columbia, Canada (1984), little has been developed in the ministerially planned systems which approaches from a theoretical (in terms of change theory and organization development) or practical perspective the methods, motivation level and results which are attained in the institutional evaluation and program review systems developed in the U.S.

Two motivations have spawned most of the recent interest in U.S. self-assessment schemes. The first, a sanction driven and less than constructive purpose, program retrenchment, has been present particularly in Western Europe in the past five years. In some instances, representatives of institutions and programs have been asked by government authorities to decide specifically where financial and any programmatic cuts will be taken. Despite arguments to the contrary (Simpson, 1985), such a motivation will rarely, if ever, result in true program review, that is, quality assessment with useful participation at the working level of the organizations to produce improvement strategies. More about this later. The second recent motivation is the intention of some of the governments of centrally planned systems to encourage some deregulation, competition, and local (institution-based) assessment in higher education. The Netherlands is a current example where the Minister of Education has recently announced that elements of competition should be introduced in the Dutch system and that quality assessment, possibly to be conducted by the universities themselves, should be introduced (Summer Conference, 1985). Whatever the reasons, however, the general interest in U.S. evaluation efforts, if somewhat ironic, is most welcome and will continue to benefit the U.S. immensely through the commentary by colleagues from other systems.

A DESCRIPTION OF THE SYSTEM

A Brief History

The evaluation of institutions of higher education in the United States did not begin in any serious and systematic way until the beginning of the twentieth century. The federal Constitution does not ascribe the control of education to the federal government. Rather, it left the matter to the various states. The most significant historical fact affecting the development of the nature of institutional evaluation in the U.S. was that for the first three hundred years of the existence of colleges and universities, the states, with the notable exception of New York, did not exercise their right to plan, develop, review and control higher education institutions within their boundaries. Rather, with very little government intrusion, institutions of different types and quality developed all over the U.S.. By the end of the nineteenth century in the absence of efforts by the states, and as growth, egalitarianism, and differentiation of institutional types occurred in response to the industrial revolution and other forces, a system of peer institutional review known as accreditation emerged. It sought to achieve the needed definition of educational terms and boundaries between the sectors, to promote improved articulation of students across these boundaries and then to list institutions and specific programs in certain professional fields which appeared to meet agreed-upon standards. Those interested in the details of the development of this voluntary peer evaluation system should consult the history by Selden (1960) and for a thorough discussion of the contemporary system the best reference source is that by Young et al. (1983).

In the three-quarters of a century since the accreditation system began, it has developed and changed dramatically. That part of the system which is program-specific, called specialized programmatic accreditation, which began about 1900 with the work of the medical profession, has grown to include over fifty professional program areas. Specialized accreditation agencies have refined their standards and have developed the nationwide capability to promote program self-assessment and the review of programs by peers so that programs which meet high professional standards can be identified and improved. The second part, the institutional accreditation system, which began its first assessments about 1920, has also evolved greatly. It has grown to include almost all types of institutions and to span the continent with six autonomous but cooperating and methodologically consistent accrediting regions across the U.S. After 1935, the evaluation scheme was altered to soften earlier prescriptive standards and to place equivalent emphasis in the process on the achievement of stated institutional intentions. The process was developed further after World War II to include the present *basic components – an institutional self-assessment in light of the accreditation standards and the institutional intentions; a review by a visiting team of trained peers from institutions not in direct competition with the institution in question; and a decision based on the foregoing steps about accreditation status and any sanctions or expectations about improvement by an elected regional accreditation commission composed of administrators, faculty members and public "lay" representatives.* Institutions undergo this cycle and now have major contact with the accrediting agency five years – with a major review every ten years and a review based on a review of plans, progress and the planning and control process at the alternate five year points. For a thorough description and analysis of this system see the book by Young et al. (1983) and regarding the self-assessment segment that by Kells (1983).

The Contemporary System

The total current picture of institutional evaluation in the U.S. is larger than the accreditation system, though accreditation still remains the centerpiece, and it is more complex, because several other major developments have occurred in the last two decades. The first is the active development since the mid 1960s of the long dormant state coordination and control systems. They were prodded into existence by the wave of growth, the subsequent decline, and the public pressure for accountability and efficiency which characterized this period. This development has not been uniform across the 50 states and includes a range of activities from simple approval of educational institutions to operate in the state (chartering or licensing), to approval of degree levels (determining what degree shall the institution offer), to one-time or even cyclical program review processes (in some states), and to budget and program approval and planning decisions for publicly supported institutions – and other variations. For a thorough review of this matter see the works by Berdahl (1971) and Millard (1980).

Other changes have occurred. Internally stimulated institutional management efforts including institutional research, program review systems, and strategic and other planning efforts are receiving much more serious attention today because resources are scarce, costs are rising, demographics continue to change and competition and even survival demand attention to these matters. It is fair to say that in the present era, for perhaps the first time in the history of institutional evaluation in the U.S., the presence of the first appreciable on-campus systems of ongoing study and planning not directly initiated by the external accreditation impetus can be seen as a significant variable in the overall evaluation landscape. That is certainly so at larger institutions, many of which have instituted cyclical program review systems. This has come about, of course, because of the obvious external pressures on institutions, because accreditation agencies have increasingly requested it over the last 10 years, and because a new breed of institutional leaders is taking over – persons who expect information for decision making on an ongoing basis and who are more comfortable with study, planning and change processes.

So, the *total* institutional evaluation system should probably be depicted as having the following components:

Basic Components of the U.S. Institutional Evaluation System

I.   *State institutional licensing and review*

This is present in all but eight or nine of the fifty states, but at different levels of scope and thoroughness. Processes range from a simple initial evaluation to permit the institution to operate, to complex and quite thorough ongoing cyclical approval of institutional authority to offer specific degrees and the like. In some states, the process is largely coordinated with and often jointly conducted with the regional institutional accreditation process (see below). Some state processes expect institutional self-assessment before the external review is made, but most do not. These state processes are currently receiving more emphasis in the U.S., with focus being placed on strengthening the initial licensing step and on expanding the cyclical program (see below) and institutional review process. For more information on this process consult the works of Richard Millard (1976, 1980) or contact The Education Commission of the States in Denver, Colorado.

II. *Regional institutional accreditation*

Virtually all non-profit and a small number of degree-granting, state-approved, profit-seeking institutions are evaluated every five years by the non-governmental regional accreditation system. This is the centerpierce of voluntary institutional evaluation and particularly the self-regulation scheme in the U.S. The institutions receive a major review every ten years (including a thorough, participative self-study process, a visit by a team of peers from non-competing institutions and an accreditation decision and any pressure to change or improve given by an elected regional accrediting commission composed of professionals and some lay citizens) and a review of changes made and plans for the future at the alternate five-year points with a team visit also a possibility at that time. In most of the six accrediting regions this process cooperates with but is not coopted by any state licensing and review system and is sometimes conducted jointly with any specialized accreditation reviews (see below) for the institution. In one of the regions in the 1970s, the former occurred in 80 per cent of the accreditation reviews and the latter in 20 per cent, Kells (1979). For more information about the regional institutional accreditation system see the reference work by Young *et al.* (1983).

III. *Institution-initiated evaluation and planning systems*

Significant, internally initiated institutional study, planning and change processes are increasingly encountered at U.S. institutions. By this is meant processes which are locally initiated and maintained, internally motivated, more or less (although increasingly) cyclical or ongoing, and usually (but not always) involving outsiders as consultants, change agent or evaluators. As this fundamental, long-needed development occurs, the relationship with and certainly the nature of the response to the outside evaluation agencies (state or nongovernmental accreditors) change because at an institution which is doing these things regularly, data are available, choices are being made and the institution knows about and is already working to correct any weaknesses. For an interesting discussion of this phenomenon on U.S. campuses see the interesting book by Keller (1982).

As indicated previously, the three part evaluation system for institutions in the U.S. is complemented by and increasingly integrated with four processes operating on the program level, the results of which complement or are considered to be integral parts of institutional evaluation in the U.S. The four complementary processes are :

a) *State level or national testing (licensing of) individual graduates of professional career programs* to certify them as qualified to practise the profession. Analysis of these results as grouped data can be used in processes to improve programs and institutions and certainly can be used on a group basis in institutional evaluation by outsiders.

b) *State mandated or induced cyclical program review processes.* Some states conduct or require such processes; most do not. Some have induced institutions to do it through the requirements for fund allocation and state-wide long range planning processes. See below and the article by Millard (1980) and the Barak (1982) book.

c) *Specialized accreditation (program level) processes.* These cyclical review processes are conducted by more than 50 recognized non-governmental professional agencies or associations operating nationally and using detailed accreditation standards developed and reviewed periodically by the profession. As not all U.S. institutions have career or professional programs, many do not deal with these agencies; some institutions are periodically reviewed by several; a few by 10-20 or more agencies. For some institutions this program review process is a very important part of the overall institutional evaluation process. For more information about it consult Young *et al.* (1983) or contact The Council on Postsecondary Accreditation, One Dupont Circle, Washington, DC 20036.

d) *Institutionally initiated and conducted cyclical program review processes.* This is the program level aspect of step III (above). It is increasingly evident at large U.S.

institutions, although recently it has spread to two year community colleges and smaller four year colleges and universities. The program review processes were often initiated first at the graduate (post baccalaureate) level or because of impending retrenchment, but increasingly they are motivated by long term improvement-oriented concerns and include departmental or program self-study steps and teams of institutionally selected outside evaluators. For more information about these processes see the works by Barak (1982), and Arns and Poland (1980).

The foregoing overall scheme, of course, is a developing one. Because the U.S. is not a centrally planned society and its higher educational system is similarly decentralized, it evolves fairly slowly rather than being subject to major or cataclysmic system-wide reforms imposed or even put into place carefully but quickly. But it has evolved substantially in recent years and it continues to evolve.

Some Trends

Most informed observers of the system described above would probably agree that it is in flux, and that several definite trends are discernible. First, with respect to the basic parts of the system (elements I-III above), while state efforts (I) are being enhanced as the external climate becomes more restrictive, the long-term inclination continues to be toward increased formalized, external, non-governmental (II) and local institutional (III) efforts and responsibility. The latter has been most recently documented by Keller (1982) and both are argued for strongly by the Carnegie Foundation (1982) in a major report entitled *The Control of the Campus.* There is a growing internal motivation for evaluation and towards *self-* rather than governmental regulation.

Other trends are seen. There is more cooperation between external agencies which interact with institutions, of particular importance when, for instance, an institution has multiple accreditation relationships. See COPA (1981), Kells and Parrish (1979) and Kells (1983*a*). There is also considerable sympathy across the system and some progress beginning to be evident for a higher reliance in the evaluation process on evidence of goal achievement, the "outcomes" or results of the educational process. See Andrews (1983), Armstrong (1985) and Kells (1984). The Council on Postsecondary Accreditation, the national, nongovernmental coordinating body for all of the accreditation efforts is working to enhance the reliability and validity of accreditation standards, a difficult, costly but long-desired item (at least by some observers). Finally, there also seems to be more concern about training and properly orienting external evaluators who operate in the accreditation system.

SOME THEORETICAL AND POLICY CONSIDERATIONS

Students and scholars of organizational analysis might well inquire about the theories and theoretical models which would support or explain the system described in this article. Certainly a more generalized view is necessary if one is to consider the implications of attempts to apply the U.S. scheme to systems with fundamentally different settings.

This observer feels that the open systems model usefully portrayed for institutions by Katz and Kahn (1978) most fully depicts the interaction of situational variables as well as constituent dimensions of higher education institutions. The model provides for the necessary importation of energy (inputs), goal/intention statements, interactions with the environment, process or functional components and output elements, and therefore is a very useful construct in examining evaluation models. The evaluation model suggested by Campbell (1977) which includes a combination of goals/ends (outcomes) tests and the analysis of functioning (or disfunction) is a useful theoretical portrayal of the desired self-assessment and evaluation team judgements employed by the U.S. accreditation system. What is not adequately enough portrayed by the "goals/ends plus analysis of functioning" evaluation model is the practical expectation that *self*-assessment or *self*-study can work as a central dimension of the system and as a spur to institutional improvement. Certainly that dimension has been questioned (Wildavsky, 1972) and the literature of non-profit, bureaucratic organizations is replete with barriers to planned change or even simple improvements in institutional processes. Self-satisfaction, fear of change, lack of awareness of real problems (Lewin, 1974), and unwillingness or inability to evaluate oneself objectively have all been cited as reasons to doubt the usefulness of self-assessment.

It is this aspect of institutional evaluation systems which requires another set of theories and strategies. It is here that work of Kurt Lewin (1974) and Ronald Havelock (1969), Jack Lindquist (1978) and a large group of organization development (OD) theorists and practitioners provide the rationale and the methods which can be and have been employed in the kind of setting which U.S. institutions provide, in order to make self-assessment work and in order to achieve improvements and organizational change (Kells, 1983). In such systems, if employees can be enticed to identify fairly closely with the organization, to narrow the gap between personal and organizational goals, to assume risks, and to see problems as tasks to be handled rather than as "finger pointing" or blaming opportunities, then true discovery of problems can occur and psychological "ownership" of the solutions will result, and change can and will take place over time. The sociocultural environment of U.S. institutions (autonomous, government-fearing, competitive, complex, diverse bureaucracies with a relatively large ability to control their own destiny) and of U.S. professionals (with great personal latitude, relatively high loyalty to their institutions, and usually relatively low levels of politicization) provides at least the potential to stimulate *self*-regulation and to affect improvement and planned change if the strategies of "discovery", psychological ownership, appropriate rewards, linkage to ideas and adequate process leadership are employed (Lindquist, 1978). While most self-study processes still do not achieve their full potential, more careful attention to internal motivation, leadership, and to the design of an appropriate process (Kells and Kirkwood, 1979 and Kells, 1983) can yield positive results. Finally, of course, political considerations can assist here. "If we don't assess and fix things our way, someone will do it their way" is a logical and powerful motivator and can yield really important information and therefore power.

The Application of the U.S. Scheme to Other Settings

While the literature of organization development does contain reports of change strategies and training interventions in highly structured government agencies and other centralized systems, most of the work on planned change strategies and organization development has employed problem solving, normative-reeducative, and empirical-rational strategies in organizational settings which permit or encourage them, rather than power-coercive strategies in institutional frameworks in which these are dominant in the organizational culture (French and Bell, 1984).

The question becomes whether an institutional evaluation scheme which in its ideal form presupposes a heavy emphasis on trustful self-assessment and nonpolitical behavior by internal and external evaluators, which expects risks to be taken, problems to be identified and solved, and which seeks primarily to improve the functioning of the institutions involved and thereby the whole system over time, can be employed in centrally planned (if not controlled) and/or in relatively highly politicized institutional settings. The limited evidence from the general management literature and the opinions of OECD officials from many of the Western, often highly planned and centralized higher education systems over the last ten years has not appeared favorable. However, despite the fact that the recent interest of quite a few countries in U.S. departmental or program review systems which this writer and others have encountered, has been based primarily on a search for more acceptable approaches to retrenchment (hardly a useful or encouraging framework for trusting, improvement-oriented self-regulation and assessment) recent, perhaps post-retrenchment, interest in deregulation, decentralization and some self-regulation holds some promise.

The retrenchment based program reviews seem to this observer to be more like attempts to conduct better triage in a field hospital or like selecting a limited number of organ transplant recipients, rather than designing systems for preventive and restorative health care. The more recent and positive motivations may over time produce the climate in which something like the U.S. methods can be adapted for more centrally planned systems in ways that yield more positive results. In a sense, some of the more centralized systems may gradually move to become somewhat more loosely coupled and – organizationally – "healthy" in an OD sense. Both are theoretically possible.

Surely the evaluations of programs and institutions by state government agencies in the U.S., while not improvement-oriented and certainly devoid of extensive cooperation or enthusiams from the institutions being inspected, have been conducted in some states for several decades and purport to meet the needs of the state. So a minimally satisfactory decision-oriented review can be conducted by a state agency using evaluation teams of peers and basic descriptive materials from the institution. One would hope for more from an evaluation system.

If centralized systems can decentralize the assessment system and encourage self-assessment of institutional and educational or program effectiveness much more can be hoped for. This can probably happen only if there is a sizeable increase in the administrative capacity at the institutional level in such systems. Without such capability and the will and power to make evaluation happen at the local level, it will falter. It will be interesting to see what happens.

July 1986 Vol. 10 No. 2

ACKNOWLEDGEMENTS

The author gratefully acknowledges the assistance provided by Eleanor Kells, who prepared the manuscript, and of Robert Berdahl, Jan Donner and Richard Millard who reviewed a draft and made valuable suggestions.

REFERENCES

Andrews, G. J. (1983). "Adapting Accreditation to New Clienteles". In:Young, Kenneth *et al.*, *Understanding Accreditation*. San Francisco: Jossey-Bass.

Armstrong, E. (forthcoming). "Outcomes Assessment and Use in the Accreditation Process". In Micek, Sidney and Kells, H.R., *Research on Accreditation*, Washington, DC: Council on Postsecondary Accreditation.

Arns, R. and Poland, W. (1980). "Changing the University through Program Review". *Journal of Higher Education*, May/June, 268-289.

Barak, R.J. (1982). *Program Review in Higher Education*. Boulder: National Center for Higher Education Management Systems.

Berdahl, R. (1971). *Statewide Coordination of Higher Education*. Washington, DC: American Council on Education.

British Columbia Council of College and Institute Principals. (1984). "Institution Evaluation Process for BC Colleges and Institutes: Policies and Procedures Manual", Vancouver.

Campbell, J.F. (1977). "On the Nature of Organizational Effectiveness". In: Goodman and Pennings, *et al. New Perspectives on Organizational Effectiveness*. San Francisco: Jossey Bass.

Carnegie Foundation. (1982). *The Control of the Campus*. Lawrenceville, NJ: Princeton University Press.

Clark, B.R. (1976). "The Benefits of Disorder". *Change*, October: 31-37.

Council on Postsecondary Accreditation. (1981). "A Guide to Interagency Cooperation". Washington, DC.

French, W.L. and Bell, C. (1984). *Organization Development*. Third Edition. Englewood Cliffs, NJ: Prentice-Hall.

Harcleroad, F.F. (1983). "Accreditation: Voluntary Enterprise". In: Young *et al. Understanding Accreditation*. San Francisco: Jossey-Bass.

Havelock, R.G. (1969). *Planning for Innovation Through Dissemination and Utilization of Knowledge*. Ann Arbor: Institute for Social Research, University of Michigan.

Katz, D. and Kahn, R.L. (1978). *The Social Psychology of Organizations*. Second Edition. New York: John Wiley & Sons.

Keller, G. (1982). *Academic Strategy*. Baltimore: Johns Hopkins Press.

Kells, H.R. (1976). "The Reform of Regional Accreditation Agencies". *Educational Record*, Winter: 24-28.

Kells, H.R. (1979). "The People of Institutional Accreditation", *Journal of Higher Education*. 50: 178-198.

Kells, H.R. (1981). "Some Theoretical and Practical Suggestions for Institutional Assessment". *New Directions for Institutional Research*, 29: 15-26.

Kells, H.R. (1983). *Self-Study Processes*. Second Edition. New York: Macmillan.

Kells, H.R. (1983a). "Institutional Rights and Responsibilities". In: Young *et al. Understanding Accreditation*. San Francisco: Jossey-Bass.

Kells, H.R. (1984). "Factors Influencing and Attitudes About Macro Level Outcome Analysis in Higher Education". *North Central Association Quarterly*, 59. No. 1. 3-8.

Kells, H.R. and Kirkwood, R. (1979). "Institutional Self-Evaluation Processes". *Educational Record*, Winter: 25-45.

Kells, H.R. and Parrish, R. (1979). *Multiple Accreditation Relationships of Postsecondary Institutions in the United States*. Washington, DC: Council on Postsecondary Accreditation.

Lewin, K. (1974). "Frontiers in Group Dynamics: Concept, Method, and Reality in Social Science, Social Equilibrium, and Social Change". *Human Relations*, 1: 5-41.

Lindquist, J. (1978). *Strategies for Change*. Washington, DC: Council of Independent Colleges.

Millard, R. (1976). *State Boards of Higher Education*. ERIC/AAHE Research Report No. 4. Washington, DC: American Association for Higher Education.

Millard, R. (1980). "The Power of State Coordinating Agencies". In: Jedamus and Peterson *et al. Improving Academic Management*. San Francisco: Jossey-Bass.

Selden, W.K. (1960). *Accreditation: A Struggle Over Standards in Higher Education*. New York: Harper & Bros.

Simpson, W.A. (1985). "Easing the Pain of Program Review: Departments Take the Initiative". *Educational Record*, Spring: 40-42.

Summer Conference. (1985). Association of Dutch Universities; Theme: "The Measurement of Educational Quality", Breukelen, The Netherlands. Background Papers. August, 19-20.

Wildavsky, A. (1972). "The Self-Evaluating Organization". *Public Administration Review*, September/October: 509-20.

Young, K. *et al.* (1983). *Understanding Accreditation.* San Francisco: Jossey-Bass.

Institutional Performance Assessment Under Conditions of Changing Needs[1]

John Sizer
University of Technology
Loughborough
United Kingdom

ABSTRACT

This paper is intended to be catalytic rather than prescriptive. It examines the changing nature of performance assessment under conditions of financial stringency, possible contraction and changing needs. It argues that the performance of an institution should be assessed in terms of its responsiveness to the needs of a complex and rapidly changing society. A portfolio approach to evaluating an institution's subject areas and developing a strategy for its future development is advocated, which would distinguish between existing and emerging growth areas, consolidation areas, and withdrawal and redeployment areas. To achieve positive motivation it is recognized that faculty and administrators at all levels should participate in a process of institutional self-evaluation and self-renewal. A case is made for the appointment of high quality managers who can build consensus within institutions and overcome the behavioural problems surrounding self-evaluation.

INTRODUCTION

Various aspects of institutional performance assessment were considered in a paper presented to the Fourth IMHE General Conference (Sizer, 1979a). This paper examines the changing nature of institutional performance assessment under conditions of financial stringency, possible contraction and changing needs. It is intended to be catalytic rather than prescriptive.

1. A shortened version of a paper given to the Fifth IMHE General Conference held on 8th-10th September, 1980.

FUTURE NEEDS OF SOCIETY

There is considerable pressure in many OECD countries for a concerted effort to be made to develop and obtain agreement within institutions on their academic policy and objectives for the 1980s and into the 1990s. In looking forward into the 1980s and on into the 1990s in response to demographic trends, should not institutions examine the environment in which they will be operating and attempt to identify what the needs of society will be given this environment? Inevitably, it will be argued that we are not very good at forecasting the future needs of society, but surely it is better to attempt to identify and satisfy future needs than to assume in a rapidly changing society that today's needs (frequently measured in terms of number and quality of applications from school-leavers) are the best and only indicators we have of future needs. Furthermore, it is often argued that because we cannot plan very effectively in the short-term at the present time, there is little point in attempting long-term planning. This argument confuses problems arising from short-term financial uncertainties with the need to examine the impact of long-term trends on an institution's portfolio of activities and to develop a strategy for the institution's long-term development.

Consideration of the trends and factors which are influencing, and will continue to influence significantly the environment in which institutions of higher education will be operating indicates that it is not simply a question of examining the impact of falling numbers on the higher education system, but that it is also necessary to recognize that society is likely to require a different mix of outputs from the system than at present. Thus Jochimsen (1979) argued at the Fourth General Conference that while "... a policy directed towards preserving, and making the necessary improvements to, the standards of efficiency at universities can be implemented only if members, professors, administrators and students join in a new effort"; an essential pre-condition for such an effort is that "policy makers and society in general can really be convinced that such higher education institutions are not only willing to fulfill, but are also capable of fulfilling, the tasks required of them from the societal aspect".

If we accept Jochimsen's arguments, a key question is: who provides the scenario documents which attempt to identify the "tasks required from a societal aspect"? Clearly, government departments and agencies should undertake macro-forecasting as a basis for decisions about higher education systems. They can provide scenario documents for use by institutions, but in the end should each institution form its own view and discuss this with the appropriate financing body? Once financing bodies go beyond the provision of scenario documents questions concerning the autonomy of universities will naturally be raised; though the State-of-the-Art Survey (Jadot, 1981) and the study of financing and control systems (Hecquet and Jadot, 1978) show that institutional autonomy has been considerably eroded already in a number of European OECD countries. Furthermore, many financing bodies may not have the expertise or resources to provide scenario documents, and some governments are averse to new initiatives which necessitate public expenditure. Nor, given the difficulties involved in preparation, should we think in terms of a single agreed scenario. If they can be mobilized, the expertise and resources required to develop scenario documents are likely to be available within institutions. As the Committee of Vice-Chancellors and Principals in the UK has argued: "Forty-five universities, each making its own informed interpretation of national needs, may well, between them, arrive at several valid versions of the best long-term pattern of research and training while the inevitable mistakes will not be on the grand scale of government miscalculations" (1980). Institutions have to decide whether to develop their own scenarios – would it be worthwhile? If they do not there is a danger that excessive weight will be given to historical data and inadequate consideration to the changing needs of society when making selective priority decisions.

Furthermore, if policy makers cannot be convinced that institutions are willing to respond to the needs of society they are likely to opt for a more interventionist approach towards higher education; there are clear signs that many governments are developing more explicit approaches which further threaten institutional autonomy.

An initiative taken at Loughborough University demonstrates the potential value of scenario analysis as a first stage in institutional self-evaluation and self-renewal. The School of Human and Environmental Studies established a Working Party, under the author's chairmanship, to consider the trends in society which are likely to make an impact upon higher education in the 1980s and 1990s and to examine the impact of these trends on the work of the School in the future. Inevitable time constraints prevented the Working Party exploring in as great a depth as it would have wished all the issues involved in a consideration of likely future trends. Given the time constraints, the Working Party adopted the following approach:

1. A comprehensive list of issues and trends was drawn up after discussions within the Working Party and consultation with colleagues in Departments with expertise in particular areas. A number of short papers relating to specific issues (eg: the impact of microprocessors) were prepared by some members of the Working Party.
2. An analysis of issues and trends identified six major broad trends: technological, demographic, environmental, social, political/economic and educational. The implications of these six broad trends, and the complexities of their inter-relationships were considered in detail.
3. Departments were asked to respond to this analysis by indicating the relevance of their *current* activities to the likely trends and their implications, and to make suggestions for *new* initiatives at both Departmental and School level.

The Working Party's Report has provided a valuable input into the evaluation of the School's current teaching and research programmes and helped in identifying opportunities for new initiatives in the future.

Certainly a consideration of the trends in society which are likely to impact upon higher education highlights the need for institutions to recognize that they must plan not only for declining numbers but also for the need for *resource mobility* on the one hand and for research in anticipation of new course demands, research and consultancy opportunities, and services to the community on the other. It may also be necessary to meet the needs of new groups of participants and new patterns of attendance may be required to meet individual needs. *Therefore should the performance of an institution be assessed in terms of its responsiveness to these changing needs of society and appropriate performance indicators be developed to measure an institution's progress in developing and implementing its strategy for resource mobility and responding to these changing needs?*

PORTFOLIO ANALYSIS

One starting point in the process of responding to changing demands is to analyse an institution's historical and current performance. If such an analysis is combined with a continuous examination of the future environment to identify society's needs, it should initiate a consideration of whether the institution should market existing courses and research facilities more effectively in existing markets; consolidate others; withdraw certain courses from the market; market existing courses and research and physical facilities in new markets; develop new courses and research facilities for existing markets; and/or develop new courses and research facilities for new markets. Such an exercise would ultimately lead the management of the institution to identify its critical resources, and to ask which is the appropriate strategy, given its current and anticipated future resources; it should stimulate institutional self-evaluation.

Thinking along similar lines, Doyle and Lynch (1979) of the University of Bradford Management Centre, have applied the *product portfolio concepts* developed by the Boston Consulting Group to the analysis of a university's competitive position. They have modified the Boston Consulting Group's planning matrix (Figure 1) (*market size* in their matrix for *market growth rate* in the Boston matrix) to distinguish between four types of courses:

'Props' (what the Boston Consulting Group call 'cash cows'). A prop is a strong course in a weak area. These are programmes in which the university has a large market share of a small market. Doyle and Lynch consider such courses are good for the university's reputation, but there are limited opportunities for expansion without a sharp decline in entry standards.

'Dogs'. These courses are in small areas nationally and the university does not even get its share of those applying. It is suggested that such courses are not a good use for the university's small resources and consideration should be given to phasing them out in the long run.

'Problem areas' (what the Boston Consulting Group describe as 'question marks'). These degree areas are strong nationally, but the university's own courses are relatively unattractive to applicants. The general problem is a weak reputation in an attractive area for expansion. Doyle and Lynch suggest often the problem is caused by a university proliferating its courses too widely and not concentrating in areas of greatest opportunity. If these courses are to be successful, they suggest the university must give them a major investment priority to build up staff, research and support services. If, however, it has many courses in this quadrant there is almost certainly a case for rationalization.

Figure 1   **UNIVERSITY COURSE PORTFOLIO**

MARKET SIZE

	Big	Small
Big	STAR	PROP
Small	PROBLEM AREA	DOG

MARKET SHARE

'Stars'. These are the university's strongest courses: in areas attracting a large number of applicants and where it has a strong reputation. Doyle and Lynch consider, in general, the university should give the highest priority to supporting the strength and reputation of departments offering these courses, and they should attract a disproportionate share of new resources.

Doyle and Lynch argue that the model offers university administrators a tool to assist in assessing demand implications and testing the viability of alternative strategic priorities. Of course, they would accept that an analysis of an institution's current course portfolio is only a starting point in determining future strategies. Not only is it necessary to forecast future market growth rates to determine whether, for example, 'today's props' will become 'tomorrow's dogs', but also to assess the institution's critical resources to determine whether these can be employed to develop 'star' positions in emerging areas. By substituting *market size* in their matrix for *market growth rate* in the Boston matrix, Doyle and Lynch *do not differentiate between high growth, low growth and declining markets*. Their model is attractive in that it relates courses to markets, but it is a *static* one. Resources tend to attach to subject areas not courses, and by concentrating on subject areas, account can also be taken of research, scholarship and community service. Therefore, in assessing a university's performance potential, do we need to compare a university's *strengths* in various subject areas relative to other institutions with the *future attractiveness* of subject areas so as to identify priority areas for future growth, consolidation and rationalization? Such an analysis might provide a starting point for internal discussions on the institution's long-term strategy for resource mobility.

The directional policy matrices employed by companies including the American General Electric Company and the Shell Group have been adapted for this purpose (Figure 2). Individual universities and external financing bodies will define "university strengths in the subject area" in different ways. A technological university may view its role differently from a long-established civic university. Thus additions and changes might be made to the list of factors for assessing university strengths in the subject area and subject area attractiveness: eg: service to the community, dependence on overseas students, service teaching to other subject areas, etc.

The matrix could be developed at a number of levels: nationally by governmental and external financing bodies, regionally by groups of institutions, and also by individual institutions. Presumably those governments that have regulated the size and type of overall intake by imposing formalized admission policies and criteria, consider they have the resources and expertise to undertake the evaluations incorporated in the matrix and so justify increased *dirigisme* in terms of societal needs. Should collaborative approaches to rationalization be welcomed by governments and external financing bodies and be seen by institutions as an alternative to increased *dirigisme?* In the United Kingdom the Committee of Vice-Chancellors and Principals (1980) has recognized "... the need to face more boldly the prospect of inter-institutional arrangements designed to promote some rationalization". In some countries institutions may well have to decide whether to compete or co-operate at the regional level.

As the Swedes have recognized in their institutional self-evaluation activity (Furumark, 1979), decentralized structures under conditions of financial stringency and possible contraction require institutions to critically study and evaluate themselves. Furthermore the absence in the UK of many of the features of the US university system, ie: the close interface with the political decision-making process, the role of laymen in university government and the management of higher education, the strength of local community links and the existence of well-recognized mechanisms for peer review, means that UK universities have to find *internal solutions to retrenchment,* ie: self-evaluation (Shattock, 1979). Similarly, peer review is hardly ever used in Sweden

Figure 2   UNIVERSITY POLICY DIRECTIONAL MATRIX

SUBJECT AREA ATTRACTIVENESS factors:

Market Size
Market Growth Rate
Market Diversity
Competitive Structure
Cost Structure
Optimal Department Size

Demographic Trends
Scientific Importance
Technological Trends
Social / Political and Economic Trends
Environmental Trends
Government Attitudes
Employment Prospects
etc.

UNIVERSITY STRENGTHS IN THE SUBJECT AREA factors:

Size of Department
Market Share
Market Position
Number of Applications
Quality of Student Intake
Graduate Employment
Cost per FTE Student
Reputation
Quality and Age of Staff
Research Record
Research Capability
Image
Publications Record
Resources : Availability and Mobility
etc.

UNIVERSITY STRENGTHS IN THE SUBJECT AREA \ SUBJECT AREA ATTRACTIVENESS	HIGH	MEDIUM	LOW
HIGH	Growth	Selective Growth or Consolidation	Consolidation
MEDIUM	Selective Growth or Consolidation	Consolidation	Planned Withdrawal and Redeployment
LOW	Consolidation or Planned Withdrawal and Redeployment	Planned Withdrawal and Redeployment	Planned Withdrawal and Redeployment

(Furumark, 1979). In other OECD countries there is a need to find internal solutions to retrenchment if institutional autonomy is to be preserved or at least not eroded further. The evaluation of subject areas by the university is a first stage in this evaluation, employing the criteria incorporated into the policy directional matrix or similar criteria.

The matrix (Figure 2) provides a starting point from which managerial judgements can be made and for discussions on regional rationalization. The decision makers in the institution need to systematically evaluate the *trade-offs* between strong and weak areas, and the administrators and academics should provide the framework and information base for this evaluation. For example, the approach of the Working Party at Loughborough, described earlier, provided a basis for evaluating subject area attractiveness beyond the static approach of the vertical axis of the policy directional matrix and the Doyle-Lynch model, and also identified a number of opportunities for new initiatives.

The *growth, consolidation* and *withdrawal and redeployment* strategies in the boxes of the matrix are examples. Institutions may not wish to withdraw from all low strength, low attractiveness subject areas, but they should recognize the dangers and costs of not doing so. There is the obvious danger of increased government intervention if institutions are not prepared to put their own houses in order, or if they are not willing to co-operate regionally. A serious risk is that under conditions of stagnation or contraction the university will not be able to support existing developments and new developments in *emerging areas* which have high future attractiveness. *Emerging areas* can be supported out of incremental funds during periods of expansion, but not under conditions of stagnation or decline. Higgledy-piggledy expansion may have been acceptable in the past, but higgledy-piggledy stagnation or decline may not lead an institution to recognize the need to redeploy resources from low strength, low attractiveness areas into emerging and existing growth areas. Thus, should institutions identify emerging growth areas as part of their study of the future needs of society, evaluate the skills and resources required to develop in these areas, and examine the extent to which the institution currently possesses or is able to acquire these skills and resources? To successfully enter these *emerging growth* areas it may be necessary to cross traditional departmental and school boundaries. It will also be recognized that existing subject areas which fall into the *growth* and *consolidation* categories should evaluate their teaching and research programmes to ensure that they remain relevant to the present and future needs of society. Self-evaluation and self-renewal also need to be encouraged in these areas.

The strategy that emerges from this evaluation of institutions' subject areas would distinguish between *existing and emerging growth* areas, *consolidation* areas, and *withdrawal and redeployment* areas. The agreed strategy would need to be translated into a detailed action plan including key result areas. Measures to assess *progress* towards implementing the strategy, particularly in these key result areas, would flow from the plan. Thus, the Swedish National Board of Universities and Colleges considers:

"Every activity evaluation project should, we think, result in an action-oriented, preferably long-range plan for future activities, including indications of alternative ways to realize the desired changes." (Furumark, 1979).

The strategic planning approach advocated here and elsewhere should enable institutions to develop a set of alternative strategies and operating plans including strategies for *long-term resource mobility*. As changes in the external environment occur the range of strategies can be narrowed down and the appropriate strategy and operating plan implemented. Under conditions of financial stringency and uncertainty, institutions may need to complement their long-term strategy for resource mobility with a short-term strategy for financial emergencies and a medium-term strategy for financial mobility. The application of these concepts to colleges and universities will be discussed by Dickmeyer (1980) in his contributed Conference paper. The existence of computer based financial planning models will facilitate the preparation and updating of such strategies. Such models do not dismiss the uncertainty surrounding university planning but assist in understanding the nature of the uncertainty. They allow administrators to test the sensitivity of the plans to variations in key variables, to evaluate trade-offs and test tactical decisions, to revise plans quickly when variations in key variables do take place, and to identify key future performance indicators relating to the primary planning variables.

Hopefully, the existence of parallel plans for short-term financial emergencies and medium-term financial mobility will ensure not only an appropriate *speed of response* to a rapidly changing external environment which is compatible with the strategy for long-term resource mobility, but also increased *flexibility* in planning. It will help to ensure an appropriate balance is obtained between the pressure to increase cost efficiency in the short-term and actions needed to be taken if the organisation is to be effective in the long-term.

"MANAGERS OF CHANGE"

Debates in United Kingdom universities in response to a University Grants Committee planning exercise based on three possible levels of funding for a University for the quadrennium 1980/81 to 1983/84: modest growth, no change, and modest decline, have highlighted the need to employ consensus building techniques and to avoid conflicts arising between the objectives, aspirations and self-perceptions of departments, schools, and other faculty groups and the objectives of the institution. At the same time acceptance has to be obtained of the need for stronger central direction of the university than heads of departments and faculty have grown accustomed to. They have also highlighted the difficulties involved in consensus building, and the behavioural problems underlying institutional self-evaluation and self-renewal. Sadly, under today's conditions institutional acceptability and consensus building can easily evaporate in the "back-alley ways of bureaucratic politics".

It is in this context that the question is frequently posed:

> Can you manage change and achieve resource mobility during a period when institutions are likely to be more concerned with coping with the pressures of revised student numbers and lower provision per FTE? In other words, will the senior academics and administrators, the managers of change, in institutions of higher education be so concerned with today's problems that they will not give adequate consideration, and make appropriate plans, to cope with tomorrow's problems, particularly when many of these managers of change may have retired before the 1990s?

Richard Cyert (1977), the distinguished organisational theorist and President of Carnegie-Mellon, has emphasized that the trick of managing the contracting organisation is to break the vicious circle which tends to lead to disintegration of the organisation, and that the management must develop counter forces which will allow the organisation to maintain viability.

Furthermore, it is important to recognize that although there are parallels with earlier periods of low growth in institutions, in many OECD countries significant changes have taken place in the status and attitudes of university lecturers. They feel there has been a significant lowering of their status in society and they have been badly treated by governments. They may face higher teaching loads at a time when their career opportunities have diminished significantly. Not only may they have less time for research, but, if there are few promotional prospects, they may well not feel motivated to undertake research of the type needed to cope with the dynamic changes in society anticipated (assuming research grants are available), and the unions that represent them may not accept, though they may recognize, the need for resource mobility and for lecturers' own retraining and redeployment. Thus, is the real danger of contraction that individuals who by nature desire excellence will begin to settle for mediocrity out of frustration (Cyert, 1978)?

Like Cyert, Sizer has argued elsewhere (1979b and c) that there is a need to appoint high quality managers of appropriate academic standing, when the opportunities arise, who can overcome institutional inertia. These managers should not only be able to plan and control efficiently the allocation of resources to see their institutions through the short-term financial pressures, but also be able to motivate people to recognize the need for long-term change, and secure their participation in its planning and subsequent implementation. By gaining acceptance for phased withdrawal from some subject areas, they need to turn fixed costs into variable costs so as to release resources to finance new faculty and new initiatives in existing and emerging growth areas which are consistent with the institution's long-term objectives. They will recognize that innovations in response to new needs and new opportunities are frequently created through the initiative of individuals. If they are to break the vicious circle that leads to disintegration, they have to create an environment which motivates individuals and fosters rather than frustrates such initiatives.

To support these managers of change, governments will have to accept that it will be necessary to develop an appropriate "incentive structure" which will facilitate and not inhibit change; for example, more resources for staff retraining and development, generous early retirement schemes, etc.

However, while Cyert (1977) considers management "... is our major hope for the future" he also recognizes that "... academics resist being managed by expert managers and seek to have an academic in the top management position. Only rarely will this approach lead to an excellent manager." (Cyert, 1978) It may be for this reason that an anonymous Registrar of a British university (*The Times Higher Education Supplement,* 1979), has expressed the view that British universities find themselves without the apparatus for that efficient and effective deployment and management of scarce resources. He considers they are

"... hung up still on the medieval and almost superstitious fear of management within universities which leaves the resource allocation processes in many of them hardly able to stand comparison with an unsophisticated game of bingo."

The IMHE Programme has made a significant contribution to breaking down this fear of management.

A recent American research study (Hills and Mahoney, 1978) suggests that university budgeting in the United States may be characterized by adherence to arbitrary rules and historical precedents and by the maintenance of stable relationships between sub-units. A bureaucratic, or universalistic, criterion, relative workload, was influential in a period of abundant resources. It may be that during periods of scarcity of resources there will be greater competition for resources and questioning of arbitrary rules and historical precedents, but this may be resisted because of its potential disruptive effects upon sub-unit relationships. Do the decision makers within institutions ask themselves whether their resource allocation formulae are compatible with their long-term objectives and strategies? Could their resource allocation processes be dysfunctional in this respect? Do the committees that take decisions about vacant posts take account of long-term strategies for resource mobility or simply concentrate on historical relative workload?

In an interesting critique of the Planning System employed at the University of Aston in Birmingham, presented to the IMHE Seminar on Institutional Planning held in Zurich in September 1979, Houghton, Mackie and Pietrowski (1979) highlighted the limitations of relative workload criteria of resource allocation under conditions of stagnation, financial stringency and changing needs. They emphasized that a quantitative system, based largely on immediate past practice and the outcome of the previous year, can only function effectively in an expanding situation. In a steady state or reducing situation, such as that now facing the university, Aston's system allows little room for manœuvre since there are no firmly established priorities in the university's plan. The matching of academic planning desires with the financial resources available can only be achieved by cutting across the spectrum equally. Thus Houghton et al conclude that "The academic plan becomes a race in which everyone wins a prize but no one gets the gold medal". Michael Shattock (1981) has examined how the end of university expansion and increasing financial stringency have affected the way universities in the United Kingdom have allocated their resources, in particular the internal changes that are taking place in systems and committee structures and the new managerial responses which have been invoked.

Over-emphasis by external financing bodies on *process performance indicators* that measure short-term effectiveness and efficiency at the expense of *progress measures* might result in incentive situations which are not consistent with the institution's long-term goals and objectives, towards which the managers of change are striving. This is not to say that short-term cost efficiency is not important and process performance indicators are not relevant. It is a question of balancing short-term cost efficiency with long-term effectiveness. Certainly resource allocation processes compatible with the institution's strategy to achieve long-term goals and objectives may be inconsistent with the achievement of improved short-term cost efficiency.

SUMMARY AND CONCLUSIONS

This paper has examined the changing nature of performance assessment in the responsive university under conditions of changing needs of society, particularly during periods of contraction and under conditions of financial stringency. It has been argued that during such periods high quality managers of appropriate academic standing should be motivating their institutions to strive to become effective in the long-term through attempts

- to examine systematically the future environment in which it will be operating and to identify threats and opportunities;
- to understand and communicate the implications of this future environment to the institution's constituencies;
- to evaluate the institution's current subject area portfolio and critical resources;
- to agree through consensus building techniques the goals and objectives for the institution and its constituent parts, and the *measures for monitoring progress* towards achieving these goals and objectives;
- to develop
    a) a set of alternative long-term strategies and operating plans including a strategy for long-term resource mobility;
    b) a strategy for medium-term financial mobility and short-term emergencies;
    c) resource allocation procedures consistent with the institution's long-term objectives; and

d) a short-term planning and control system based on measurable information and performance indicators, backed up by a nationally organised
scheme for inter-institutional comparisons.

To achieve positive motivation institutions of higher education are having to
recognize that faculty and administrators at all levels should participate in all aspects of
performance assessment, hence the growing interest in institutional self-evaluation and
self-renewal.

A case has been made for the appointment of high quality managers when
opportunities arise who can build consensus within institutions and overcome the
behavioural problems surrounding institutional self-evaluation. It will be recognized
that there are at least three alternative models: ie: the dominating, dictatorial
vice-chancellor or rector; the high quality manager of conflict; and the 'dirigiste'
government department or central body. Not only are these alternatives likely to be
incompatible with the democratic nature of institutions, but they may create more
behavioural problems than they solve and are unlikely to maintain institutional vitality
and cohesiveness.

March 1982 Vol. 6 No. 1

REFERENCES

Committee of Vice-Chancellors and Principals (1980). Memorandum to the UK Government's Select
Committee on Education, Science and the Arts, 1st February.

Cyert, Richard (1977). "Academic Progress and Stable Resources". A lecture given at NCHEMS, Denver,
Colorado, November 7, p. 17.

Cyert, Richard (1978). "The Management of Universities of Constant or Decreasing Size". *Public
Administration Review,* July/August.

Dickmeyer, N. (1980). "Balancing Risks and Resources: Financial Strategies for Colleges and Universities". A paper presented to the Fifth IMHE General Conference, Paris, 8th-10th September.

Doyle, Peter and Lynch, James E. (1979). "A Strategic Model for University Planning". *Journal of the
Operational Research Society,* 30.7:603-609.

Furumark, A.M. (1979). *Activity Evaluation in Higher Education – A Swedish Project.* Stockholm, Sweden:
R & D Division of the National Board of Universities and Colleges.

Hecquet, I. and Jadot, J. (1978). *The Impact on University Management of Financing and Control Systems
for Higher Education.* Summary Report of a Joint Project of the IMHE Programme (OECD/CERI)
and Association des Universités partiellement ou entièrement de langue française (AUPELF). Paris:
IMHE/CERI/OECD.

Hills, F.A. and Mahoney, T.A. (1978). "University Budgets and Organisation Decision Making". *Administrative Science Quarterly,* 23: 454-465.

Houghton, K.N., Mackie, D. and Pietrowski, C. (1979). "The University of Aston in Birmingham". A
case study presented to the Seventh IMHE Professional Seminar, Zurich, 10th-12th September.

Jadot, Jean (1981). "Survey of the State-of-the-Art and Likely Future Trends of University Management in
Europe – A Summary Report". *International Journal of Institutional Management in Higher Education,* 5.1: 49-71.

Jochimsen, R. (1979). "Managing Universities in the Eighties: Introductory Remark". *International
Journal of Institutional Management in Higher Education,* 3.1: 5-10.

Shattock, M.L. (1979). "Retrenchment in US Higher Education: Some Reflections on the Resilience of the
US and UK University Systems". *Education Policy Bulletin,* 7.2. Institute for Post-Compulsory
Education, University of Lancaster.

Shattock, M.L. (1981). "University Resource Allocation Procedures: Responses to Change". *International Journal of Institutional Management in Higher Education,* 5.3: 199-205.

Sizer, John (1979a). "Assessing Institutional Performance: An Overview". *International Journal of Institutional Management in Higher Education,* 3.1: 49-75.

Sizer, John (1979b). "Performance Indicators for Institutions of Higher Education under Conditions of Financial Stringency, Contraction and Changing Needs". A keynote address to the Annual Conference of the Society for Research into Higher Education, Brigthon Polytechnic, 19th-20th December.

Sizer, John (1979c). "Performance Assessment and the Management of Universities for the 1990s". A paper presented to the Conference of University Administrators Annual Conference, Edinburgth, 5th-7th April.

The Times Higher Education Supplement (1979). The Registrar of a Northern University, "British Universities: What Next?", 28th December.

Le Comité National d'Evaluation:
An Innovation in French Higher Education

André Staropoli
Le Comité National d'Evaluation
France

ABSTRACT

*The creation of the Comité National d'Evaluation des Universités
in May 1985 is an "innovation of the greatest consequence" in
French higher education. Chaired by Laurent Schwartz, Fields
Mathematics Medal, its fifteen members are all eminent people
and include nine "representatives of the scientific community".
In this article, the Committee's Secretary-General explains its
objectives, organisation and methods of work. It has some novel
features, notably its national coverage, its permanent character
and its freedom to decide which institutions to evaluate, what
special commissions to set up and who should receive its reports.
Other features it shares with its counterparts in a number of
countries, as is consistent with the requirements of the
international scientific community. The Committee has already
begun its first evaluations and has on the whole been well accepted
by the French universities.*

AN ORIGINAL IDEA

On 10th May 1985, the President of the Republic formally inaugurated the Comité National d'Evaluation. It was his intention, in doing so, to mark the importance of this new body, which he himself called an "innovation of the greatest consequence".

The Comité National d'Evaluation occupies a unique position among French institutions: attached to the Ministry for Education, but reporting direct to the President of the Republic, it is left free to choose the universities it will evaluate; it is also free to make its conclusions public.

The Committee's mandate is in itself an innovation. Any evaluation is a tricky undertaking which raises many complex and sensitive problems; that of a university is especially difficult. That is probably why no real evaluation has ever been carried out in France as it has in many other countries.

The Comité National d'Evaluation has no regulatory powers; it has no part to play in central government; it is not concerned with monitoring management. But it does issue authoritative value judgments on the quality of research and education, and on the way in which the university fulfils its assignment. While it may reasonably be expected that its verdict will be followed by effects, it is for the Minister for Education and his department to decide what those effects shall be.

The President of the Republic made this quite plain when he said: "I trust that the Committee's report will have positive effects; in arriving at the decisions incumbent upon them, the relevant authorities will have to take account of the opinions it contains".

Lastly, the relationship to be established between the Comité National d'Evaluation and the universities must bring about a change of mentality. For evaluation is justified and possible only if it embodies three principles:

- Peer judgment, the oldest and most fundamental of the university's attributions and rights. In this regard, the composition of the committee guarantees its competence, prestige and experience.
- The independence of the universities must entail real responsibility; evaluation itself is only the necessary complement of that responsibility. But the Committee, for its part, must fully appreciate the constraint placed on the university and the intrinsic responsibility of the supervisory authorities.
- Higher education must be of excellent quality; some degree of emulation guarantees that quality. Public service cannot, of course, be reduced to the provision of certain services, and this applies particularly to the university, which provides education and awards diplomas according to criteria set by itself and plays its part in research and training activities. But citizens are entitled to know the value of their institutions (their strengths and weaknesses), and how they operate; this is now taken for granted and demanded.

OBJECTIVES OF EVALUATION

A point of detail first: French higher education has always been extraordinarily complex, and this is compounded by the question of research (largely fundamental research, which in many countries is carried out in the universities). In France, however, the institutional system is different. Research is partly attached to university structures and premises and partly separate, with its own administrative, management and evaluation structures.

At the same time, alongside the universities there are the schools of engineering or commerce; while some of these depend on the Ministry for Education, others are placed under the authority of one or more other Ministries – Industry, Defence, Agriculture, Public Works, etc.

The Comité National d'Evaluation does not confine its investigations solely to the universities and the research laboratories they house, which often depend on major research institutions, notably the CNRS (Centre National de la Recherche Scientifique) and the INSERM (Institut National de la Santé et de la Recherche Médicale). It is responsible for all public scientific, cultural and professional institutions (a new appellation written into the legislation on higher education). The Decree of 21st February 1985 stipulates that here "the agreement of the Minister concerned shall then be requested by the Minister for Education; any Minister may also request the Committee to evaluate the activities of higher education institutions for which he (or she) is responsible".

Evaluation itself concerns "all the activities and means deployed by institutions in the context of their scientific and educational policy. The Committee gives its opinion on the results of the contracts (covering several years) concluded with the Ministry for Education. It reviews doctoral education and procedures for authorising research. It considers the performance of co-operative programmes conducted jointly with outside partners; in particular, it evaluates the operation of public interest associations and offshoots...".

The Committee's recommendations aim "to put university operation on the right lines".

A key question is raised, especially in academic circles, by the creation of the Committee: under cover of the name "evaluation" is it not in fact a special inspectorate that is being set up – in other words, a central government agency to monitor the implementation of the regulations?

On this point the reply is unequivocal. By its composition, structure, form of organisation and work, the Committee is quite different from an inspectorate. There is no question of it somehow duplicating either the Inspection Générale des Finances, the Cour des Comptes (Audit Office) or the Ministry for Education's General Inspectorate.

Neither will the Committee do the job of central government departments or evaluate the work of individuals, the latter task being the prerogative of the Conseil Scientifique des Universités.

ORGANISATION OF THE COMMITTEE

The Comité National d'Evaluation has to give an opinion on the general operation of the system overall and of its parts, in this case the "components" of a university, i.e. training and research units, departments, institutes, etc.

Evaluation of an institution must therefore be based on evaluation of its components. To this end, after consulting the President of the university and obtaining his consent and that of his principal Councils, the Committee will appoint two or three experts to examine each component in situ and to report back to it direct.

These assignments will be carefully prepared; the experts must have access not only to the information held by central government departments, but also to the reports and opinions of major research institutions. Additional information will, in particular, be provided by the university itself and the heads of the component units, less in the form of replies to adminstrative questionnaires or detailed statistics than by making available existing documents and the information necessary to a clear understanding of how the main departments or laboratories are run.

For the evaluation itself must cover every facet of university life, starting with research and education, through continuing education and training, the students' situation, their origins, the courses they are following and their future career, social life on the campus and management, to relations with the outside world – in short, policy in all its aspects, with its aims and constraints, ambitions and obstacles, so as to be able to gauge its strengths and weaknesses.

The Committee is a permanent body, and each of its members will devote a by no means inconsiderable part of his or her time to its work. This is another new departure; all in all, the Committee members will be working for it half-time.

To help it perform its two fundamental tasks of research and processing available information and to look after logistics and organise assignments, the Committee has its own secretariat and budget, provided by the Minister for Education.

Under its Secretary-General, this team comprises three field officers for each major scientific discipline – social sciences and humanities, exact sciences and biomedical sciences; a financial director; and a liaison officer responsible for the information system which is to link the Committee with its principal partners – the central office of the Ministry for Education, other ministerial departments, the main research agencies, consultancy bureaux and centres and, of course, the higher education institutions themselves.

Secretarial tasks proper, logistic support, organisation, external relations and publication of reports, will be the task of a small staff directly responsible to the Committee.

The Committee can also call on part-time consultants, notably in areas of science for which it does not itself have sufficient expertise.

THE COMMITTEE AND ITS FUTURE

It is hardly possible as yet to describe in any detail the evaluation methods which the Comité National d'Evaluation intends to use, and much too soon to say whether it will be able to carry out its assignments successfully.

Nevertheless, five months after its official inauguration, the Committee is already operational. It has its own premises, a small team and a budget, and is busy working out the methodology it will apply.

The backing it has received, from the President of the Republic down – from the Prime Minister, the Minister for Education, the Secretary of State attached to the Minister for Education, responsible for the Universities, and the Secretary of State attached to the Minister for Economic Affairs and the Budget, as well as from the Director-General of Higher Education and Research and from top civil servants, has enabled it to acquire the means of independent action.

It has been given support by the Minister for Research and Technology, and effective help by the Directors-General of the CEA (Commissariat à l'Energie Atomique), the CNRS and the INSERM.

The Committee has on the whole been well accepted in the world of higher education and research and, most importantly, by the university Presidents themselves. Significantly, more than a dozen institutions have already applied to be evaluated, some of them being dependent on departments other than the Ministry for Education.

Any criticisms have stemmed either from scepticism or from the fear that, contrary to the spirit and letter of its mission, the Committee may attempt to judge individuals or be over-dependent on the administrative authorities.

The Committee has endeavoured right from the start to set itself a number of ethical rules as to its relations with institutions and with central government, the choice of experts, the principles of evaluation and the preservation of university custom. It has been able here to draw on experience abroad, notably in the United Kingdom and the major American universities, but also on a whole range of other interesting experience.

The Committee has already drawn up a programme and a work schedule – ambitious, certainly, but still reasonable – and three evaluations were undertaken in 1985.

The Committee also intends to consider a number of major transversal – not to say national – problems for which an appropriate procedure (examination, commission, considered opinion) will be established. It has been approached several times on certain serious issues that are currently worrying the world of higher education and research. Some in essential aspects of university life are hard hit by financial restraint and public opinion is now becoming much more demanding of higher education, prompting often grossly exaggerated criticism.

The Comité National d'Evaluation will therefore have to prove its determination and its independent thinking. It is in this respect, above all, that it must live up to the expectations its creation has aroused.

July 1986, Vol. 10 No. 2

Academic Program Review and the Determination of University Priorities

Frederick E. Balderston[1]
University of California, Berkeley
United States

INTRODUCTION

The broad aims that universities serve — chiefly, original scholarship and the education and certification of young people for major responsibilities — require universities to be organized internally according to academic expertise (the basic disciplines and the major professions); to protect academic freedom and autonomy as indispensable to learning; and to enforce high standards of performance upon their members, both students and faculty. These standards of performance reflect conceptions of academic quality that prevail in a nation and in the wider world of advanced scholarship in each field.

In most of Europe, nearly all of the support for the universities' operating budget comes from the national government, most of it in the main budget approved by the Ministry of Education and Science. In the public universities of West Germany and the United States, the state government provides a basic academic budget, but this is supplemented by substantial Federal funding of research projects and, in varying degrees in different states, by income from student tuition and fees. The great American private universities, not having budgetary support from state governments, rely on their income from private endowments and gifts and also on tuition income and Federal research money. Whatever the mix of sources, society does not make available to any university enough resources for it to do everything that every academic group or individual professor might want. Howard Bowen has pointed out that the cost of education in any institution rises to whatever level of resources is made available (Bowen, 1982).

Selective priority in the allocation of resources within a university is difficult in the historic internal pattern of autonomous or semi-atonomous academic administration of schools, departments, or faculties; but selective priority is necessary, given a limited budget, if a university is to obtain the most worthwhile results.

Salary levels, staffing patterns, and other costs vary widely between universities in different countries (and also between fields within the same university) but the general shape of the relationship between costs and results is pretty well agreed: in a given academic field, the quality that is achieved (both in teaching and research), the volume of activity, and the efficiency with which resources can be employed, are all related, and there is a threshold of minimum scale of the program for both quality and efficiency. Teaching and research are conducted together, especially at the more advanced levels, and while there exist strong complementaries between the two, there are also trade-offs. Given the subtlety of the relationships, it is often difficult to infer what specific impact a change in resources will produce; often, budgets are adjusted in accordance with changes in the number of students, using historically-derived budgetary standards: the quality of academic operations is an unknown variable.

In the countries of Western Europe and in the United States and Canada, demographic trends in the number of those reaching college-going age will cause enrollment declines, of varying severity and with some difference of timing, for the next decade or more. These, together with a quite general climate of fiscal constraint in the Western democracies, will make it necessary for universities to concentrate on reallocations and efficiency gains as the main method of financing changes and improvements during the next decade. The "zero-sum" university, like the zero-sum society, is not an altogether happy prospect: only with workable compromises will it be reasonably harmonious.

In this context, good decision-making on resource allocations according to a scheme of selective priority needs: first, a good data-base, including strong and credible evidence of the importance of academic programs (to the university and to society) and the quality of these programs; second, a basis for judging how effectively these programs are using the resources already available to them; and, finally, a mechanism for arriving at wise choices and implementing them successfully.

In some instances, the allocation decisions are made within the individual institution from a fixed pool of resources already available to it; then the problem is to determine which programs or activities should be more heavily supported (or cut least) and which should be reduced significantly or even eliminated. In other instances, the allocation problem is a broader one — over a whole multi-campus university system, such as the nine-campus University of California or the system of thirteen Dutch universities. Then, there exist two alternative approaches: to reduce budgets of some campuses differentially more than others: or, to look across the system at discipline areas or broad program categories, in order to identify the weak units in those disciplines that may be candidates for consolidation or elimination. Whether the allocation problem is for an individual institution or for a system, the twin considerations of quality and efficiency form the basis of intelligent management of the problem of allocation. Thus, judgements of the quality of academic programs are needed.

Two experiences of evaluation of academic programs are discussed below to illustrate different approaches. These are: the recent assessment of research-doctorate programs in the U.S., conducted by a consortium of four national academic organizations; and the experience of the University of California with program reviews, 1981-84.

THE U.S. NATIONAL ASSESSMENT

The Conference Board of Associated Research Councils, composed of the National Research Council, the American Council of Learned Societies, the American Council on Education, and the Social Science Research Council, undertook a thorough-going quality assessment of doctoral programs, and the results were published in a five-volume publication: An Assessment of Research-Doctorate Programs in the United States (Washington, D.C.: The National Academy Press, 1982).

A distinguished committee of academic scientists and humanists, chaired by Lyle V. Jones, designed and executed the study, and several large foundation grants provided the financing for it.

The assessment covered 28 academic disciplines and four fields of engineering. It focused entirely on graduate (doctoral) education. The committee decided to omit some academic fields, because it did not have staff resources to cover every possible specialty. It also had to resolve numerous problems of classification of academic programs within the boundaries of the disciplines.

The committee asked each university that was known to conduct doctoral education to identify each academic program within the 32 categories, to indicate whether that program had produced at least five recent doctorates (if not, it was considered too small to be rated at all), and to provide several types of institutional information as to each academic program. (A given university might have two or more distinct and separate doctoral programs within the same discipline; in fact, this occurred with surprising frequency, especially in certain of the biological sciences). Every university having one or more academic programs in a given discipline was listed for rating.

The committee developed a careful methodology. It defined a total of sixteen quality indicators or measures. Thirteen of these were objectivistic in nature, with data sources from the respondent universities or from national data-banks (for example, number of faculty in the program; number of published articles). Three of the measures were secured by means of elaborate surveys of the judgments of peer-evaluators in each discipline. These measures were: the judgment of faculty quality; the judgment of the program's effectiveness for graduate study; and the judgment of the extent of improvement in the program within the past few years.

The committee and its professional staff took elaborate precautions in conducting the survey for each discipline. Each peer-evaluator was requested to provide rating judgments of only a limited number of programs, to minimize biases from evaluator fatigue: evaluators were asked to supply information about their own graduate education so as to check for possible "sentimentality" bias; and evaluators were given the option of not rating a given program if they did not feel that they knew enough about it. The committee sought to assure that it received a substantial number of peer evaluations for every program.

The committee reduced each of the main survey ratings to a standardized measure with a mean of 50 and a standard deviation of 10, so that the reader could quickly identify how far up in the distribution for that variable a given program was found to be. In the publication, the committee showed the complete distribution on each key measure as well as the value of that measure and relative rank for each university. Some fields had many more programs than others — the "smallest" fields, such as art history, had about 100 programs of sufficient size to be rated; the largest, such as chemistry, had about 300 programs.

Besides discussing its methodology with commendable thoroughness, the committee provided some comparisons between the new ratings of faculty quality and the ratings of an earlier, less comprehensive survey. The first big survey of the quality of doctoral programs, in 1966, was sponsored by the American Council on Education and conducted under the leadership of the well-known labor economist Alan Cartter, then Vice-President of ACE. A few years later, ACE repeated the survey and published the 'Roose-Andersen ratings'. These were the ones used for comparison with the 1982 survey. In general, there was fairly high correlation between the ratings that programs received in 1982 and those they had received more than a decade earlier: but there were also numerous individual instances of significant gain or loss of reputation for faculty quality. Critics of reputational ratings had long deplored the possible unfairness of ratings based on general impressions about a given university program; and they had pointed to the possible damage that undeservedly low ratings might inflict on a program whose faculty leaders were working hard to do a good job. The committee conceded the limitations of human judgments at the base of its survey data, but it disclosed fully its efforts to avoid superficiality and bias.

The committee also took a stand against combining the sixteen indicators into a single, overall measure of academic quality. It felt that while it could publish the individual measures, it could not arrive at a scheme of weights for these measures so that they could be combined together in a manner with which the academic profession would agree. Thus, it is left to the individual reader of the publication to deal with this problem in whatever way seems appropriate to the occasion.

This quality assessment is clearly the most thorough and reliable yet conducted for U.S. doctoral education. It cannot be ignored by university faculties and presidents, for it contains invaluable clues to the strengths and weaknesses of each institution. The assessment also provides the prospective doctoral student with information about quality that can assist in the selection of a doctoral program in his or her chosen discipline.

At the time, the assessment does not tell a university what should be done. For example, if there is a low rating for a given discipline at a particular university, and if this is confirmed by other evidence that the president and faculty can assemble, should that university:

— Invest resources heavily in the weak program to improve it, or
— Prepare to phase it out or consolidate it with other programs, as a lost cause ?

The assessments do not say which course of action ought to be taken; that is the proper business of the institution and those concerned with its welfare. (There is a third possibility, namely, that the university could simply go on as before, ignoring the evidence of a weak program. While this may happen, it ought not to happen, in the broad interest of academia and of society.)

PROGRAM REVIEW IN THE UNIVERSITY OF CALIFORNIA

The University of California, founded in 1868 as the land-grant university of the state of California, now has nine campuses and approximately 140 000 students. Its Board of Regents and President are responsible for overall policies and for negotiations with the state government concerning the basic academic budget. Besides this state support, the university receives substantial Federal support for research through project grants to faculty members on the various campuses. It also has private endowments and receives annual gifts that provide helpful supplementary support. Student tuition is treated by the state of California as an offset to the state budget appropriation, but other student fees support a wide range of student services.

A scheme of decentralized administration confers wide authority upon each campus chancellor and his administration. Through its instrumentality, the Academic Senate, the faculty shares internal governance of the university in all significant academic matters: appointment and promotion of faculty; approval of courses and curricula; and the setting of standards of admission and the requirements for university degrees.

In the early 1970s, the central administration of the university initiated a small number of cross-campus program reviews, by appointing panels of members to undertake studies of program areas (e.g., the schools of education and programs of teacher training on many of the campuses). The campus chancellors were not in favor of this cross-campus approach because it interfered with decentralization. The academic Senate was not brought into the process, and it too was unhappy with the arrangements for the activity. For a number of years, cross-campus program reviews were not undertaken, but significant budget cuts from the state government in the late 1970s prompted the President and the Academic Senate to establish a new procedure for joint sponsorship of cross-campus program reviews. A Program Review Steering Committee, consisting of the chairpersons of the important standing committees of the university-wide Academic Senate, plus the Vice-President for Academic Affairs, had the tasks of receiving requests for cross-campus program reviews, writing the specific definition of the assignment for a program review panel, and designing the general composition of the panel (in particular, the number of academicians from outside the university as against those inside). The office of the Vice-President for Academic Affairs then solicited nominations for the panel from the campus chancellors and the Academic Senate, and then he appointed the panel and provided technical staff support to it. When the panel finished its work and filed its report, the Program Review Steering Committee determined whether the report satisfied the original charge to the review panel. Then, the report was circulated to the campus administrations and to the Academic Senate for critical review. As a final step, the Vice President issued a statement summarizing actions and recommendations on the basis of the report and its findings.

The procedure made both the Administration and the Academic Senate responsible for the undertaking. That this approach was agreed to at all was testimony to the forebodings of the Administration and the faculty leadership that very hard choices would soon be unavoidable. Universitywide program review had to be seen in the accompanying context of potentially severe budget cuts and of the possible necessity of program eliminations and reductions and the possible dismissal of long-service administrative staff and ladder-rank faculty. In fact, in parallel with the discussions concerning program reviews, President Saxon called attention to needs for a policy on programmatic displacement of faculty and on phase-out and consolidation of academic programs.

On December 9, 1981, Academic Vice-President Frazer requested, on behalf of the Universitywide Academic Planning and Program Review Board, that the President and the Academic Senate appoint the Program Review Steering Committee that was called for in the policy statement, so that a series of Universitywide program reviews could be started as soon as possible. This committee commenced work in 1982. The first review focussed upon Engineering, with special reference to the question of whether programs and enrollments in that area should be expanded. The panel's report, issued in July 1982, received widespread comment over a period of months from administrators, Academic Senate committees and faculty groups in engineering throughout the University. Vice-President Frazer wrote to the Chancellors and the Chairman of the Academic Council on March 7, 1983 to indicate final disposition of several of the review panel's action recommendations.

Subsequently, review panels were instituted and completed work on reviews of Law (August 1982, with a supplement later), Foreign Languages (January 1983) and Humanities (February 1983). A review of schools and programs in Education was still under way as of May 1984.

The Humanities review panel was designed to utilize as a prime part of its information base the humanities portions of the campus graduate enrollment plans that were, at the time, under submission. That review and certain others, however, were not able to obtain and use the academic program review documents that existed on most of the campuses. The divisions of the Academic Senate and the campus administrations expressed justifiable concern about the violation of confidentiality in connection with judgmental information about individual faculty or faculty groups that might be in these documents, or about the release to any other body of academic assessments that had been solicited from experts under promises of confidentiality. The Program Review Steering Committee proposed in its 1982-83 annual report to the Systemwide Administration and the Academic Senate that, to avoid breaches of confidentiality, each campus provide to the designated review panel a summary of the available academic review reports that had been prepared on that campus in the academic area in question. As a practical matter, however, the difficult work of preparing such summaries and the reluctance of campus Senates and administrations to come forth with assessment information made it quite problematical to rely on campus-level program review reports as a basis for universitywide efforts.

In the course of this experience, the Academic Vice-President and the Steering Committee were asked on numerous occasions why a particular academic area was "singled out" for review and whether it was anticipated that, in due course, most or all academic areas would be reviewed. The response was that areas had been selected for review when significant questions of academic and budgetary priority were felt to be impending, but that, in principle, no academic discipline or field of professional education should be considered exempt from assessment, either because reductions and consolidations might become necessary or because expansion to additional campuses might be proposed.

The procedural complexities of finding and appointing review panels to undertake these reviews, and the strain on very limited staff resources in the Systemwide Administration, imposed severe limits in any case on the number of reviews that could be done. Even if reviews were undertaken according to broad designations of the areas to be reviewed ("engineering", "foreign languages", "humanities"), it became unrealistic to expect that the broad span of academic programs in the University of California would ever be fully covered. In fact, the pace of these reviews slowed appreciably, so that only one new program review (that for Education) was begun during 1983-84.

That such a deliberate and tentative rate of activity is not always necessary is indicated by the manner in which rapid and searching review took place when the 1981-82 health sciences and professions budget had to be cut by several percentage points. The Health Sciences Subcommittee of the Academic Planning and Program Review Board, and the cognizant campus administrations, worked with the Systemwide Administration to sort out priorities across the health sciences over a period of months rather than years. It is true that the size of the cut was small enough to permit absorption without raising the spectre of major program eliminations; but it *was* an absolute reduction, and it was very painful to face. Perhaps the higher degree of cohesion among the health sciences and professions, and the urgency of the budget adjustment, had something to do with the relative success of this very difficult effort.

Several committees of the Universitywide Academic Senate called for a "stock-taking" of the experience with program reviews. Vice-President Frazer and the Academic Planning and Program Review Board agreed that an assessment of the successes and failures of these efforts would be desirable. Vice-President Frazer's office produced a draft report in September 1983. Numerous comments on the draft were received. Clearly, this limited experience was in any case a minor subplot in the much larger drama of University budgeting and University internal and external politics.

VARYING VIEWS OF THE NEEDED REACH OF
UNIVERSITYWIDE PROGRAM REVIEWS

One view, probably more widely held among campus administrators and faculty members than any other, is that Universitywide program reviews are a dangerous nuisance: a nuisance because they require some tending with nominations of names and cooperation in supplying data, and potentially dangerous if they actually arrive at implementable and implemented conclusions.

A second view holds that program reviews in areas of discretionary development of academic programs — in particular, the establishment of professional-degree programs and professional schools and colleges — may indeed be necessary, for decisions about these must go forward to the State. However, program reviews of the academic disciplines that are typically within the span of Letters and Sciences should not be undertaken. Why not? Because all of the basic academic disciplines must in any event be present on a university campus:

they reinforce each other and interact with each other. If it be argued that a given·field is too small or at present too weak to mount a satisfactory doctoral program, this cannot be a reason for cutting off that discipline and consigning its faculty members in a permanent way to the oblivion of purely undergraduate teaching.

A third view of Universitywide program reviews is that, if they are to be undertaken as a basis for significant priority determinations, *all disciplines and professions* should expect to be included in a reasonable expeditious cycle of review. This view, in contrast to the one previously stated, holds that there are possibilities for adjustment and consolidation in many basic disciplines as well as for review of professional-degree programs and schools. In any case, it is argued, there would be a faulty view of the possibilities for retrenchment if some areas are intensively examined and others (either by exemption or for lack of time and energy) are never examined at all.

The large scale on which program reviews would have to be conducted, if this view were to prevail, does deserve comment. The recent nationwide *Assessment of Research-Doctorate Programs in the United States,* sponsored by the Conference Board of Associated Research Councils and published by the National Academy Press in 1982, covered 28 major academic disciplines and four subdivisions of engineering. If one were to add eight more areas of the graduate professions and perhaps eight additional, less sizable "letters and science" disciplines, the total would be 48 reviews. Perhaps the number could be reduced by grouping disciplines together; but, in any event, the range of the number of reviews to be undertaken would likely be between 30 and 50. At a rate of six per year (more than were previously completed in the highest year of activity in recent experience), 30 reviews would need five years of time and work.

Here are a few general conclusions about the experience:

1.   At each campus, the administration and the Academic Senate had on-going responsibility for monitoring the quality of academic programs. The campuses were reluctant to share their detailed information about quality of programs with the office of the Vice-President for Academic Affairs in the central administration or with cross-campus review panels, partly because this information was collected under conditions of confidentiality, and partly because it would have been potentially threatening to the campus to do so. The Program Review Steering Committee proposed that the campus administration and Academic Senate prepare summaries, omitting confidential information about individuals, but the impasse over information was not resolved. Cross-campus review panels had to go over the same ground that had often been covered at the campus level.

2.   Announcement that a cross-campus review in a particular field was to be conducted tended to raise the level of anxiety. Faculty leaders and Academic Senate committees raised questions about the 'singling out' of just a few fields for review. There were two possible responses. First, it would have been possible for the Program Review Steering Committee to set up a plan for reviewing all the major disciplines and professions over a period of years. However, with the procedures that were required to be used, and with the limitations of staff support, no more than five or six reviews per year could have been managed. Thus, it would have taken at least six or eight years to complete a cycle. A second alternative was to point out that a review would be undertaken in a particular field only if there was a policy issue of some urgency facing the university as a whole; for example, the university faced pressure in 1982 to expand the number of student places in its engineering programs, and this issue led to the cross-campus review of engineering. During the 1981-84 experience, these reviews continued to occur in response to fairly

immediate policy pressures. Thus, the process as it was conducted could not have
led to a systematic accumulation of evaluative judgments about program quality
throughout the university, so that all fields could be compared in a selective
priority scheme.

3.   The campuses were of varying size and stages of development. Berkeley and Los
     Angeles had already reached their planned enrollment ceilings. Their academic
     departments in the disciplines had reached critical mass in size, and these depart-
     ments were, for the most part, strong in accumulated reputation. Both of these
     campuses also had a good representation of professional schools. By contrast, the
     newer and smaller campuses of the university had started a build-up in the early
     1960s but had been forced to slow down before completing their development.
     In any case, it takes time to build up a reputation for high quality in a given field.
     If severe retrenchment were to be forced through big budget cuts, and if it were
     based on the comparative ranking of academic programs, there was fear that
     excessive weight of retrenchment might fall on the smaller campuses.

4.   In January, 1984, the Governor of California announced a budget that provided a
     very welcome improvement in the support given to the university. A great sense of
     relief swept over the university. Very soon after the proposed new budget for
     1984-85 was announced, the Chairman of the Academic Senate called on the
     President to abandon plans for final adoption of the retrenchment policy directives
     on program eliminations and faculty lay-off that had been under discussion. It
     was apparent that in the absence of an immediate fiscal threat, there was little
     stomach for pursuing these difficult and painful questions.

5.   In contrast with all this, the university did carry through, in a few months during
     1981, an extensive review of the medical schools and other health science programs
     in order to achieve a one-year, three-percent reduction of their budgets. This was
     done by a special committee of faculty and administrators which worked inten-
     sively with the campus administrations.

Journalistic accounts of the 1982 ratings tended to concentrate heavily on Measure #08,
the peer ratings of faculty quality. In his report to The Regents of the University, however,
Vice-President William Frazer discussed both this measure and the extent of improvement in
program quality, noting that numerous programs on the smaller campuses had high marks on
the latter measure. A composite index for each of the 32 fields has also been prepared within
the University. This gives equal and significant weights to the faculty quality measure and to
a peer judgment of program effectiveness in graduate education, and it also gives some weight
to the program improvement rating. On this composite index, a total of 108 University of
California doctoral programs were equivalent to the composite index rating of those programs
in the top 20 nationwide, and 69 programs were not within that cutoff value.

These program numbers do reflect some problems of defining the boundaries of each
discipline and determining what are separate individual doctoral programs. The universities
themselves reported data on what they regarded as separate programs. A given university
campus may have more than one identifiable doctoral program in the same field or discipline;
in an extreme example, the Davis campus had three programs in botany (Berkeley also had
three).

In the continuing struggle to maintain and enhance academic quality, Vice-President
Frazer pointed out that the nine campuses of the University of California were, as a group,
by far the strongest system in the United States. The younger and smaller campuses suffered
the inherent biases of such rating schemes in favor of program age and large program size, but
even so the younger and smaller campuses had appreciable numbers of programs of high standing.

Yet there remains the difficulty that many doctoral programs in the University are not now of high nationwide standing, even on the indications of the composite index, which is somewhat more generous to smaller programs.

The 1982 assessment could serve as a starting point for a new effort to focus upon selective strategies for improvement of the quality of the University. To be effective, such an effort would need to consider ways of strengthening the capabilities of the University as a whole. Each individual campus, acting on its own, would not be likely to succeed in coping with the implications of a serious new address to the problem of academic excellence.

THE ALTERNATIVE ACADEMIC DESIGNS
OF THE UNIVERSITY OF CALIFORNIA

Each newly-established campus of the University has engaged in a struggle for its own self-definition and its autonomy. The Los Angeles campus began as "the southern branch" of the University, and its rise to eminence took 50 years. The scars of this fierce effort, which each new campus has repeated as it was initiated, have tended to condition the institutional attitudes of administrators and faculty members. The development of effective decentralization in most areas of university administration through the policies adopted in the 1960s and 1970s has been a victory for good sense and a vindication of the need for each campus to have a significant measure of control over its academic operations.

There has never been a serious proposal, however, to take the argument of autonomy to its logical conclusion and declare the institutional independence of each University campus. Large and difficult constitutional and political steps would be required for such a change. The political leadership of California has, if anything, gradually moved in the opposite direction, toward stronger integrated control of higher education through increased reliance upon the California Postsecondary Education Commission. Within the University, even the most zealous advocates of campus autonomy do not press for a breakup of the University.

Thus, the issue is how to cope with the operation of one, multi-campus University system. The Academic Senate addressed this issue with considerable care in the report of its Special Committee on Long-range Educational Objectives and Planning. This report, to the University-wide Academic Assembly in May 1975, discussed a number of possibilities for strengthening academic quality throughout the University. Among these were: greater emphasis on inter-campus cooperation to mobilize academic strengths; promotion of faculty contacts and mutual understanding through periodic conferences within each discipline; and the adoption of a more specific and specialized academic mission for each campus, so that it could concentrate on achieving the highest academic performance in its selected areas of graduate education and research. It was proposed that each campus identify a cluster of related fields, and that the University as a whole be organized to maximize these quality clusters and to promote inter-campus co-operation wherever that would strengthen academic operations.

The Report received sober consideration by the Academic Assembly, and its recommendations were for the most part adopted or referred for further study; few were rejected out of hand. What has happened since?

President David Saxon took office in July 1975. The underlying tendencies toward campus autonomy were, step-by-step, reinforced. Saxon and his staff in the Systemwide Administration were punctilious in consulting the Academic Council and other instrumentalities of the Academic Senate. At the same time, the Council of Chancellors became a more and more significant internal decision-making forum of the University. Until the severe budgetary strains of the late 1970s brought home the possible need for significant program reductions on budgetary grounds, the Saxon administration sought to avoid, as much as possible, interventions in the campus conduct of academic activities.

Earlier and modest efforts toward institution-building on a Universitywide basis, such as the All-University Faculty Conferences that Clark Kerr had initiated, were abandoned. At the same time, reliance on the chancellors for their judgments tended to produce the "7 to 2" syndrome, whereby Berkeley and Los Angeles as the large comprehensive campuses saw the University's interest in one way and the other campuses saw it in another.

President Saxon repeatedly emphasized his intention of protecting the high academic quality of Berkeley and Los Angeles in the face of severe budgetary difficulties, but the fact that most of the non-health science budget was allocated to these two campuses gave the other campuses incentives to look for ways whereby to avoid disproportionate impact of budget cuts on their own campus budgets. An outcome of the evolutionary developments during the Saxon administration is that the chancellors at Los Angeles and Berkeley joined with their chancellorial colleagues in advocating the barest minimum of Presidential attention to academic program priorities. As to resource-allocation policies, the chancellors have appeared to unite on the idea that the closer the University can come to administration by formula, the better — provided that the formula is reasonably generous to the interests of the campus that the chancellor in question is obligated to defend.

The present concept of academic organization of the multi-campus University of California first developed in a conscious way when Clark Kerr undertook three enormously significant tasks. First, he promoted the formulation of the California Master Plan for Higher Education, which anchored the University's role through the differentiation of functions between the University and the other segments of public higher education. Second, seeing the huge expected growth of higher education enrollments, he negotiated for the establishment of University campuses (Irvine, Riverside, San Diego and Santa Cruz) and the broadening and enhancement of Davis and Santa Barbara. Third, his administration contemplated only two major subdivisions of the University academic budget: "health sciences", and "general campus". Each new campus was intended to be distinctive in style, but each was mandated to aspire to become a comprehensive university in the course of time. At the time, President Kerr's administration included a group of university deans for oversight of developmental possibilities, and his administration asserted academic priorities in many ways. But steps toward greater campus autonomy, initiated during Kerr's administration in order to provide the authority for more effective management of the stressful campuses during the 1960s, continued thereafter. The Systemwide Administration's capability for administering resources according to academic priorities became atrophied. What remained as to concepts of academic organization for the younger campuses was the idea of the "general campus" — a hunting license toward comprehensiveness, inhibited by resource limitations and by externally-imposed requirements for approval of new degrees and new schools or colleges. A more effective, selective approach would call for a campus and the Systemwide Administration to arrive at well-defined agreement for a profile of related areas of doctoral programs, professional degree programs, and advanced research; this would provide the campus with a surer future basis upon which to claim priorities for support. Self-assessments and careful negotiation with the Systemwide Administration, and incorporation of its commitments in its academic plans, would enable a campus to focus its energies. Universitywide program reviews might be of modest assistance in the stages of this process.

CONCLUDING OBSERVATIONS

Quality assessments across universities can be undertaken, and they can be undertaken in a systematic and responsible fashion, as the recent effort in the United States demonstrates. For some purposes, such as the planning of an internal reorganization and strengthening of a faculty or school over a period of time, much more than a general judgment is needed, for the planning of faculty recruitment for specialities needed and the shaping of the distinctive focus of the program require detailed study and evaluation. Thus there is not a need for judgments of academic quality, but a whole series of possible needs that depend on the decisions to be made.

Strange to say, however, some of the most significant determinations of budgetary priorities have been accomplished under the spur of urgency and without as much systematic evidence about the quality of academic programs as one might think was essential. Academic program review appears to have a secondary role in a much larger drama of adjustment in universities' resources and resource priorities. (For an account of the "10 percent cut" in the Dutch universities, see Acherman (1984).)

Deeper in the foundations of academic life is the question of what "quality" is: how a sense of striving for intellectual achievement is built up, and how it translates into the standards of performance that are applied to students and to the selection and advancement of their mentors, the professors of the university. At their best, these standards embody a respect for competence in depth and for originality, and they demand that the scholar demonstrate appropriate achievement at each level of development: from student to junior research contributor to senior professor. This sense of the obligation to achieve (and the excitement of achieving) is more fundamental to the vitality of academic life than all the budget schemes, the regulations, and the formal apparatus. One interesting aspect of it is that, across the boundaries of nations and individual cultures, serious scholars in a field can quickly recognize each other and share common enthusiasms. Some aspects of this attitude of striving for excellence are drawn, no doubt, from the attitudes and interests of surrounding society. But wherever they can, the leaders in a university need to nurture these values and standards, for they are at the heart of academic quality.

Several basic tensions nearly always exist in the context of priority-setting in universities. There is inevitable tension between institutional autonomy on the one hand, and the pressures toward economy and efficiency of the larger system of education for the society. Universities are important places, and they are a locus for the critical thinking that a society needs but often finds uncomfortable, so there is tension between the political establishment and the free engagement with ideas that a university stands for. Because government is an important patron (often, indeed, the sole patron) of the university, government can use its financial power in ways that universities fear as an intrusion into their own areas of necessary discretion in decision-making; there are inevitable battles between contemporary universities and the governmental agencies that allocate funds to them and set the conditions for expenditure of these funds. Within each university, there are tensions between old disciplines and new areas of study, and between "growth" fields and those fields that are, for one reason or another, facing loss of popularity with students or decline in budgetary support for other reasons. Finally, the social responsiveness of the university (to changes of enrollment interests of students and changes of needs for university research and services as expressed by the surrounding society) stands in tension with the self-directing efforts of the academy for the long-term — that is, for the preservation and enhancement of scientific knowledge and of the culture.

Universities face real difficulties in finding courses of action that mediate between these tensions. Their members make strong claims for individuality, and this often results in what

James March described as an "organized anarchy" rather than a system of tight control. But universities prosper when they have the full confidence of the surrounding society as effective contributors to its long-term welfare. The trouble is that even the definitions of "quality" and "efficiency" are difficult to agree on in philosophical terms and still more difficult to translate into practical guides for action. In this sense, quality and efficiency are little miracles when they happen in universities; but they are miracles worth trying for.

November 1985 Vol. 9 N° 3

NOTES AND REFERENCES

1.   In September 1984 The Netherlands Institute for Advanced Study at Wassenaar held an international symposium on problems of University management. This paper is a revision of a lecture presented to that symposium. The author is indebted to NIAS for partial support of this work, but he alone is responsible for the content.

Acherman, Hans A. (1984). "Termination of degree and research programs". *International Journal of Institutional Management in Higher Education,* 8:1, 67-78.

Balderston, Fred. "Academic excellence in the University of California, 1980-1995: Program reviews and campus missions". Berkeley, CA, unpublished.

Bowen, Howard R. (1980). *The Costs of Higher Education: How Much do Colleges at Universities Spend Per Student and How Much Should They Spend?* San Francisco: Jossey-Bass.

Conference Board of Associated Research Councils. (1980). *An Assessment of Research-Doctorate Programs in the United States.* Washington, D.C.: National Academy Press, 5 volumes.

In't Veld, R.J. Lecture, "Annual Report 1981-82" Wassenaar, The Netherlands: Netherlands Institute for Advanced Study, 81-95.

Peer Review and Partnership:
Changing Patterns of Validation in the Public
Sector of Higher Education in the United Kingdom

John Brennan
Council for National Academic Awards
United Kingdom

ABSTRACT

*This paper describes the external system of course validation in
the non-university sector of British higher education. It is a system
under review as institutions seek greater autonomy and the state
seeks greater control and more effective quality assurance. The
implications of the changes in the system currently proposed are
explored with reference to relationships within institutions and the
balance of power between academic networks and institutional
hierarchies.*

INTRODUCTION:
UK HIGHER EDUCATION OUTSIDE THE UNIVERSITIES

There are more students enrolled in the United Kingdom outside the universities than
there are within them. Not all are studying at the level of the bachelor's degree but even on this
restricted definition of higher education 42 per cent of full-time students take their degrees in
the so-called public sector institutions. There are substantial numbers of students taking
higher degrees including doctorates and, at all academic levels, a high proportion of part-time
students.

The public sector of higher education consists of over 150 institutions, most of them
owned by the local education authorities (LEAs). The LEAs are responsible for state
provision of education at all levels, excepting the universities. Most of the other colleges in the
public sector are church-owned. Although there are 152 institutions with some kind of stake in
higher education, the bulk of the provision is concentrated in 30 English and Welsh
polytechnics, a small number of major Scottish institutions, and around 10 other English
colleges. Only the polytechnics and the equivalent Scottish colleges are large broadly-based
institutions comparable in size to universities.

Almost all of the major institutions in the public sector have experience of degree level
work which stretches back over two decades. Although the polytechnics were not designated

as such until the late 1960s and early 1970s, all of them were formed from established colleges, many of which already possessed reputations for degree level work in certain fields. Since the 1970s the polytechnics and other colleges have expanded considerably and today cover almost the whole range of subject provision, including the humanities and social sciences as well as technological subjects.

One of the most important differences between the university and non-university sectors of higher education lies in the locus of responsibility for the maintenance of academic standards. Authority to award degrees is vested in each university through the grant of a Royal Charter. No public sector institution possesses a charter and the courses which they offer lead to qualifications awarded by external bodies. At degree level, 89 per cent of awards are made by the Council for National Academic Awards (CNAA), which is the only non-university institution to possess a Royal Charter for this purpose. The remaining 11 per cent of degree awards are made by universities, several of which have developed close ties with smaller local colleges, particularly those concerned with teacher education. Courses below degree level lead to awards of professional bodies or the Business and Technician Education Council (BTEC).

There are plenty of precedents in higher education, particularly during periods of rapid expansion, for new institutions to serve periods of tutelage to other more experienced institutions. The latter award the qualifications and take ultimate responsibility for academic standards. The present system of external validation in the public sector is unique because *a)* it is nationally organised, and *b)* it seems unlikely to disappear or develop to permit the kind of academic autonomy enjoyed by the universities. However, the system is under criticism. These take two main but to some extent contradictory forms. One is that it is unnecessary because the major public sector institutions are now sufficiently experienced to take full responsibility for their own academic standards. The other main criticism is that external validation is ineffective in maintaining standards, that the quality of some courses is unacceptably low. The first criticism comes chiefly from the institutions themselves, particularly their managements, and the second, often in coded form, from government ministers. Coupled with both criticisms is a view that external validation as practised by the *CNAA* is bureaucratic and costly of resources.

In April 1984, the Secretary of State for Education and Science, Sir Keith Joseph, announced the setting up of a Committee of Enquiry into Academic Validation in Public Sector Higher Education. The Committee, chaired by Sir Norman Lindop, formerly Director of the Hatfield Polytechnic, reported in April 1985. The establishment of the Committee followed a period of protracted conflict between the Minister and the *CNAA* about the academic standards of a sociology degree course at one of the London polytechnics. The Minister had received evidence to suggest that the course was ideologically biased and that standards were low. The *CNAA* validators had given the course a favourable report and the *CNAA* could not be persuaded that punitive action was required. The result was the Enquiry, the broad remit of which was to

> "identify and examine key issues for the effective and efficient maintenance and improvement of academic standards in the way those responsible for the academic validation of first and higher degree level courses in the public sector in Great Britain discharge their responsibilities, having regard to the validation arrangements of sub-degree higher education courses in the public sector, and distinguishing as necessary between different branches of learning, and to recommend changes as appropriate". (Lindop Report, p. 1)

Although the origins of the Committee of Enquiry lay in a concern over academic standards, it provided the opportunity for the advocates of greater institutional autonomy to put forward a more broadly-based critique of the *CNAA* validation system. Before looking at the Committee's report and the debate which has surrounded it, it is necessary to describe the main characteristics of *CNAA* validation.

CNAA validation is a system of peer group evaluation carried out by faculty drawn from universities, polytechnics and colleges. The faculty form a substructure of committees and boards within the *CNAA* which are responsible for the approval and the continued maintenance of standards of courses in the different subject fields. Institutions submit documented proposals for new courses to the appropriate committee or board which makes an initial quality appraisal. If the appraisal is positive, a visit to the polytechnic or college by a sub-group of members of the board takes place. The visit is the occasion for discussion with and appraisal of the faculty group which devised the course. Once a course is approved, it may operate with little interference from *CNAA* except for periodic review which takes a simplified form of the initial approval procedures. *CNAA* is not involved in the examining of students although it does have ultimate responsibility for the appointment of external examiners. These appointments invariably confirm recommendations made by the institutions themselves. The role of the external examiner is to moderate marks awarded by the internal examiners and to ensure the comparability of standards. It is a system also found in UK universities. The framework for the external validation of courses has survived without fundamental change since the establishment of the *CNAA* in 1964. It is a system in which it has been comparatively difficult to start a new course (only about 50 per cent are approved at the first attempt) but it has only rarely caused the closure of an established course.

EXTERNAL VALIDATION AND THE ATTITUDES OF FACULTY

Faculty members operate in at least two work arenas. One is the institutional setting provided by the employing university or college. The other is the academic network of faculty working in the same subject field. The latter stretches far beyond the individual college and forms an 'invisible college' which, according to Halsey and Trow in their study of British academics, is the more important reference point for the majority of faculty. Loyalty is to the subject and academic status is defined primarily in terms of a person's standing in the subject network. The focus of the subject network is research activity. It is the recipient and evaluator of the academic production of faculty members. The institutional arena is more concerned with academic reproduction, with teaching and the design and delivery of courses. Inevitably success and rewards in one arena frequently have pay-off in the other. Thus, promotion within the institution is often gained as a result of prestige acquired in the subject network. Appointment to a prestigious institution may enhance status within the subject network. The significance of the *CNAA* system of external validation has been to involve the external academic network of subject peers in course-related matters and, moreover, to give it great power within the institutions.

The work of faculty as teachers and administrators is the subject of peer group evaluation by *CNAA* subject boards. As a consequence, the work is less privatised and more collaborative and has entered into the institutional system of rewards and incentives to a much greater extent than in the universities. Individual faculty have been able to deliver to their institutions not only publications and research grants but validated courses and *CNAA* praise.

Academic work outside the universities has traditionally been subject to a variety of external and institutional controls. In most cases the LEAs are the employing bodies and sometimes they have taken on particularly active roles in the management and day-to-day operation of institutions. Lines of managerial control and principles of accountability have been given greater emphasis than in the universities. The institutions themselves operate in a complex system of governmental and quasi-governmental controls. In the early days of its operation *CNAA* subject boards were regarded by faculty as powerful allies against a range of non-academic, and sometimes apparently anti-academic, forces within the institutions. For example, *CNAA* could be relied upon to demand that appropriately qualified staff and other resources were provided to mount new courses, that teaching hours for faculty were set at levels that were comparable to those found in universities. *CNAA* could be a considerable nuisance to institutional managements. But partly as a result of pressures from *CNAA*, institutions in the public sector gradually became more collegiate in organisation and power shifted from managements towards the academic boards of institutions. With the support of *CNAA*, institutions gained greater freedom from the maintaining LEAs.

In recognition of this trend and in response to pressures from institutions for greater autonomy, *CNAA* announced in 1979 a policy of 'Partnership in Validation'. The essence of this policy was that validation should take greater account of the institutional context of courses, the strengths and weaknesses of institutional structures and their bearing on an institution's capacity to take greater responsibility for maintaining standards. The policy was meant to be a recognition that *CNAA*'s concerns about quality and standards were fully shared by the institutions themselves. Thus, a policy of 'partnership' was proposed. What the policy failed to take properly into account was the disjunction of the institutional and the subject peer group arenas and the divided loyalties of faculty members. Partnership was meant to give greater powers to the institutions, not necessarily to the faculty within them. It represented a shift in control away from the external peer group represented by the *CNAA* subject boards to the institutional arena.

One near universal effect of the Partnership policy was the growth of internal systems of course monitoring and validation. This was partly a result of *CNAA* promises that more effective internal evaluation would lead to a reduction in external requirements. The promises were not always delivered. The subject-based boards of *CNAA* were not impressed by the results of the internal procedures for monitoring and validation. Although these made use of faculty from outside the institutions, they were institutionally based and managed. The focus of internal validation tended to be on the organisational characteristics of courses rather than the intellectual content of the curriculum which was less accessible to faculty from outside the subject.

'Partnership in Validation' brought additional validation. Often complex and time-consuming internal procedures were added to an already extensive apparatus of external control. The contrast with the universities was great. Without any form of external control other than the external examiner system, internal procedures for the approval of courses were simpler and much less onerous than those found in the public sector. Insofar as the referent for academic standards was university courses, the polytechnics and colleges became increasingly reluctant to accept the costs in time and resources and the status implications of dependence on external authority.

THE LINDOP REPORT

The Lindop Committee, with a membership drawn heavily from the universities, concluded that the system of external validation in the public sector was unnecessarily complex and time-consuming. It found that standards were generally high, but considered that the effort devoted to monitoring and maintaining them was so great as to be counter-productive. The resources consumed by validation could be used more effectively and more directly to enhance the quality of academic work. It was also felt that a lessening of external controls would assist in raising institutional and faculty self-confidence. The Lindop Committee was of the view that the most effective guarantor of academic standards was 'the academic strength and responsibility of staff' coupled with a system of external examinerships as practised by the universities. However, the recommendations of the Committee were less clear-cut than its conclusions.

The Committee envisaged a scaling-down of the *CNAA* but not its abolition. Its recommendations attempted to give everyone what they wanted. Institutions which wanted university-style autonomy should be eligible for it. Institutions which were content with the present system could remain with it. Options between the two extremes were to be available:

"There should be a range of different forms of validation available, including external validation of individual courses and groups of courses, accreditation of institutions and possibly of subject areas, and complete self-validation. It would be for each institution to apply for that form of validation which it considered would best meet its particular needs." (Lindop Report, p. 81/2)

The designation of an institution as entitled to award its own degrees would be determined by the Secretary of State by whom the designation would be reviewed from time to time.

Although critical of *CNAA* validation, the Lindop Committee expressed its support for the principle of external peer review which underpinned it. In the debates which have followed, commitment to external peer review has been near universal. What has differed has been the interpretation placed upon the concept and the conditions regarded as necessary for its effectiveness. Government decision on the implementation of Lindop's recommendations is still awaited, but already major changes are being set in hand to transform the *CNAA* system of validation. The chosen model is one of accreditation where the principle of Partnership in Validation is given radical extension to bring together internal and external validation and to put both under the operational controls of the polytechnics and colleges.

THE CNAA RESPONSE TO LINDOP: AN ACCREDITATION MODEL

Accreditation of institutions by the *CNAA* would involve the delegation to institutions of the power of course approval and the authorisation of institutions to confer degrees and other awards in their own name. Such changes would require modification to the Charter and Statutes of the *CNAA*, but even without this, *CNAA* has decided to negotiate validation agreements with the major institutions in the public sector which would give them a measure of 'de facto' autonomy equivalent to that sought through accreditation.

The accreditation model would transfer the powers presently held by *CNAA*'s committees and subject boards to the academic boards of the institutions. The procedures for course validation and monitoring established by the academic boards would be the mechanisms through which the new powers would be exercised. An element of externality would be maintained through the presence in internal validation of faculty external to the institution, possibly though not necessarily members of *CNAA* subject boards.

Changes currently under consideration are more concerned with the locus of authority for validation than the processes through which authority is exercised. Internal validation is based very heavily on *CNAA* methods and procedures. Faculty members prepare an account of the operation of a course and the validating group, internal or external, subjects that account to critical scrutiny. The onus is on the course team to demonstrate the success of their course. The validators must look for evidence of failure.

The public sector institutions of higher education in the United Kingdom continue to place great emphasis on the collective maintenance of academic standards. Standards are not to be taken for granted, and it is the academic peer group through which evaluation is achieved. There is a movement away from an exclusive use of external faculty drawn from the academic network of the subject group to the involvement of faculty from within the institutions but who are outside the subject network. The shift of validation authority from subject to institutional arena inevitably involves some change of focus. Intellectual concerns tend to give way to operational concerns. This is not necessarily a disadvantage as the student experience of a course is often affected most directly by operational matters. The most important requirements are that validation is seen to be both competent and neutral. There is a danger that internal validation will fail in these respects. Faculty members may be reluctant to accept judgements on their academic work from people outside of their subject network and may suspect that such judgements are influenced by internal rivalries. The presence of external subject specialists in the validating group can provide some reassurance although their role can easily become ambiguous. Are they there primarily to subject the work of their peers to critical scrutiny or to protect them from institutional attack?

THE FUTURE

Despite its reservations about the *CNAA* system of validation, the Lindop Committee found that it was valued by large numbers of faculty across many institutions. The opportunity to discuss academic work with colleagues engaged in similar work elsewhere and to do so in a systematic and public manner with a focus on course design and pedagogy as well as on research and subject development was widely regarded as useful and worth preserving. How far these characteristics will be maintained in the new forms of validation is not yet clear.

The Lindop Committee emphasised that the quality of public sector higher education was high. Whatever contribution external validation had made to this quality in the past, the Committee was not persuaded that the maintenance of academic quality in the future required the continuation of external controls. Standards were maintained within the universities without such elaborate machinery. The imposition of such machinery on large and experienced institutions within the public sector could easily be regarded as withholding recognition of status and achievement. The aspirations of institutions for autonomy were understandable and not easily resisted. Higher education no longer needed academic policemen who only looked at one half of the higher education community.

In the longer term, the maintenance of external peer group review of academic work as practised by the *CNAA* is likely to depend on the success and completeness with which the powers of the *CNAA* can be transferred to institutions. So long as participation in external peer review can be interpreted as a denial of respect and status, it will be resisted whatever its benefits. If critical appraisal of academic work before those who are knowledgeable and appreciative of such work has value, it has value for all who are involved in higher education, irrespective of status or institutional location. The future of academic validation in public sector higher education in the United Kingdom will in the long run be determined by its future in the universities.

July 1986 Vol. 10 No. 2

REFERENCES

HMSO (1985). *The Report of the Committee of Enquiry into the Academic Validation of Degree Courses in Public Sector Higher Education* (The Lindop Report).

Halsey, A.H. and Trow, M. (1971). *The British Academics*, Faber.

CNAA (1979). *The Development of Partnership in Validation.*

A Ten Year Perspective on Faculty Evaluation

Richard I. Miller
Ohio University
United States

ABSTRACT

This article reviews the use of faculty evaluation in the USA over the ten year period from 1974-84, with these positive changes noted: (1) Significant increase in its use; (2) broader data base is evident; (3) functional "systems" are emerging; (4) survey instruments are better, and (5) court cases have improved the quality of faculty evaluation.
In the next ten years, these directions are expected: (1) Better and more equitable faculty evaluation systems will be developed; (2) faculty evaluation will become more rigorous; (3) more sophisticated, computerized systems will become evident; (4) more flexibility and individualization in faculty evaluations will be made; and (5) more faculty evaluation decisions will be made in the context of institutional, college, and department priorities than in the past.

Ten years ago, the United States was fresh from the memory of the tragic student shootings at Kent State University. During the 1965-1970 period of student riots and protests and for several subsequent years, state legislators reacted in many states by cutting budgets, passing punitive legislation, and insisting that state governing or coordinating bodies take a sterner hand in campus management.

In 1974 the United States was in the throes of a strong recession that particularly affected the private colleges. The recession meant fewer students, less money for collegiate operations, and need for fewer academic personnel; therefore, assessing teaching effectiveness became more important as a means of making more equitable decisions about retention, promotion, and tenure.

The 1974-1984 period in the United States saw double-digit inflation, economic slowdowns, and worsening economic pressures on our colleges and universities. But most of our institutions of higher education were coping through the generous use of creative frugality. Recent evidence (1984) from research by the National Center for Higher Education Management Systems (NCHEMS) indicates that "during the past three years, fewer than

20 per cent of all colleges and universities experienced declining enrollments", and more institutions experienced enrollment declines than revenue declines.[1]

An element in coping strategies included more equitable and effective ways of making academic personnel decisions on promotion and tenure, and merit. This "belt-tightening" affected all types and sizes of our colleges and universities, and lessons learned have been conducive to better management. Our institutions of higher education are definitely better managed in 1984 than in 1974, but there is still room for much improvement.

CHANGES OVER THE TEN YEARS

The changes in faculty evaluation in United States colleges and universities over the 1974-84 span have been both positive and questionable.

Positive changes

1.   *The use of faculty evaluation has significantly increased over the past ten years, and no end is in sight.* The "high point" mentioned in 1974 is significantly higher in 1984. Several surveys have probed the extent to which faculty evaluation is used in both formative (development) and summative (promotion and tenure) decisions. Generally speaking, one can generalize from these disparate studies that about two-thirds to three-quarters of United States colleges and universities have some systematic way for evaluating academic faculty so the question is whether or not a *systematic* approach is used.

The use of *faculty development* programs has increased more dramatically than summative systems. Approaches to faculty development are not new; in fact, gatherings of scholars to discuss matters of mutual interest pre-date Ancient Greece by a thousand years or more. The use of other faculty development approaches such as pedagogical assistance, technological aids, career guidance, and personal counseling are relatively new. These dimensions are areas where the most noticeable improvements in faculty development were made during the 1974-1984 period. However, the extent to which colleges and universities are using their faculty evaluation systems for developmental purposes is not known. Judith Aubrecht concludes that "very few institutions are making good use of their faculty evaluation systems for developmental purposes"[2].

2.   *A broader data base for making faculty evaluation decisions is evident.* Data from Peter Seldin's very useful, new book[3] indicate an expansion in the number of significant sources of data for evaluating teaching. See Table 1.

In Seldin's 1973 study, as indicated in Table 1, only three sources – colleagues' opinions, chair evaluation, and dean evaluation – earned a mean score rating of less than 2.00. But in the 1983 study five sources – the same three plus systematic student ratings and self-evaluation – earned the same low rating. This increase in the number of sources with low mean scores suggests that private colleges increasingly are considering a wider range of sources in evaluating faculty performance. Although evidence is not available for other classifications of US postsecondary institutions, I would judge that Seldin's data, which focuses on private, liberal arts colleges, would be relevant for other types as well.

3.   *Functional "systems" for faculty evaluation have developed.* Ten years ago we were thinking much more about faculty evaluation in terms of a number of separate pieces rather than as parts of an integrated system. A system considers each part and how it meshes with the whole, which can be greater than the "sum of the parts" – to use a basic Gestalt tenet.

Table 1

TESTS OF DIFFERENCES IN MEAN SCORES OF SOURCES OF INFORMATION CONSIDERED
IN EVALUATING FACULTY TEACHING PERFORMANCE
IN PRIVATE LIBERAL ARTS COLLEGES, 1973 AND 1983

Sources of Information	1973 (N = 410) Mean Score	1983 (N = 515) Mean Score	t^a
Systematic student ratings	2.20	1.45	13.57^b
Informal student opinions	2.04	2.35	-6.40^b
Classroom visits	2.98	2.48	8.99^b
Colleagues' opinions	1.76	1.69	1.42
Scholarly research and publication	2.30	2.28	0.31
Student examination performance	2.95	3.03	−1.47
Chair evaluation	1.22	1.26	−0.87
Dean evaluation	1.19	1.33	-3.40^b
Course syllabi and examinations	2.56	2.21	6.41^b
Long-term follow-up of students	3.13	3.13	−0.08
Enrollment in elective courses	2.79	3.09	-6.07^b
Alumni opinions	3.09	3.05	0.97
Committee evaluation	2.17	2.06	1.38
Grade distributions	3.05	3.04	0.23
Self-evaluation or report	2.58	1.95	9.24^b

a)   The test used was a t-test for differences in independent proportions.
b)   Significant at 0.01 level of confidence.

The noticeable trend toward developing evaluation systems reflects the increasing sophistication in using faculty evaluation. More people know much more about evaluation today than ten years ago. Also, the much greater use of computers has made systems easier. And some collective bargaining agreements have included detailed information on the system approach.

An evaluation *system* might include these components:
–   Explicit instructions for administering the classroom teaching evaluation instrument to students.
–   Information on turnaround time for the results.
–   Who sees the results?
–   How will the components, such as research and public service, be evaluated?
–   What is the weighting among the evaluative components?
–   What is the role of the various constituencies in the decision-making process: colleagues, chairperson, designated committees, dean, VPAA, and others?
–   What grievance procedures are available to faculty members?

4.   *Survey instruments for appraising classroom teaching performance have substantially improved.* Some earlier forms enjoyed widespread use and acceptance such as the Purdue Rating Scale that was developed by Remmers, and the various rating scales for classroom teaching that were developed at the University of Washington – both pre-World War Two vintage.

More recently developed instruments are machine scored and/or optically scanned, and they tend to focus on more relevant questions as contrasted with the "kitchen sink" approach that typifies many earlier efforts. This earlier approach followed the dictum, "When in doubt about the value of a question, include it". As a result, earlier evaluation forms tended to be longer and to include too many extraneous questions.

Students who watch a teacher perform in a classroom for 50-60 hours per term, if asked questions that they can answer based upon their general background as well as the classroom activities, can give *valid* and *reliable* answers. Students are the best judges of *a)* teaching methods (pedagogy); *b)* fairness, which primarily concerns testing; *c)* interest in me; *d)* interest in the subject; and *e)* global questions, such as: "How would you rate this teacher in comparison with all others that you have had thus far?".

There are other questions, however, that colleagues are *best* able to answer. These are: *a)* the teacher's mastery of content; *b)* selection of content; *c)* relevance of content to continuity of the course sequence; and *d)* the relevance and quality of the course syllabus and related materials. Two questions – *a)* course organization, and *b)* course workload – can be asked of both students and colleagues.

5.   *Court cases have improved the quality and equity of faculty evaluation.* The rash of court cases on irregularities and inequities in the evaluation of faculty may have peaked in the United States but a steady stream of such cases may be expected to continue. In the late seventies in the State University of New York (SUNY) system, the threat and actuality of faculty suing the administration became so commonplace that one administrator, when threatened with a suit by a faculty member, replied: "Get a ticket and stand at the end of the line!". On the whole, the court cases have had a significant impact upon improving the process, equity, and quality of faculty evaluation over the 1974-1984 period.

6.   *The use of research/scholarship in evaluating total faculty performance has increased.* Kenneth Eble speaks about "...a return to what a majority of faculty probably regard as 'traditional' values. I refer to the increasing weight given to research, publication, and professional activities"[4]. The survey of private and public liberal arts colleges reported by Peter Seldin indicates that the importance of research/scholarship in evaluating faculty performance has increased. He suggests that "public colleges in particular may be emphasizing research and publication in the drive to impress state legislatures and other public bodies that control the purse strings"[5].

Another reason for the increased use of research/scholarship in evaluating overall faculty performance might be related to better policies and procedures for evaluating this dimension. Today many colleges and universities have detailed explanations for this process whereas such statements were quite uncommon in 1974. Again, a general increase in sophistication in the field of academic evaluation may play a part.

Questionable changes

As one would expect, not all perceived and documented changes in faculty evaluation over the 1974-1984 span have been positive.

1.   *The "rush-to-press" has seriously flawed some evaluation systems.* Mandates that allow insufficient time for faculty and administrator reflection and investigation have a high mediocrity rate. The recommended time needed for developing and/or extensively re-studying a current evaluation system is one academic year plus a summer.

2.   *An anti-intellectual backlash has hindered development of some well-designed plans for faculty evaluation sytems.* Anyone who has gathered chalk dust on his/her sleeves knows there is *The Art of Teaching* – to use the title of a thoughtful little book by Gilbert Highet. He writes: "I believe teaching is an art, not a science. It seems very dangerous to me to apply the aims and methods of science to human beings as individuals... Teaching is not like inducing a chemistry

reaction: it is much more like painting a picture, or making a piece of music.... You must throw your heart into it, you must realize that it cannot be done by formulas, or you will spoil your work, and your pupils and yourself"[6].

We live in social contexts in which all of us are judged by some standard by someone. The teaching-learning process is difficult to capture with words or on a rating scale yet objective treatment of the process is much fairer and more defensible than mystical pronouncements about it. It would be a genuine mistake, however, for those advocating more objective and systematic faculty evaluation systems to take lightly this and other objections to faculty evaluation, and especially to take lightly the objections to student ratings of classroom teaching.

3. *Excessive reliance upon quantification can be detrimental.* The "if you can't count it, it doesn't exist" point of view has lead to excessive reliance on numbers on rating scales and numerical weightings. Certainly some quantification is desirable and necessary if only to be able to process large amounts of data, but these data need always to be buttressed with systematic and reasoned judgement. Perhaps the quantification problem and its humanistic amelioration was stated most succinctly by A. Enthoven: "It is better to be generally right than precisely wrong"[7].

THE FUTURE

What future directions will faculty evaluation take? The statement on the front of the National Archives Building in Washington, D.C. is relevant. With respect to the future nature of faculty evaluation, "The Past Is Prologue".

1. *Better and more equitable faculty evaluation systems will be developed.* These systems will include, in my opinion, better instrumentation, and better ways of using faculty evaluation criteria. Lawrence Aleamoni, with respect to the future, writes: "I feel that faculty evaluation will be a very comprehensive, well-defined system by the year 2000, with explicit criteria and guidelines for evaluation decisions. These systems will be predominantly computer based, with explicit recommendations for improvement provided along with time lines to achieve improvement"[8].

2. *Faculty evaluation will become more rigorous.* External forces and pressures will provide the impetus for this increased rigor. Caution must be exercised, however, so that this likely trend will not make professors overly conscious about their evaluations. Such lurking thoughts can deter innovation and freshness in teaching.

3. *We can expect to see more sophisticated, computerized systems.* Here again a caveat: The system is a *means* to formative and summative evaluation and not an *end* in itself. We should not become over-enamored with the systems themselves. Their success will depend upon being cost-effective, providing some formative assistance, having the technical competence on the campus to maintain and "tinker" with the system, having sufficiently simple printouts so as to be readily understood by non-machine oriented faculty members, and being credible.

4. *We can expect to see more individualized and flexible systems.* A few current systems allow the individual faculty member to decide upon criteria for student evaluation of their teaching from a data bank of possible questions. Other systems, such as the one developed by this writer in 1972, allows each faculty member, in concert with the departmental chairperson and within constraints imposed by the needs of the department and directions and nature of the university or college, to determine professional work load and the weightings for the chosen criteria[9].

The view of the future held by Robert Menges requires "flexibility" in evaluation. He writes: "Most present evaluation systems, because they are the result of compromise, are inherently conservative"[10]. Continuing with the individualization theme as a future trend, Lawrence Aleamoni contends that "every new faculty member will be able to construct a contract indicating how much time and effort will be devoted to teaching, research, and service and what criteria will be used to judge his or her effectiveness in each of those areas"[11].

5.   *To an increasing extent, at least in the next ten years, we likely will see faculty evaluation decisions made in the context of department, college, and university priorities.* George Geis makes this point in the following way: "Evaluation of faculty... should be viewed in the larger perspective of the evaluation of the purposes of institutions of higher education"[12].

The institutional vitality has been a controlling reality for many colleges and universities that have undergone fiscal problems. With more fiscal austerity likely in the decade ahead, this future direction should not be surprising. In one sense it may be unfair because it can penalize a faculty member for being in the wrong discipline at the wrong time, yet institutional health may depend upon making selective cuts in human and material resources. Where these circumstances are found, the administrative leadership needs to make decisions based upon the good of the larger whole as personified in institutional priorities.

And, finally, we need to keep in perspective what evaluation is all about. It is really to serve students through providing better teaching and learning in a unique societal institution known as a college or university. Its products and its on-going activities account for most human progress and inventions; its traditions and mores cause frustrations and misunderstandings among its critics; its freedoms provide an essential bulwark for the democratic way of life; and its concern for idealism and ideas has kindled the hopes and dreams of millions who found themselves during college days.

July 1986 Vol. 10 No. 2

REFERENCES

1. NCHEMS, (1984). "Decline: Separating Facts from Fallacies". *The NCHEMS Newsletter.* No. 87, June: 8.

2. Aubrecht, J.D. (1984). "Better Faculty Evaluation Systems". In P. Seldin, *Changing Practices in Faculty Evaluation.* San Francisco: Jossey-Bass: 88.

3. Seldin, P. (1984). *Changing Practices in Faculty Evaluation.* San Francisco: Jossey Bass: 50-51.

4. Eble, K.E. (1984. "New Directions in Faculty Evaluation". In P. Seldin, *Changing Practices in Faculty Evaluation.* San Francisco: Jossey Bass: 97.

5. Seldin, *op. cit.*: 74.

6. Highet, G. (1950). *The Art of Teaching.* New York: Alfred A. Knopf. In preface.

7. Enthoven, A. (1970). "Measures of the Outputs of Higher Education: Some Practical Suggestions for Their Development and Use". In Lawrence and Associates (Eds). *Outputs of Higher Education: Their Identification, Measurement, and Evaluation.* Boulder, CO.: Western Interstate Commission for Higher Education.

8. Aleamoni, L.M. (1984). "The Dynamics of Faculty Evaluation". In P. Seldin, *Changing Practices in Faculty Evaluation.* San Francisco: Jossey-Bass: 78-79.

9. Miller, R.I. (1972). *Evaluating Faculty Performance.* San Francisco: Jossey-Bass.

10. Menges, R.J. (1984). "Evaluation in the Service of Faculty". In P. Seldin, *Changing Practices in Faculty Evaluation*. San Francisco: Jossey-Bass: 114.

11. Aleamoni, *op. cit.*, p. 79.

12. Geis, G.L. (1984). "The Context of Evaluation". In P. Seldin, *Changing Practices in Faculty Evaluation*. San Francisco: Jossey-Bass: 107.

Evaluating Basic Units:
Seven Fundamental Questions

Rune Premfors
University of Stockholm
Sweden

ABSTRACT

This article provides a set of hints for the would-be evaluator of basic units in higher education. Evaluators should be explicit about the motives, object, organization, criteria, methods, dissemination and impacts of evaluation efforts. Without an understanding of the complex nature of basic units, formal evaluations may be counterproductive.

INTRODUCTION

Basic units in higher education may be defined as "the smallest component elements which have a corporate life of their own" (Becher & Kogan, 1980: 79). Obviously their size, structure and tasks vary immensely, within and between national systems of higher education. Some are organized on the basis of traditional disciplines, while others, by contrast, cover e.g. educational programs or substantive research problems. Some comprise undergraduate and postgraduate training as well as research (and even "community service"), while others specialize in one or two of these activities (Premfors, 1985).

In a word, basic units come in widely varying shapes and forms. I will, however, in the ensuing discussion, start from the assumption that any attempt at evaluating basic unit performance will have to confront a set of generic questions. What follows may be seen as a set of hints for the systematic planning of any evaluation enterprise. These hints for the would-be evaluator of basic unit activity concern seven aspects: motives, object, organization, criteria, methods, dissemination and impacts. I will comment on each in turn although they are obviously intimately related; answering one of these generic questions in a particular fashion largely determines the type of answers one may provide for the rest.

Motives

Why evaluate? The answer may seem obvious. Evaluation is typically defined as an attempt to measure how well the actual accomplishment of an activity or program matches the anticipated accomplishment (see e.g. Quade, 1982: 262). But as is often observed in the general evaluation literature, motivation may and does vary greatly. For example, a distinction is often made between evaluations which primarily aim at *accountability* or control and those which emphasize *organizational learning* (for a useful discussion, see Cronbach et al., 1981). The former may be seen as an effort to strengthen (or at least confirm) hierarchical control, while the latter may form part of ongoing processes of *self-evaluation*.

Although these two types of motives may to some extent be combined, there is obviously at some point a fundamental tension between them. Any would-be evaluator of basic units should already at the outset, I believe, be aware of his/her basic motives since these are bound to affect almost every other aspect of the evaluation effort.

Object

What is to be evaluated in basic unit life? A Swedish observer (Hermeren, 1983: 58) has suggested that basic units, viz. ordinary university departments, may be viewed as:

- a teaching unit
- a research unit
- an administrative unit
- a social unit

An evaluation may be focused on any of these functions or on all of them. The general evaluation literature makes the quite obvious distinction between *comprehensive* and *partial* evaluations; the latter is without doubt more common than the former.

Partial evaluations of basic unit performance are, in my experience, by far the most common. Most of them seem to be focused on *either* research *or* administrative problems. Such evaluations may obviously be both legitimate and useful. I am prepared to argue, however, that some of the key problems in basic unit life stem from the interaction of the four basic functions mentioned above. This may be illustrated by reference to the oft-discussed relations between teaching and research (they are without doubt in *competition* in important respects), between administration and research ("all these meetings!", etc.), and between social concerns and the other functions (e.g. employment security vs. performance). Rarely or never, I believe, may basic unit performance be improved without addressing the necessary *trade-offs* between the various functions. The would-be evaluator should bear this in mind in designing his/her study.

Organization

Who should perform an evaluation? Whether evaluations should be external or internal in relation to a particular organization is a constant matter of debate in the general evaluation literature. Advantages and disadvantages with either form are discussed. It has been noted, for example, that while *internal* evaluations may be quickly initiated and performed, may draw on already existing familiarity and expertise and may provide for effective feedback, they may also be wanting in terms of objectivity and methodological expertise.

The peculiar features of higher education organizations alert us to the limits of such simple schemes of advantages and disadvantages. In particular, we may ask what is "external" and "internal" respectively to basic units in higher education. The most common form of systematic evaluation in such settings is undoubtedly various forms of *peer review*. Practices in connection with peer reviews illustrate that we are confronted with a peculiar organization where there are two parallel, and sometimes conflicting, systems of authority. Much has been written on this duality (from Corson, 1960 to Clark, 1983); the point here is just to remind our would-be evaluator that he or she, in organizing the evaluation effort, must realize that basic units are part of this "crisscrossing matrix" (Clark) which is higher education organization.

Criteria

What criteria should be used in evaluating basic unit performance? Obviously, any evaluation enterprise may derive criteria from a number of *sources*. We may distinguish between at least three kinds:

- authoritative goal statements
- interest group statements
- theoretical statements

Evaluations which start from some source of the first-mentioned type are probably most frequent. If no formal statement exists, the starting point may, rather, be some "common understanding" of what the major goals of a program or an activity are. More often than not, however, it turns out that such authoritative goal statements are neither as authoritative nor as operational as is needed for systematic evaluation efforts. The evaluator must, through various strategies, "circumvent" this problem (Premfors, 1981). One radical way of coping with a situation where authoritative goal statements are lacking is to derive criteria from various interest groups. This of course only solves the problem of identifying authoritative goals; goal statements by interest groups are probably as vague and conflicting as those derived from authoritative sources. A third way of coping, as indicated above, is to derive evaluation criteria from "theory". However, while evaluations of basic unit performance may no doubt be informed by relevant theory in the behavioural and social sciences, I strongly doubt that it will help our would-be evaluator very much in his or her effort to cope with the problem of finding appropriate criteria. No major aspect of basic unit life, I would argue (and certainly not the fundamental trade-offs mentioned above), is covered by existing theory in a way which makes it "authoritative" or relatively undisputed. Nor are, as we shall see, existing methods of evaluation.

Methods

What methods should be used? The general evaluation literature is very much concerned with methodology and methods. A major debate has concerned, to put it rather crudely, the issue of quantitative versus qualitative methodological approaches. A kind of *modus vivendi* has been established where it is recognized that the choice of method depends on evaluation object, criteria, etc. A simple but important distinction has been made between *summative* and *formative* evaluations, where the former type is concerned with products (output and outcome) and the latter with processes. It seems obvious that summative evaluations are more likely to contain quantitative measures and techniques, while this is less probable in connection with formative studies. The latter should, by contrast, draw on the more qualitative approaches of organization and decision approach. Any comprehensive evaluation effort had better use a mixture of methodological approaches and techniques.

A comprehensive evaluation of basic units means, I would argue, a great challenge to our would-be evaluator. There are in fact some tool kits available, but they have typically been assembled for partial evaluations. The tools for the evaluation of teaching and learning are probably best developed. No doubt this is due to the many quantifiable aspects of this major function of basic units; after all, examinations are evaluations, and students come in large numbers. At the same time, teaching is – much in contrast with research – a rather "private" process. This obviously explains the spread of "external" evaluation, such as course evaluations by students.

With respect to the evaluation of research, there is currently a rather intense effort to develop various methodological approaches and techniques. This occurs in many national contexts and, not least, through international organizations (for example, OECD recently organized a Workshop on Science and Technology Indicators in the Higher Education Sector). The discussion mainly centers on the possibilities of using various bibliometric indicators for evaluation purposes (see e.g. Moed *et al.*, 1985 and Narin, 1985). As in the general debate on research evaluation methods, there are sceptics and believers with respect to their applicability to higher education institutions (including basic units). A lesson learnt from this general debate is the *varying* usefulness of measures and techniques, depending very much on the patterns of publication and communication existing in various specialities, disciplines and fields of research.

As almost always, the only reasonable conclusion is that various formalized, quantitative methods should be used with caution. This seems to be particularly important in connection with research, an activity which is to an unusual extent characterized by unpredictability, fragmentation and non-uniformity (Ziman, 1985). And again, any comprehensive evaluation of basic units – comprising at least teaching, research and administration – will profit even less from simple, partial measures and methods.

Dissemination

Who is the intended user or consumer? This question is obviously closely related to the first (Motives) and fourth (Criteria) ones. But it also has a more "technical" aspect: how should evaluation results be effectively disseminated? Again, this has been a major topic of debate in the general evaluation literature. The starting point has often been a wide-spread feeling of frustration among evaluators in the face of pervasive evidence of non-utilization; many have argued that there exists a "utilization crisis". The recipes for coping with this problem have varied greatly: from rather mundane recommendations to write more readable reports to quite sophisticated schemes for "utilization-focused" evaluations (Patton, 1978). Most commonly, evaluators argue in favour of a better "integration" of users in the evaluation process itself, and at an early stage ("when the report is written it is usually too late"). Not surprisingly, some writers have also argued that the needs of systematic evaluation should, to some important extent, and beforehand, determine the contents of programs (e.g. Wholey, 1983 and Rutman, 1980).

All these recipes are of course useful. Our would-be evaluator of basic unit performance should think before acting, be reasonably clear about who the intended user is, and communicate results as effectively as possible. But he or she had also better be prepared for some worse-than-normal difficulties. The fragmentation, non-uniformity and often highly abstract nature of work in higher education sets definite limits to dissemination efforts. Often only peers will truly understand; too much "popularization" will simplify beyond the point of distortion. After all this is why the organization, when it works, is characterized by a dual authority structure.

Impacts

What impacts may be expected? This question of course indicates that we have travelled full circle. The expected impacts should in essence correspond to the motives behind our evaluation enterprise. In the end, then, we should be able to tell if basic unit performance (in part or as a whole) matches expectations. Some evaluations will chiefly be used as mechanisms of control by higher organizational levels; others will primarily become part of processes of self-evaluation. Irrespective of this, our would-be evaluator had better think hard about other possible impacts of his or her evaluation effort, impacts which may not be part of (explicit) motives.

A satisfactory discussion of possible "hidden" impacts would require a separate article (a good one is Larsen, 1985). Here, I will only briefly mention two important impacts of this kind. First, there are good reasons to believe that formal evaluations in higher education display a "conservative" bias. Most approaches and methods used aim at assessing the quantity or quality of *past* work. Rarely do such evaluations focus on the *potential* contributions of individuals, groups, basic units or institutions. This observation may seen to border on the trivial, but I think it is far from that. The more we resort to formal evaluations, the more we will see of the Matthew effect which Robert Merton identified years ago (Merton, 1973): "to those that have shall be given...".

Second, evaluations may foster "unnecessary" conflicts. It may seem evident that systematic evaluation efforts should preferably specify the contribution of each and every member of a basic unit. But we should not expect that this kind of "individual accountability" necessarily will lead to improved performance. Believing so would be to subscribe to a rather naive theory of individual or group motivation. Some people will inevitably suffer,and thus probably perform worse, in a context of increasing conflict. Although we have little certain knowledge about the circumstances which foster creativity in teaching and research, I for one believe that a creative milieu should include different personality types. Some would fare badly in formal evaluations, but may nonetheless be of key importance to the overall performance of, for example, a basic unit.

CONCLUSIONS

So much for my seven hints to would-be evaluators of basic units in higher education. The message is simply, first, that any evaluation enterprise should, before it is undertaken, provide reasonably explicit and well-argued answers to seven fundamental questions: Why evaluate? What should be evaluated? Who should evaluate? What criteria should be used? What methods? Who is the intended user? and, finally, What impacts may be expected?

But, second, I also hope to have conveyed another message. This is, in brief, that evaluating basic units is an extremely difficult undertaking. Without being informed by an understanding of the complex and peculiar nature of this core organization of the higher education enterprise, a widespread use of formal evaluations may be counter-productive: we will *not* learn more about their effectiveness and we will *not* be able to contribute to more effective performance. At best it will simply be a waste of scarce resources; at worst it will be detrimental to the rather delicate mechanisms which make for creative work inside basic units.

July 1986 Vol. 10 No. 2

REFERENCES

Becher, A. and Kogan, M. (1980). *Process and Structure in Higher Education*. London: Heinemann.

Clark, B. (1983). *The Higher Education System*. Berkeley and Los Angeles: University of California Press.

Corson, J. (1960). *The Governance of Colleges and Universities*. New York: McGraw-Hill.

Cronback, L. et al. (1981). *Toward Reform of Program Evaluation*. San Francisco: Jossey-Bass.

Larsen, B. (1985). "Forskningsevaluering – problemer og muligheter", in Egil Fivelsdal (ed.), *Naerbilleder af forskning*. Copenhagen: Nyt fra Samfundsvidenskaperna.

Merton, R. (1973). *The Sociology of Science*. Chicago: University of Chicago Press.

Moed, F. et al. (1985). "The Use of Bibliometric Data as Tools for University Research Policy". Paper for OECD Workshop on Science and Technology Indicators in the Higher Education Sector (10-13 June, 1985).

Narin, F. (1985). "Measuring the Research Productivity of Higher Education Institutions Using Bibliometric Techniques". Paper for OECD Workshop on Science and Technology Indicators in the Higher Education Sector (10-13 June, 1985).

Patton, M. (1978). *Utilization-Focused Evaluation*. Beverly Hills and London: Sage.

Premfors, R. (1981). *Genomförande och utvärdering av offentlig politik*. University of Stockholm: GSHR Report No. 12.

Premfors, R. (1985). *Evaluating Basic Units in Higher Education*. University of Stockholm: GSHR Report No. 33.

Rutman, L. (1980). *Planning Useful Evaluations: Evaluability Assessment*. Beverly Hills and London: Sage.

Quade, E. (1982). *Analysis for Public Decisions*. New York: North-Holland.

Wholey, J. (1983). *Evaluation and Effective Public Management*. Boston: Little, Brown.

Ziman, J. (1985). "Criteria for National Priorities in Research". London: Imperial College, Department of Social and Economic Studies (mimeo).

Methods for the Evaluation of Research

Michael Gibbons
University of Manchester
United Kingdom

Before embarking on this discussion of the evaluation of university research, it is important to keep in mind that it is not a new activity. Evaluation has been a central element in the life of science since its institutionalisation began and a great deal of it is going on all the time. Evaluation is taking place, in one form or another, every time a research council or government agency awards a grant or contract; when reports are submitted, papers published and invitations to international meetings extended. Evaluation is present when professors are appointed; in the examination of doctoral dissertations and in the awarding of undergraduate degrees. Evaluation is omnipresent in scientific activity. The principal question is whether it is adequate to the current situation in which research in general and research in universities in particular finds itself.

To the question, "Is anything *further* needed ?", the answer is unequivocally "yes" ! The reason is that the evaluation methods which are currently operative in science are most effective at the *project level,* that is, at the level of the individual or research team. However, the further development of science depends upon more effective evaluation procedures at higher levels of aggregation. There is, at the present time, far from adequate evaluation of research activity at the programme, research council, university and national levels. While it may not have always been so, it is increasingly the case that the quality of research at the project level is a function of the ability of the higher levels of the research system to manage its activities; that is, it depends upon the effectiveness of its research policy. This is so because contemporary research requires a stable environment − at the very least, continuity of funding − if it is to function properly.

Current interest in the evaluation of research stems, in part, from the general slow-down in the growth of resources for science and, in part, from a growing awareness of the difficulty of extending the methods of evaluation from the lower to the higher levels of the research system from evaluation at the micro - (or project) level to evaluation at the macro - (or programme) level. The technique of evaluation at the micro-level varies slightly from country to country but in all countries the peer-review system occupies centre stage. This method works better in some situationsthan others. For example, peer-review is particularly well adapted to:

  i) Scientific fields which are sufficiently well developed to have an international community, a number of journals and conferences for its members to utilise, and a clearly articulated reward structure;

 ii) Scientific fields in which problems −that is, what is worth working on −are decided by the community itself; and *iii)*   When research is carried out in an economic context of at least modest growth.

Conversely, when these conditions are not met the peer-review system is apt to work less well. Thus, problems may be expected to arise:

  i)   When resources fail to keep pace with inflation;
  ii)   When research is deliberately oriented to social or economic needs;
  iii) When multidisciplinary research is needed;
  iv)   When, as is the case in big science projects, every reviewer is also a user of the facility being evaluated; and
  v)   When judgements about future prospects rather than past performance are important.

In these situations various attempts have been made to modify or extend the peer-review system as, for example, by including in the process representatives from industry or government laboratories. So far at least, there is little consensus about the effectiveness, or otherwise, of doing this.

Thus, in considering the evaluation of research — where one is thinking primarily of the type of research being carried out in institutions of higher education — there are two different problems to be dealt with. The first is that the mechanism of peer-review is only partially adapted to the evaluation of the quality of projects and/or the competence of individuals and teams and that it seems to work better when evaluating the performance of well-established scientific areas. The second problem is related to the need to evaluate research at higher levels of aggregation. As one moves upward from the research project level purely scientific considerations must take their place alongside extra scientific factors such as economic and social need, defence of the realm and international prestige. And, as these extra-scientific considerations intrude, so the range of interests involved in decision-making broadens.

Both problems are related to, and affected by, resource constraints. The economic context of many OECD member states has been characterised by the slowing down (if not contraction) of economic growth. In few cases have governments chosen to remedy the situation by the prior and general application of funds to scientific research. Instead, budgets for research have remained static and those responsible for allocating resources have had to fund new areas of science by reducing activity in already funded areas. This has raised, in acute form, the problem of comparing one scientific field with another and in this situation evaluation by peer-review is all but powerless. There are no ways in which physics and chemistry and biology can be ranked on purely scientific criteria, except perhaps by subjective judgements about the likelihood, or otherwise, of a significant breakthrough in one discipline or another.

To a large extent, this problem is being solved (or rather by-passed) by the super-position of criteria of industrial relevance over purely scientific considerations. This decision eliminates the need to compare disciplines by judging them in relation to some pre-established industrial need such as information technology, biotechnology, microelectronic applications etc. In terms of evaluation, this has meant enlarging the peer-review system to include in the scientific decision making process itself industrialists who are competent in research but who may have slightly different perspectives on the problem areas that are worth exploring. This is a significant development because, in those case where it is successful, it is bringing forth a different type of science. The division of research into pure, and therefore long-term research, and applied, and therefore short-term research, is giving way to strategic research — that is, to basic research oriented to a technological objective. In strategic research, the distinction between long and short-term research is abandoned in favour of a distinction between research which is strategic and that which is non-strategic. To make this more than a whitewash — a simple re-labelling of existing scientific activities — requires time and a great deal of thought but, in my view, governments in their support for research over the last decade have been moving steadily in this direction. They attacked first the outposts of their own research establishments and met little resistance. They are now marching on the citadels of pure research, that is, upon the universities.

In many European countries, universities are now being asked to set up research committees and to present their plans for research through which they will indicate what type of institutions they intend to become. From the government side, studies of the competence of the research groups are beginning to emerge and no doubt these assessments will play a role in the future allocation of research resources to individual university departments. In the meantime, the number of collaborative research programmes between government and industry is increasing. As a result, those resources available for pure research are being further and further restricted while scientists and universities which are flexible enough to hitch themselves to strategic programmes are prospering even as the nature of the research questions begins to change.

As the context of research begins to develop the nature of the universities' principal evaluation mechanism – the peer-review system – will have to adapt as well. At the very least, one should expect the increasing involvement of non-specialists in what have until now been purely specialist considerations. This will have to become less arbitrary than it is currently as industrial researchers as well as university and government scientists try to identify networks of projects which bear upon one or other national programme. What will quality mean in this context ? Who will evaluate it ?

The way forward involves developing a range of methods of evaluation in which an important element in each evaluative study will be the choice of the appropriate "method mix". Of the general methods currently available one can identify five which have some relevance to the evaluation of research:

    i)   Comparisons of intentions with outcomes;
    ii)   The use of control groups (i.e. the comparison of supported versus non-supported groups);
    iii) Cost benefit analyses;
    iv) Case-studies (detailed histories of different programmes);
    v)   Monitoring.

Each technique will have its appropriateness to the specific problem under investigation. But in each case there is a need to develop better numerical input and output indicators. Of the two it is the development of reliable time-series output indicators for research that are of crucial importance. As with empirical research generally, the meaning given to a set of numerical data is a function of the framework of analysis being used. So, one will need different types of indicators for an evaluation based upon a comparison of intentions and outcomes than for one based on cost-benefit techniques.

Of particular interest is the use of monitoring in the evaluation of research. Apparently, monitoring is not used nearly as widely as might be expected, partly because it is an aspect of the normal political process whereby all programmes are routinely scrutinised but also, and more significantly, because monitoring is " primarily an analysis of implementation and administrative management". The close relationship between monitoring and evaluation is crucial and it is perhaps worth clarifying a little what is meant by these terms. Monitoring answers the questions, "What is happening ?" or, more usually, "What happened ?". Evaluation, by contrast, is addressed to the question, "Has this *policy* made any difference ?". On the basis of this distinction much of what has been classed as evaluation is, in fact, monitoring. As an example, consider government policy for the UK aircraft industry between 1945 and 1968. In his analysis, Gardiner[1] estimates, using a cost-benefit type of model, the flow of receipts *from* government to industry at £1505.4M at input prices, while receipts *by* government in 1964 had totalled only £141.9M at the same prices. On the basis of the distinction made above between monitoring and evaluation it is clear that Gardiner has monitored a policy and given a partial account of what happened. The question of whether the policy of giving industrial subsidies to the aircraft industry made any difference and to whom remains largely unanswered. Even though the rate of return on capital was low, it could be argued that during the period, the industry was able to completely modernise its plant, or that it was able to hold together a first class team of specialists while senior management looked for new markets. If either of these were true, the policy could be said to have made a difference to the functioning of the industry and then the question of whether this was for the better or not could be addressed. It should also be clear that if the difference is judged to be a positive improvement, it does not follow that it would be possible to show any congruence between this outcome and the policy intentions that initiated the change.

A FEW NEW DEVELOPMENTS IN THE LITERATURE[2]

Though there has been more empirical work aimed at monitoring than at evaluation, there are, currently, a number of interesting developments in the literature relevant to the theme of evaluating strategic research. In citing the work of Martin and Irvine at SPRU, Maurice Kogan at Brunel University and Peter deLeon at Rand in America, clearly no claim can be made to being comprehensive. Nonetheless, each represents a genre of method which can cast some light on the problem of evaluating university research.

i) The work of Martin and Irvine[3] in the UK provides an excellent exemplar of what can be achieved by dint of careful analysis in the evaluation of the output of basic research. The authors are careful to avoid the obvious dangers of selecting a single variable to evaluate scientific performance. Rather, they make use of three indicators of output: publications, impact (measured by citations), and international peer-ranking. What is important and novel about this, methodologically speaking, is that it tries to develop a set of interrelated measures which, if they all point in the same direction, increases the reliability with which one can rank the performance of scientists engaged in similar sorts of scientific work.

Still, the work of Martin and Irvine has not escaped criticism from the scientific community whose performance the indicators aim to evaluate. This criticism falls into two broad categories, one methodological and the other political. With regard to method, it is not clear to what extent publications, citation indexes and peer-rankings measure three independent aspects of performance. If they are not independent, then what interpretation can be attached to their convergence ? With regard to the second, scientists in particular have been concerned about the use that might be made of performance indicators in the allocation process. To put the matter bluntly, if somewhat superficially, will a low ranking, internationally, be used more to terminate programmes and shut laboratories than to promote new development ? This is a real difficulty for the scientific community and for policy analysts but it does not follow that such measures, because they are imperfect, are therefore useless. The key problem for this type of work is how the numerical indicators are to be integrated into the decision making process and at what levels.

ii) In the evaluation of research, knowledge of the relevant decision making processes are vital as the recent work of Kogan[4] and his colleagues at Brunel on the implementation of the Rothschild reforms in the Department of Health and Social Security (DHSS) in the UK has amply demonstrated. In the 1971 White Paper, the British government backed Lord Rothschild's recommendations that public resources for scientific and technical research be allocated on the basis of the "customer-contractor" principle. The customer (a government department), knowing what its needs are, commissions the appropriate research from the appropriate laboratories in the public or private sector. A corollary of this was that the directors of government research establishments had to structure and to justify their programmes in terms of departmental objectives. Kogan *et al.* studied in detail what happened in the DHSS to the relationship between the customers and the contractors — that is, between the scientists and the policy makers — as they met in the annual attempt to align scientific resources and departmental requirements. The analysis showed that the "market-type" of collaboration between scientist and policy maker originally envisaged by Rothschild quickly deteriorated into a form of adversary relationship in which the norms and values of the two different constituencies became polarised.

iii) Whereas scholars such as Martin and Irvine have focussed their attention on the perception of individual scientists, engineers and administrators, and whereas Kogan *et al.* have concentrated on the relationships between functional groups, Peter deLeon[5] directed his attention to the relationships existing between sets of institutions. In a study of national nuclear reactor programmes in six countries, deLeon has identified four factors which may have much wider applicability to the development of heuristics for the evaluation of research, particularly strategic research. The main conclusions of his study were:

1. In each national programme several important institutional actors were vying for centre stage and each at different times having greater or lesser roles to play during the development and diffusion of the technology;

2. Because there were multiple actors and each had its own particular organisational goals, there are multiple objectives (which may or may not be harmonious with one another) simultaneously being pursued;

3. Each technological development can be characterised by a number of attributes that were influential (by being present or absent) in defining the course of a technical development. In this framework, technological development is based upon a series of interactions between a set of institutional objectives and a set of technological attributes which define and characterise these same developments;

4. A changing set of political, economic and technological conditions may be expected during the course of a major technological development. This suggests different stages of development may present different types of problems. In particular, deLeon points out "the transition between periods (of development) are especially critical because they suggest how readily the development can move to new and more appropriate objectives or is bound by outmoded ones". (deLeon, 1980: 291);

5. Finally, there is a close parallel between the set of relationships that characterise a given stage of development and the sort of continuous interaction between technological opportunities and market needs characterising innovation within a business enterprise. As Rothwell and Zegveld[6] have pointed out, there is a clear need for policy to take on board what is known about technological innovations. Clearly in the area of strategic research, there is plenty of room for further study of the extent to which successful scientific development is influenced by the close and continual involvement of scientists with developing technological goals.

CONCLUSIONS

The first conclusion which should emerge from this discussion is that evaluation has two interrelated aspects: the use of various methods to monitor the outcome of research policies and programmes and the application of some scale of value to determine whether the outcome is of benefit to a group or to society as a whole. The evaluation question, "Has the policy made any difference ?", carries with it the implicit assumption that, if it has had any effect at all, it has made matters better or worse. If one accepts this distinction between monitoring and evaluating policy its is clear that as far as government policies for research are concerned there has been more of the former than the latter. The works of Martin and Irvine, Kogan *et al.* and deLeon are concerned mainly with monitoring the outcomes of policy though their results have implications for evaluation.

One of the more promising approaches, as far as evaluation is concerned, emerges from the work of Kogan *et al.* They have analysed the process of *implementing* a policy. There has been much talk, among OECD member states, of the importance of orienting research to national needs. But, as far as I am aware, Kogan is among the few who have tried to observe the problems of implementing programmes to attain such an objective. Kogan and his colleagues have discovered that the relevant variables are not just numerical measures of output, but the mode of decision making. If Rothschild has failed to make a difference in British R & D policy, it is because of organisational factors – because of the sharp functional division within the Office of the Chief Scientist whereby scientific and policy matters are kept isolated. This research not only offers some insight into the question of what difference Rothschild's policies have made in the commissioning of research but, more importantly, gives some idea of what steps might be taken to improve its implementation.

Kogan's research, in fact, provides a test of deLeon's model. To evaluate research policies, one assumes that multiple actors and multiple objectives are involved: central and local government, firms, banks, etc. do not all have the same purposes in mind when they support research. But deLeon's work gives us a further insight that actors and objectives shift over time in rough relationship with the stage of development of the project. Seen in this context, the weaknesses and dangers of a "snapshot analysis" emerge: recommendations based upon the interaction of objectives and actors at a given point in time – say early in the project – may not be relevant at a later stage. During the implementation process different combinations of actors and objectives may become dominant.

We are now in a position to suggest that the problems of monitoring and evaluating policy are questions about *implementation.* Much of the literature and practice of policy-making takes a "top down" view of the process and treats administrators as agents for policy makers while tending to play down power relations, conflicts of interest, and value differences between individuals and agencies responsible for policy making. In other words, implementation is conceptualised as "putting policy into effect". The problems of implementation are from this "managerial perspective" defined in terms of coordination, control and obtaining compliance with policy.

But, as deLeon and Kogan have shown, this is a faulty view of implementation: policy does not implement itself, and attention needs to be directed at the processes whereby policy is translated into action and at influencing these processes. Implementation may be viewed as a process of interaction between the setting of goals and action geared to achieving them. But one can go further and regard implementation as the ability to forge links in the causal chain leading from objectives to action. This is not a once-for-all single effort, but a continual and collective one. As Dunsire[7] argues, implementation is a complicated job of "creating and establishing links between separate bodies making a chain, not just using one; a chain which, in principle, might be made up of sets of institutions or groups for each implementation exercise, though the more often a chain is forged, the more easily it is forged the next time until it may become virtually permanent". (Dunsire, 1978: 131).

It is suggested in this paper that the thrust of evaluation studies should be directed not at monitoring outcomes, but at affecting the process of implementation — the forging of links between different institutions and groups. This is particularly crucial for strategic research where the principal institutions which are supposed to be the beneficiaries of the policy are located in government and industry. Here the implementation process is crucial. One plausible explanation of the faltering performance of government research policies may be traceable to the failure to " forge the appropriate links" with the industries, industrialists and scientists concerned. Viewed from the outside, it sometimes appears as if these policies were intended to implement themselves. If policies to promote strategic research are left to implement themselves, the breakdown of communication which will inevitably result may lead to the development of the sort of adversarial relationship between sponsors and researchers that has been discussed above. And, as so often happens in such situations, everyone loses — the universities, industry and, of course, the nation itself.

March 1985 Vol. 9 No. 1

REFERENCES

1.   Gardiner, N. (1975). *Economics of Industrial Subsidies.* London: HMSO/Department of Industry.

2.   For a further discussion of some of these issues see M. Gibbons (1984) *Policy Studies Review,* Vol. 3: 3-4, 476-482.

3.   Irvine, J., Martin, B. and Schwarz, M. (1981). *Government Support for Industrial Research in Norway: A SPRU Report.* A report prepared for the Industriforskningsutvelget by the Science Policy Research Unit, University of Sussex.

4.   Kogan, M. *et al.* (1981). *Government's Commissioning of Research: a Case Study.* Department of Government, Brunel University.

5.   deLeon, P. (1980). "Comparative Technology and Public Policy: the Development of the Nuclear Power Reactor in Six Countries". *Policy Studies,* 11: 285-307.

6.   Rothwell, R. and Zegveld, W. (1981). *Industrial Innovation and Public Policy.* London: France Pinter.

7.   Dunsire, A. (1978). *Implementation in Bureaucracy: The Execution Process,* 1. London: Martin Robertson.

Resource Allocation Based on Evaluation of Research

Rune Fransson
The Karolinska Institute
Sweden

ABSTRACT

At the Karolinska Institute, Sweden, a resource allocation model for medical research has been in use since 1979. The main purpose of the model is to allow the research activity of the different departments to have a direct effect on the allocation of resources. The author describes the background, experiences and effects of the model.

INTRODUCTION

The Karolinska Institute, Stockholm, Sweden is a university specialising in professional training and research within the medical field. At the Institute there are only two faculties, the Medical and the Odontological. In spite of that, the Karolinska Institute is one of the largest universities in Sweden measured in financial terms. The professional training of physicians and medical research constitute the dominating fields of activity.

The Institute has a long tradition in medical research and will be celebrating its 175-year jubilee next year (1985). During this time the Karolinska Institute has gained an internationally recognised position as a medical centre of research. Development has, during most of this time, been characterised by increasing activity and economic growth. At the end of the 1970s the Karolinska Institute experienced, as did most other western universities, a financial stagnation or decline. It was necessary to seek new ways of developing activity without the aid of new resources.

ORGANISATIONAL SURVEY

There are about 3 500 students in undergraduate training at the Karolinska Institute at present, of which about 2 000 are studying for the medical profession. As at other Swedish universities, the admission of students to basic education is strictly regulated by the government and other higher authorities. The possibilities for a particular university to influence the enrolment therefore are very limited. Furthermore, undergraduate education is almost entirely financed by regular federal grants.

Concerning the number of students involved in post-graduate education, however, every university has the liberty to enrol as many students as are judged possible to train, within the limits of its resources. The number of post-graduate students at the Faculty of Medicine at the Karolinska amounts to about 700.

Research at Swedish universities is, to a varying extent, financed by regular federal grants. About 60 per cent of the medical research at the Karolinska Institute is financed from other sources — e.g. grants from research councils, private research grants, own funds, etc. — and therefore the Institute has, to quite a large extent, the liberty to determine the policy, the size and the growth of the research organisation.

Student training, and research within the medical field is carried out within 75 different departments, of which 17 are theoretical/basic scientific and 58 are clinical, associated with different hospitals within the region. The number of persons employed at these departments amounts to about 2 200. Of these 135 are professors.

MANAGEMENT AND RESEARCH POLICY

The direct and overall responsibility for medical research and post-graduate education lies with the Medical Faculty Board.

The basic objective of the Faculty Board is to develop research at the Institute as a whole within the framework of a system with relatively strong and autonomous research departments. More precisely this means that the different departments are allowed a certain latitude in determining policy and the dimensions of its research, in the generation of resources, etc., whereas the Faculty Board, e.g. through the allocation of resources, tries to stimulate activities within new and important areas that fit into the general research policy of the Institute. The Faculty Board has of course other tasks, e.g. the quality aspect of research and post-graduate education, but policy questions and incentive tasks are emphasised at the sacrifice of the controlling and managing functions.

When determining the research policy of the Institute, certain important new fields of research have been identified. By allocating limited additional resources and through reductions within other areas it has been possible to generate certain basic resources for these areas. For this work, at the macro-level, there are no uniform or systematic models for research evaluation. Until now the policy for medical research within the Institute has been worked out by the Faculty Board on the basis of consultative committees. The members of these committees are successful researchers within a certain number of main areas. All of them have international contacts on a large scale and a great knowledge of medical research in other countries.

In a situation of financial stagnation one important instrument for stimulating and initiating new research is missing, namely the access to uncommitted resources. Therefore at the end of the 1970s it was judged necessary to find a way to redistribute resources that would ensure that new research fields that developed in times of resource shortage, were allowed a reasonable economic basis from which they could evolve by their own power.

RESOURCE ALLOCATION BASED ON RESEARCH ACTIVITY

As mentioned before, one of the primary tasks of the Faculty Board is to initiate and stimulate research within new fields. During the economic growth in the 1960s it was possible to build up new research units and departments. During the stagnation in the 1970s it was found necessary to finance such new actitivies by redistribution of resources from existing departments. By selected reductions it was possible to generate certain resources for special projects within important fields. It was obvious, however, that even if certain basic resources could be made available to these groups or departments by such redistributions, there would be a resulting imbalance in resource allocation to these areas compared to the departments that had been established during a period with a more favourable economic climate.

Even within the established institutions there was a shift in research activity that should have been accompanied by a change in resource allocation. A higher degree of flexibility in resource allocation was thus desirable. At the same time it was clear that it would not be possible for the Faculty Board to annually analyse the development within each of the 75 re-search units and on this basis make revised budget decisions. For this purpose a redistribution model was created that to a certain extent was generalised and simplified.

The starting points for such a model were as follows:

—   There should be a stronger and clearer link between research activity and resource allocation;
—   The allocation of resources should be based on previous research activity and be influenced by the activity in a direct and specific way that had been agreed on in advance;
—   The redistribution of resources based on the model should be gradual and long-term. The model derived at should not result in dramatic changes in the resource allocation. Those kinds of changes should require special decisions by the Faculty Board;
—   The model should not require that quantitative goals for each department be set up annually but should instead be a comparison of activities between comparable departments;
—   Each department should represent a basic unit in the model.

From the fiscal year 1979/80 a model based on the described principles was put into practice. Data concerning the following factors were collected from all departments:

—   Scientific papers published during the last two years;
—   The number of foreign visiting researchers during the last two years;
—   External research financing, i.e. grants for research from research councils, private research grants, etc. during the last three years;
—   The number of doctoral theses at the department during the last two years;
—   The number of active post-graduate students at the department the last year;
—   The number of courses for post-graduate students given at the department during the last two years;
—   The number of teachers at the department who obtained senior lectureships during the last two years;
—   Budget for research and post-graduate training the previous year.

The data collected were compiled thus. The different activities were measured and given a value. The total sum of these values was related to the budget of the department which gave a quota. In the computerised system that was used for the calculation the average department was given the quota 1. The other departments could thus be compared with the average depart-ment. That is to say, a department with a quota less than 1 had a research activity that was less than the average related to its budget and vice versa.

The allocation of resources was affected in the following way. The budget one year was multiplied with the quota of the department and the result indicated the budget the following year. An example: a department that according to the model had the quota 1.2 had an increase in allocation of resources of 20 per cent the following year; a department with the quota 0.8 had a decrease of 20 per cent.

As a principle this formula was used:

Budget year 0 x Quota = Budget year 1

A number of restrictions were adopted in order to limit the effects of the model in accordance with the objectives of the Faculty Board, namely that the redistribution of resources should be gradual and long-term.

The theoretical/basic scientific departments constituted one group in the model and the clinical departments another group. The research activities in the theoretical departments and in the clinical departments respectively were not compared due to the different conditions for research between the two groups.

From a theoretical point of view, a number of objections could be raised against the model. It is a very simplified and generalised model for the evaluation of research. It is focused on quantitative data and disregards the qualitative aspects.

It was proved, however, that even if an additional number of more sophisticated variables were added to the model, the relationship between the departments was not altered significantly. A few, simple variables were thus indicative of the true picture.

Furthermore, the data collected were judged and estimated qualitatively. Certain factors were also judged to have an inherent, qualitative aspect. Grants from the research councils, for example, were considered to indicate projects of high quality and credibility, considering the hard competition in acquiring such grants.

Despite fundamental objections the model proved valuable as it enabled the transfer of resources to departments and research units that, according to the general view of the Faculty Board and the Faculty in general, were successful in their research, both qualitatively and quantitatively.

It is worth mentioning that the model supported a development where departments with a high degree of activity were allocated additional resources. The opposite view, that weak departments should be allocated more resources to increase research activity was consequently not supported. There are of course cases where such an approach would be justified, especially when it comes to departments conducting research within areas judged to have future potential but not yet conducting extraordinary work. Additional resources to these areas can then be allocated by special decisions.

EXPERIENCES

Resources for research at the Karolinska Institute have, during the past five years, been allocated according to two main principles.

One is to initiate new research fields and create a basis for future development.

Complementary to this general and strategic planning and allocation of resources, the described model for redistribution of resources based on research activity has been introduced. The main effects of the model are as follows:

  —   The budgetary work of the Faculty Board can be concentrated on main issues;
  —   The recurrent and systematic accounting of the research of the different departments has increased insight on development;
  —   Awareness of resource utilisation has increased;

—   Use of the model has redistributed about SKr 5 million from departments with low research activity to departments with a greater research activity during the past five years.

The redistribution of SKr 5 million might be considered insignificant within a group of departments having more than SKr 300 million at their disposal for medical research. To the individual department, however, the redistribution has been an important resource increase at a time when these have been gradually decreasing, among other reasons due to inflation.

CONCLUSION

Even though it is very important to develop new methods for the evaluation of research it is the opinion of the author that with the help of relatively simple and quantitative models it is possible to achieve certain positive effects on the research activity provided the models fit into the total framework of controlling instruments existing within an organisation.

It is also the author's belief that it is a combination of different instruments for research evaluation and resource allocation that makes a research management system successful.

March 1985 Vol. 9 No. 1

NOTES

1.   The views expressed in this article are those of the author and do not commit the Karolinska Institute.

Evaluation and Funding of
University Research: Where does the Need Lie?

Jean-Marie Archambault
University of Quebec at Trois-Rivières
Canada

ABSTRACT

As a means of preparing the ground for decision-making, evaluation is directly associated with the planning function. This is particularly so with university research, where the allocation of resources is usually based on an evaluation of research activities. In Quebec, funding is gaining significance in the evaluation of university research. While the model of peer evaluation currently used has its limits with respect to the planning of research resources, it is nonetheless vital for the equilibrium of the science structure and the university's mission. This statement is illustrated by reference to a pilot exercise in research evaluation carried out at the University of Quebec at Trois-Rivières which set the objectives of research quality and resource planning side by side.

Societies driven by a desire to innovate, to excel and to satisfy their environment very reasonably try to find out what their achievements are worth. A gratifying or helpful process, evaluation is an essential stage in the assessment, criticism and adjustment of activities to improve their quality and value. The importance of evaluation as a management and decision-making instrument is now increasingly recognised. Alkin (1969) placed emphasis on decision-making in his definition of evaluation. Stufflebeam (1980) supports this view; the role of evaluation is to clarify issues and help produce optimum decisions. This definition has necessarily affected the way evaluation is applied, or the uses to which it is put; and it is clear that, in troubled economic times such as those facing industrialised societies since the beginning of the 1980s, evaluation will be put directly at the service of the planning function. We propose to examine research evaluation in the context of the growing weight of the funding system, by considering university research in Quebec.

In the early 1970s Quebec noted that in many areas of research it was lagging behind the rest of Canada. A science policy began to emerge in Quebec around this time; significantly, the evaluation of research was one of the major concerns. The CORU committee (Lalancette et al.,

1974), whose aim was to take stock of the objectives of university research in Quebec, specified in its very first recommendation that "compliance with the standards of the scientific community (must) continue to be one of the prime objectives of university researchers in Quebec".

What is in fact the position ten years later? This question is especially pertinent because wide-ranging analysis of the science structure has recently been carried out in Quebec[1]. On the evaluation of research, the findings are surprising, to say the least. Opinions on the university and government sides differ substantially.

The universities broadly claim that few activities are better or more thoroughly evaluated than research. Peer evaluation is an excellent guarantee of quality and ensures that researchers share the same standards and that research circulates freely within the scientific community. That, for example, was the stance taken by the Conference of Rectors and Principals of the Universities of Quebec in the Council of Universities study (1984) on the impact of federal funding. Moreover, when questioned by the Council about ways of solving the main problems of research and researcher training, the universities made absolutely no criticism of peer evaluation.

The Council of Universities and the government bodies, on the other hand, were by no means satisfied with the evaluation of research. In its 1979 Green Paper on research, the Government of Quebec pointed out that it had to rely to a considerable degree on intuitive impressions in order to describe the state, performance and objectives of the university research system. The Commission d'étude sur les universités (Committee of Inquiry on the Universities) (1979) came to the same conclusion. By 1984 dissatisfaction was even clearer; the study by the Council of Universities on the impact of federal funding deplored the absence of full and reliable indicators for evaluating the state and needs of university research.

These are significant observations at a time when the Government of Quebec is considering a new method of financing the universities. There is good reason to think that, if it had adequate evaluation data on the university research system, the Government might opt for a different funding model. Giving the universities a separate budget allocation for research is one possibility, and another is that the grant agencies might be more or less phased out in favour of a system under which research would develop still more selectively and resources would be pooled.

This is unlikely to leave university research evaluation practices intact. Major aspects of the workings of university research, and indeed the very mission of the university, would be called in question.

The principal challenge in evaluation is to assess the many different facets of an activity equitably, obviously a substantial task in the case of university research owing to this function's many ramifications.

These begin with the scientific community. Research takes place on the frontiers of knowledge and yields innovations which shape our science and culture. It cannot afford to be imperfect, and must submit to severe quality assessment. The intrinsic value and scientific originality of projects are involved here, as well as the ability of the researchers, while the value of prospective advances must be taken into account as well.

Research is also of socio-economic importance. Because it prepares strategies for social and economic change and concerns the greater well-being of individuals and the community, it must be to the point, effective and *profitable*. On this score evaluation is in the throes of redefinition in the light of the new criteria brought forward by the crisis in technological values (e.g. need for short-term solutions, future relations with industry, promotion of industrial innovation and marketing, job creation).

Another no less important ramification couples research with university life. The fact that it takes place in the university produces obligations towards the university structure: to give support to institutional growth sectors, to renew teaching content, to breathe new life into graduate studies, to fuel the teaching body and to provide intellectual fresh air. Thus, when an evaluation committee approves a research project it makes a contribution to the university as a whole.

Evaluation by peers respects the balance among all these factors. Proof of this is provided by the evaluation grids used by the research funding agencies; panels weight their judgements, according to a wide range of criteria. This form of evaluation has proved functional and relatively watertight in practice. Assessments could well vary, no doubt, if the same project was referred to different panels. But the model will rarely be wrong about projects which do not meet the conditions for valid research.

It is hard to imagine how university research could work without peer evaluation.

There is a danger, surely, that phasing out the grant system would kill off healthy competition between researchers, and hence put a serious damper on scientific emulation. Would it not inevitably downgrade the research function? Stripped of supervision by the scientific community, research would surely become hothouse projects, sheltered from the intellectual challenge that peer evaluation provides. It is to be feared, too, that without peer evaluation, the community will lose every means of assessing research in the round, in all its ramifications with the scientific, socio-economic and university environment. In such circumtances research could well become introspective and develop on its own and for its own purposes. It must not be forgotten that the evaluation practices of the FCAC Fund have played a great part in Quebec in facilitating the partnership of university education and research and in increasing research's contribution to researcher training. The universities have no right to take risks there; the separation of research and teaching would undoubtedly sap the vitality of spheres of university excellence, ultimately penalising society itself. The same could happen with disciplinary equilibrium. The importance of the grant agencies for the harmonious development of research in every discipline cannot be overstated. The creation of peer committees and sectoral allocations within the general funding open to all disciplines promotes this equilibrium. Lastly, if research were removed from the critical inspection of peers, it could well congeal into a purely *politicised* system. We are already questioning the way the grant system is coming under growing *political* influence as a result of sweeping changes in technology[2]. The worst must be feared if the scientific community can no longer act as arbiter here.

Peer evaluation may nevertheless be inadequate when it comes to the planning and fair sharing of resources for research.

To begin with, the peer committee is formed largely in terms of disciplinary expertise, and is probably ill-prepared for the task of allocating research appropriations. While committee members will be familiar with the research costs in a given area, they will not necessarily have all the information they need to judge exactly how much a specific project requires. Given the variety of grant systems, any one committee will have only a very incomplete view of the resources provided for a particular research sector, at university level. The committee will also have too little information about an institution's circumstances, so it cannot properly assess the physical and material context in which a project is to be carried out. As a result, most universities are obliged to top up outside grants from internal resources[3].

Criticism is also levelled at peer committees for dividing research appropriations too finely and for allocating money more according to the quality of the applications than to the budget estimates they contain. Furthermore, the present system of grant aided research is not conducive to continuous planning. Every year researchers are at the mercy of committees' decisions on their grant applications.

In addition, the results of peer evaluation provide few reliable indicators for assessing the performance of the university science structure and for informing decisions on the future directions of research. In Quebec, this method of evaluation applies only to directly-funded research. For work which is not grant-aided, to our knowledge the Quebec system makes no provision for special evaluation, except when reports for publication go before reading committees. The non-aided component, therefore, is not properly taken into account when university science potential is appraised. In any case, the results of grant allocation need to be interpreted with the utmost caution. By no means all the grants are proportional to the quality of projects or to the vitality of research sectors. The estimate of teacher participation in a project does not necessarily show the amount of time that teachers actually spend on research. What is more, grant agencies do not all use the same criteria to determine the size of grants. Total grant achievement depends among other things on the programmes concerned (on their objectives and the budgets allotted to them), and it must always be remembered that grants vary according to the discipline concerned.

For reasons of precisely this kind the University of Quebec at Trois-Rivières readily agreed to participate in a 1978 pilot exercise in research evaluation geared to quality and rationalisation of resources for research[4].

The stated objectives of the operation were:

- to check the scientific value of research activities;
- to rationalise the allocation of human, material and financial resources;
- to identify research-related problems and to determine their probable cause with a view to finding a solution;
- to see that a special research effort was made in areas geared to the development of the University of Quebec at Trois-Rivières;
- to check that research contributed to researcher training and teaching;
- to see that there was a balance between fundamental, applied and experimental research;
- to establish a balance between grant-aided and sponsored research;
- to evaluate the socio-economic importance of research.

For the purposes of this study, the University had to carrry out two evaluations in one. It had to assess both the intrinsic value of its research activities and the efficiency of its research management and funding machinery in relation to the institutions' functions and priorities, using methodology and instruments specially devised by Gagnon (1976).

The pilot exercise was in three stages: collection of data on research activities, intrinsic evaluation of research projects[5] and programmes[6], and compilation of the results obtained in the second stage in order to get an overall view of research in the sector[7] evaluated.

1st stage. Information was collected on forms filled in by the directors of the research projects and programmes selected for evaluation. These forms ensured that the activities were uniformly treated. The project form contained 43 questions on the field of study, state of progress and basic concepts, the research results expected and obtained (e.g. publications, reports, patents), the project's relationship to a research programme and to the university's development policy, its socio-economic spin-off, its contribution to university teaching, the characteristics of the team and the research experience of its members, as well as the human, physical, material and financial resources involved. The programme form contained 35 questions on the programme's objectives and management unit, the list of projects in the programme, the common factors of projects (objectives, methodologies, resources), the complementarity of the researchers, the relevance of each project to the programme, progress of work, socio-economic spin-off, links with institutional priorities, and resources involved.

The forms were distributed in two research sectors, A and B, chosen for the purposes of the exercise. These sectors held scope for analysing both individual and group research geared to university policy and supporting graduate curricula. Sector A was chosen because it was an emerging area. The evaluation covered ten projects and one research programme. Sector B was chosen as a traditional area with a significant research activity. Twelve projects and three research programmes were evaluated in this sector.

The directors of the pilot exercise held a preliminary meeting with the teachers concerned in each of the sectors in order to explain the context, objectives and stages of the evaluation and to familiarise them with the information forms. The heads of the two sectors were asked to have the forms filled in by the teacher; one week was allowed for this. Once the forms had been filled in, the directors of the exercise held a second meeting with the teachers in each sector in order to see how this stage had gone and look at any particular difficulties; it was also an opportunity for teachers to suggest changes in the forms.

Data collection was spread over a period of four months in sector A, from October 1977 to February 1978. Although the operation began at the same time in sector B, circumstances delayed return of the completed forms until the end of September 1978.

2nd stage. Once the data had been collected, the projects and programmes were evaluated by peers from both inside and outside the university. A committee of peers was formed for each sector. The committees were so composed that each project and each programme could be evaluated separately by three peers.

The directors of the pilot exercise held a briefing for the committee members to inform them of the procedure for evaluating activities. The information forms on the projects and programmes were distributed at this meeting, with two sets of assessment forms, one for projects and the other for programmes. The assessment forms had score-grids for assessing separately each objective. The generic indicators were:

PROJECTS	PROGRAMMES
— Scientific value of the project — Value of the project for researcher training and teaching — Socio-economic significance of the project — Relevance of the project to institutional policy — Relevance of the project to the programme to which it belongs — Degree of integration with other projects in the programme — Project resources	— Value of the programme for teaching and researcher training — Socio-economic significance of the programme — Relevance of the programme to the unit's objectives — Relevance of projects to programmes — Degree of integration and programming of projects — Relevance of the programme to institutional policy — Dissemination of research results — Programme resources

The assessors were allowed two weeks to make their individual evaluations and the full committee then met, with the directors of the exercise, to reach a consensus on each project and programme.

3rd stage. The results of the evaluation of the projects and programmes were then compiled, for each sector, using a special scoring grid. The directors of the exercise transposed the committees' quantified results to these grids. This stage was left to the university, which drew conclusions on the following points:

-       scientific value of research in the sector (quality of projects evaluated);
-       amount of research in the sector;
-       state of human, physical and material resources in the sector;

—   proportions of private sponsorship and official grants in the sector;
—   relevance of research to university development policy;
—   proportions of fundamental, applied and experimental research:
—   value of research for researcher training and teaching;
—   relevance and integration of projects with the programmes;
—   relevance of the programmes to their management units;
—   socio-economic value of the research.

The pilot experiment took a little over two years to complete. Given the confidentiality of the information no official report was produced, but meetings were held with heads of each sector to take stock of the general problems relating to the organisation of research and the solutions considered for further improvement. From this angle the experiment was extremely profitable. The university learned more about the needs of its researchers in the sectors concerned and in science in general. The broad range of factors included in the evaluation gave a fairly comprehensive picture. The teachers, for their part, had a better understanding of the evaluation of research (benefits and requirements). No one was reluctant to take part, and all found the experiment of considerable intellectual and practical benefit.

The directors concluded that the evaluation scheme could be applied operationally as it stood, provided some instruments were made more flexible. They acknowledged that success was closely tied to the precision and quality of the descriptive information given by researchers, in what proved the most tiresome and problematical section of the exercise. Moreover, disproportionate time, cutting into research, was needed to fill in the forms. The operation also called for considerable supervision. If it had been applied right across the university, normal work would certainly have been disturbed. Yet for its results to be of value for decision-making and planning institutional research as a whole, evaluation needs to cover every sector. The university was ultimately sceptical about the need to continue the exercise or extend its scope, deciding to leave the matter in abeyance and concentrate on the traditional machinery for internal[8] and external evaluation. The last word has not yet been said, but a device that will one day describe Quebec's university research system and rationalise it any better than the present resource allocation system seems, in some quarters, a utopian prospect. In any event, we should not delude ourselves that there are forms of research evaluation which can get over the need for rational and concerted allocation of resources. If they find the scale of a university a stumbling block, it seems ambitious, to say the least, to expect them to cope with the entire university science structure.

For all that, research has to be evaluated. A free, autonomous function it may be, but the universities have a responsibility to see that this asset, which belongs to all, is beneficially exploited.

It is a responsibility they clearly accept. They are devising internal evaluation and allocation machinery to adjust resources to institutional circumstances. Furthermore, given the indirect costs of research, they need practically to double the amounts received from all outside sources.

A single system of research evaluation probably cannot cover every aspect of quality, relevance, planning and resources. Universities and grant agencies should stick resolutely to the evaluation of quality, and see that research is not duplicated-something the peer system ensures fairly well. This is a basic rule for avoiding wastage in science, and safeguards the university's mission. But the planning of research is also legitimate, partly as a matter of distributive justice. Peer evaluation appears inadequate in this respect. Using a modified form of the present research evaluation system is not supported by the results of the pilot exercise we have described. Instead, alongside that system we should apply evaluation research, as defined by Nadeau (1975), i.e. "research which applies the scientific method to problems that have administrative consequences". Researchers would have to enlarge this *research on research* method and provide decision-makers with expertise to improve the planning of resource allocation at ground level.

Acknowledgements: The author wishes to thank Mr. François Durand, who helped to research and draft this article, and who was also an observer in the pilot exercise.

NOTES AND REFERENCES

1. The appearance of the Quebec Government's 1980 White Paper on science policy capped broad consultations on future prospects with scientific circles in Quebec. Then, in 1983, researchers were associated with two studies, on the impact of federal research funding on the university system and the other on the 1985-1988 development projects of one of the main grant-making agencies in Quebec, the FCAC Fund.

2. This was the gist of the author's public statement at the Symposium of the "Association des administrateurs de recherche universitaire du Québec" on 27th September 1984.

3. During the consultations on the impact of federal funding, several universities deplored the structuring effects of outside research grants on the university system, pointing out that the universities had no control over the situation.

4. The University of Quebec had then recently put a research evaluation policy on record in its report on *"Lois et politiques de l'Université"*, requiring each institution to evaluate its research activities. This policy was based on the principle of continuing evaluation, and its main objective was to ensure the quality and relevance not only of research projects and programmes but of institutions' research sectors as well.

5. Project: a set of research activities (such as observation, data collection, synthesis, conceptualisation, technical operation, critical analysis) that are necessarily interrelated and designed to yield a research product.

6. Programme: a set of projects based on the pooling of facilities and resources and geared to obtaining a new product regarded as useful for achieving one or more defined objectives in a given research sector.

7. Sector: Field of development of one or more scientific sectors within a subject area (e.g. aquatic environment biology, psychosociology of leisure).

8. The university applies the peer evaluation model internally for its annual distribution of institutional research funds. General policy is laid down by a sub-committee responsible for planning and co-ordinating research in the university. Actual distribution of funds is assigned to a peer committee representing the university's various research sectors.

November 1985 Vol. 9 N° 3

REFERENCES

Alkin, N.C. (1969). "Evaluation theory development". *Evaluation comment,* UCLA Vol. 2, N° 1: 1-7. Commission d'étude sur les universités (1979). "Livre premier: le réseau universitaire". *Éditeur officiel du Québec:* 50-56.

Conseil des universités (1984). "Avis au Ministre de l'Éducation sur l'état et les besoins de la recherche universitaire et de la formation de chercheurs au Québec à la lumière de la performance des universités dans les programmes fédéraux". *Opinion,* 83.29: 28-37 and 63.

Gagnon, P. (1976). "Instrument méthodologique pour l'évaluation de la recherche à l'Université du Québec à Trois-Rivières: fiche d'identification et fiches d'appréciation des projets, programmes et secteurs de recherche". *Internal report,* University of Québec.

Government of Quebec (1979). "Pour une politique québécoise de la recherche scientifique". *Éditeur officiel du Québec.*

Lalancette, J.M., Bélanger, M., Lemieux, V., Parent, J., Robson, J., Roy, L. (1974). "Rapport à la commission de la recherche universitaire", published in "Rapport intérimaire du Conseil des universités sur les objectifs de la recherche universitaire". *Conseil des universités:* 45.

Nadeau, M.A. (1975). "L'évaluation vue dans la perspective des programmes". *Série documents,* Laval University, 9:7.

Stufflebeam, D. (1980). *L'évaluation en éducation et la prise de décision.* Victoriaville: NHP.

Excellence Versus Relevance:
The Evaluation of Research

Mary Henkel
Brunel University
United Kingdom

ABSTRACT

This article is based upon a case study of the evaluation of research carried out by "hybrid research communities": research units developed by the English and Welsh Department of Health and Social Security. It describes the process of review of policy oriented research by scientists and policy makers. It highlights the problems of attempting to separate criteria of academic excellence and of policy relevance and presents a case for evolving multiple evaluative frameworks for the assessment of disciplined inquiry that seeks to advance policy and practice.

This article examines a case of the review of publicly financed research in which the norms of excellence and of relevance came into conflicts, namely, the programmes incorporated in research units funded by the English and Welsh Department of Health and Social Security (DHSS) between the mid 1960s and the end of the 1970s. The study shows how notions of excellence are not exclusively related to abstract academic norms of scientific validity but, in many important zones of disciplines enquiry, become saturated by the objectives and, hence, the relevance of the research.

The case of the DHSS research units is particularly relevant to present policy debates about the evaluation of university based research because it presents a good example of the development of "hybrid research communities" (Weigart et al., 1977; Elzinga, 1986). Hybrid research communities develop their own reputational systems whilst sustaining a wide range of research frames. If such a range is acceptable to both the policy systems ("customers") and the academic community, a wide and eclectic range of evaluations can be endorsed as valid. An alternative view (for example, Elzinga, forthcoming) deplores the "epistemic drift" in which academic values and criteria are subverted by those derived from notions of "relevance". On this view, the evaluation range would be correspondingly narrower.

The case study exemplifies such other issues as whether the "customers", the policy makers who commission research, are able to articulate an authentic "voice" and whether they, in both voice and mind, change as a result of their interaction with researchers. The conclusion reached is that the difference between academic and customer criteria narrows as the relationship between them develops; perhaps a case of convergence caused by the nature of the exchange or perhaps because there need be no deep seated or strident conflict between the two sets of values.

The Case

Between the 1960s and the end of the 1970s, the DHSS attempted to establish a resource incorporating both utility and excellence: a range of funded research units in the emerging field of health services research. At first, wishing to promote the contributions of research to the planning and organisation of the health service, the Department funded researchers in fields such as community medicine and mental health. It hoped to build up a strong, independent and even critical network for the generation of new knowledge and methodology in their field, on which they could also draw for advice.

By the beginning of the 1970s, the DHSS's White Paper, *Framework for Government Research and Development* (Cmnd 5406, 1972), was envisaging a more directive strategy. On the basis of a clear distinction between fundamental and applied research, the Department would seek to commission applied research on the Rothschild "customer-contractor"principle. It established machinery to identify research priorities and individual and opportunistic links were to be replaced by specific commissioning of research identified by the Department as important to it. By 1978, the economic straitjacket was pulling tighter, and the Department adopted a new approach and the central preoccupation became "scientific accountability".

The needs to seek out and to nurture, to give both freedom and direction, to insist upon policy relevance and upon the highest scientific standards, emerged with differing force at different times. These various needs created tensions about the funding of DHSS research units and their relationship with the Department.

The Department built research unit contracts round named directors and made them subject to renegotiation if the Directors left their institutions for any reason. It thus asserted its faith in individual scientific leadership, although contracts normally rolled for six years, with interim reviews. Some continuity was therefore established but not the full security of tenured academic appointment.

The field in which units worked varied greatly; units' terms of reference sometimes extended beyond research to include, for example, dissemination and training. They spanned health services and personal social services research. Those research fields are still evolving from different starting points and the DHSS's sponsorship has been perhaps their most powerful defining force. They span the study of the needs of people dealt with by health and personal social services and the systems created to meet those needs.

In 1979, the Department set out to make the major quadrennial review of the funded research units more rigorous. The primary purpose was to enhance the scientific accountability of the Office of the Chief Scientist (OCS). It was felt that the review process ought to make a more systematic contribution to setting priorities in research policy. The starting point was significant for our current concerns; in the revised procedures, scientific merit was to be assessed separately from policy relevance and determined through the quadrennial visits to the research units by the Chief Scientist which included scientific advisers. Until that time, visiting teams had included representatives from the policy divisions of the Department. Under the new arrangements, for fear that scientific judgements would be confused with judgements about policy or practice usefulness, visiting parties were to comprise only scientists. The Department was then to conduct separate reviews of customers' needs for units' work once the report of the Chief Scientist was cleared.

The Department wanted an external evaluation of the new procedures and two researchers observed the Chief Scientist's visits to five units and then followed the process of their review in the Department.

The units had varied histories demonstrating the difficulty of finding a single evaluative frame for them and their fields differed in the degree of consensus reached about methods and concepts. Older units had broadened their scientific base and were facing the implications of that for their organisation and modes of working. Two units were strongly committed to scientific norms of precision, logic, reliability, validity and generalisability. Both were interested in the development of instruments and methods in their field, and one in the development of explanatory theory. The other units all placed value on stated scientific norms but their emphasis was elsewhere. One tended towards "illuminative studies" and action research, although it was also concerned with theory development. One moved between large scale survey work, hypothesis testing and action research and was interested in the generation as well as the testing of theory. The main focus of the fifth was the promotion of research and self-evaluation in the field of general practice.

All five units did work beyond research. Most considered that there were integral links between research, service, education and dissemination and one had practitioners working in a combined practice and research role. Some were actively concerned with the role of research in changing service delivery or professional practice. They were clearly "mission oriented".

The Review Process: The Chief Scientist's Visits

The formats of academic visitations are significant for what they say about the relative power of the visitors and those visited. First, the selection of the visiting party was considered by interviewees of all parties to the visits to be potentially the strongest influence upon and source of dissatisfaction about the process. Visiting parties did not necessarily mirror the unit's specialist interests, although most members were specialists in the unit's field. Specialist knowledge could be supplemented through external referees. Normally at least one member of visiting parties was a scientist from outside the unit's field of work and thus tapped into the evaluative criteria asserted over the whole range of research units.

Most problems of match between the visitors' expertise and units' concerns occurred in units with the widest span of interests or disciplines. Questioned about possible sources of bias, participants drew attention to the close knit or controversial nature of many specialist scientific networks and to the strong commitments that might divide different schools of thought. In health and personal social services research controversies about the nature of validity or generalisability often go to the root of the work.

Directors were expected to give an overview of their total research programme, to outline research in progress or recently completed and set out the objectives, design, methodology and, where appropriate, the conclusions of each project. The director also included a forward look placing the unit's work in the context of research in that policy field and outlined proposals for future work.

The setting, selection of work for examination on the day, mode of presentation and style of hospitality were chosen by the unit; while the essential components of the visit were set by the Department. These were: a short preliminary private meeting of the visiting panel; encounters between researchers and visitors that allowed for pursuit of questions raised for the panel to discuss their judgements; a final meeting with the director and senior staff.

The length of the visit varied little and took no apparent account of the differences between different units' size and range of work. The day was dominated by the clock and many participants were oppressed by a sense of rush. Nor were there arrangements for the visitors to meet together for systematic discussion the night before the event.

The event itself was unequivocally formal. Dress was by near universal consent quasi-"sub fusc", saving the odd red tie and tweed or corduroy suit. Exchanges between the visitors and the research unit staff were almost without exception characterised by a measured politeness. Only the use of first or surnames differentiated between established and new relationships. And even the most aggressive examinations emerge as elements of a ritual comprising distinctive stages and components.

The "art form" of interchange between researchers and the visiting party was that of a viva voce examination. An adversarial mode of encounter in which scholars are challenged to defend their work is well established in the scientific community. Weaknesses or uncertainties are exposed and theoretical bases or methodology may be held up to scrutiny against alternative approaches.This was the predominant mode adopted in visits observed, although some advisers were more persistent and confronting than others. In three visits, one adviser adopted, or moved in and out of, a contrasting "interactive" style in which he or she displayed personal interest in the work and invited some sharing of the problems entailed. But this was not the expected mode.

Questions were aimed at determining whether basic scientific criteria were met. Was the logic of the inquiry sound? Were the aims clear, and the methodology appropriate? What evidence was there that the researchers had the capacity, time and resources to complete the research successfully? Were the confidence limits of the research clear? Were the data sufficiently controlled for the results to be generalisable?

Project presentations were followed by private meetings of the visiting party. Discussions in the private meetings revealed that the purposes of the Chief Scientist's visits were to aid development as well as to reach decisive judgements. The style of visits ensured, however, that, contrary to the expectation of some units, the latter prevailed. Differences of value and about the theoretical bases of research could not be fully explored, nor could some of the most intractable of the research problems be shared and analysed with the units.

Where problems were recognised, the implications were usually not fully acknowledged. The limitation of random allocation studies in circumstances where the internal process of practitioner-patient systems remains ill-analysed, the intellectual and managerial problems of researchers in a new field, and the minefield of the theory – dissemination, practice relationship – such factors were not in the end allowed to weigh heavily against the requirements of scientific control. It was not that the evaluation process was too rigorous but that it did not allow for appreciation of complexity and therefore risked narrowing the research base.

The dynamics of different visiting parties varied.Shared values seemed more important to advisers than conflicting ones. Interviews with advisers following visits for the most part confirmed this impression although there were dissenting voices. One adviser saw a danger that Chief Scientist's visits could collude to reinforce illusions of certainty. Many were concerned that the complexities of evaluation were not fully taken account of in the visit procedure.

The Concept of Scientific Merit and the Process of Evaluation

A central issue that emerged concerned the epistemological assumptions inherent in the process of the Chief Scientist's visit. Focus on the concept of scientific merit was less simple than at first appeared.

In interviews, some advisers elaborated the complexities of judging the quality of work, if that judgement were to extend beyond basic technical competence. Several stressed the personal nature of scientific judgements; one spoke of the need to combine individual values with a deep knowledge of the stage of development and intellectual strength of one's field, and of how the collective view of scientists in particular fields is continually shifting. The differential development of concepts and instruments of measurement between fields was emphasized by three interviewed. In a "preparadigmatic" field (Weingart et al.), unwarranted assumptions were sometimes made about what was taken for granted, about appropriate methodology and about criteria of quality. Lines of controversy might not be clearly demarcated. The balance to be struck between theory generation and theory verification could be more than usually uncertain. Tight control of data in evaluating, for example, care of the mentally handicapped might be useless if the data were inadequate to develop the concepts of quality of care in this field.

Anxiety was expressed by some advisers as well as by the directors that the selection of advisers did not take account of the criterion of scientific coherence. Others considered that the assessment process was subject to excessive reduction of evidence and that assessment of the unit as a whole was unsystematic of even arbitrary.

The sense of injustice among some unit directors derived from their belief that the work of their units was not fully understood: that the strength of the unit's academic networks and influence was understated; that the links between research in the unit had been seriously underestimated; that the scientific constraints deriving from its overall function had not been appreciated or that the balance of the unit's work had been misunderstood.

The decision to made "scientific merit" the sole focus of visit threatened the basic assumptions of some research units. Such units, often with the encouragement of the DHSS, concentrated upon policy relevant research that made no pretensions to influence the course of science. They feared that their work would be subjected to criteria quite different from those prevailing when they began it.

Some of the presented work certainly tested the definitions of science. The units themselves differed in their thinking about scientific rigour and policy research. Some were clear that research must remain within the established parameters of controlled investigation. Their task was to develop instruments of measurement that could extend their work without transgressing those parameters. They emphasized the unity and the boundaries of scientific method. Others had been more influenced by the critics of positivism and their impact on definitions of social science and social research. Their work reflected too a broad-based anxiety about the efficacy of research undertaken to evaluate policy relevant programmes of all kinds.

Some researchers in the units whose visits we observed were vulnerable to criticism that they were falling short of scientific standards. Some units worked within terms of reference that were neither science nor research: for example, an epidemiological reporting system, the provision of a referral system for mentally handicapped babies, and the building up of a research information service. Those whose research, service, dissemination and information or communication functions were integrally linked with each other, found that the scientific visiting parties mostly rejected the essential nature of these links except where they were incorporated within research projects. This judgement could be, however, in conflict with needs stated by the DHSS policy makers.

It seems then that while, with few exceptions, the researchers regarded themselves primarily as members of the scientific community, they had different views about science and about the relationship between science and policy research.

Scientific Merit and Policy Relevance

Most unit staff considered that their assessment had been confined to science, but a significant minority thought that criteria other than those of science were applied. Testing the strength of the principle of separating scientific merit and policy relevance entailed two questions. Ought science to be assessed by scientists separately from the policy makers whose concern is with its usefulness to them? Can science be assessed independently of an understanding of the policy questions that it is tackling and of the constraints upon it? The judgements of some of the participants in our study were clear. One spoke of the danger that "*alpha* judgements of scientific advisers could be subjected to the *beta* assessments" of policy makers if they helped to determine scientific merit. He and others considered policy and science to belong to different universes, although views about their respective nature and contributions varied.

These responses highlight important differences within health and personal social services research. Three distinct categories of research can be described in which the relationship between science and policy is different. There is, first, research upon, for example, the epidemiology of diseases of the central nervous system. Such research has important implications for policy makers but the questions, the causal theories, the hypotheses about treatment, and the methodologies all belong to established fields of medical and health science: a separate system from that of policy.

Such work can be contrasted with the application of established disciplines, theories or methods to a policy problem; for example, the application of micro-economics or epidemiology to resource allocation or assessing the impact of social policies on the health of children. Here science can be seen as different from policy but as directly instrumental to policy questions. Research in such fields is usually multidisciplinary. There is no established discipline or research field with a prior claim on it. It is domain-based research and not separate from policy. Good research in such work depends on the development of both method and theory and their interdependence.

Most of the advisers interviewed were unhappy about the exclusion of policy issues from the Chief Scientist's visits. Some thought a division between scientific content and the relevance of research to be artificial. Policy researchers would incorporate criteria other than scientific merit which is not always a sufficient yardstick of the quality of policy relevant research.

The advisers in all visits emphasized the criterion of "importance" for scientific or for policy development. Two advisers noted that motivation to influence social development affected the degree of importance of researchers' work. Scientific quality was thus promoted by social motivation and values other than the "purely" scientific might be entailed.

Some advisers who accepted the separation of scientific merit from policy relevance in principle nevertheless thought it unworkable. One considered that the degree of certainty required, the available money and the relevance or urgency of the research, had always to be balanced. Science was not an independent variable. Others, too, argued for a greater emphasis upon the context of research, even if policy and science were seen as separate concerns.

It has been contended here that different forms of policy relevant research entail different relationships between policy and science. In some, criteria of policy relevance and scientific importance are difficult to keep separate. In most, judgements need to be informed by an understanding of the economic, policy and scientific context. In some cases, the knowledge systems of advisers will not be distinct from those of policy makers; accordingly the judgements made by advisers may extend to the formulation of policy problems as well as to the methods by which they are tackled.

The principle that the assessment of scientific merit and policy relevance ought to be separated is not destroyed by these arguments. However, an over-rigid application of it may lead to distorted judgements.

The Concept of Scientific Merit and the Adversarial Mode

The adversarial mode adopted in visits is entrenched in the scientific tradition. The automatic self-regulation of science through the operation of universally accepted norms has, however, been convincingly challenged (Mulkay, 1977 and 1979). Yet Chief Scientist's visits are broadly based upon this idea.

Criticism of the evaluative style of the visits focussed on the illusion that any such occasions could ever be wholly rational, objective or directed towards a single purpose. It was said that such encounters tested adversarial skills and not scientific ability. The complexities of group judgements of scientific quality were thought to be insufficiently acknowledged.

Nor, it was thought, did Chief Scientist's visits fully conform to notions of peer review. Scientists do not feel they belong to a republic of equal citizens. Visiting parties were constituted largely of professorial or other senior researchers, while the seniority and experience of unit staff were widely varied. The multiple focus of most units, and the application of general scientific as well as specialist criteria, ensured that reviews were not peer in the second sense: review by those working on one's own specialism. The visiting parties combined scientific authority with the power of a system whose decision could mean life or death to the units. They were part of a governmental process. Finally, advisers from new research fields may have been anxious to assert that they were peer of their fellow advisers. Their membership of a visiting party might symbolise recognition for themselves and the work they represent, and help them in the struggles in their field about dominant norms. Advisers rejected the view that such motives propelled members of their visiting party "to perform" before their colleagues, but acknowledged that it could have been so.

Modelling Alternatives

Alternatives models for Chief Scientist's visits could be formulated. Possible evaluative structures include the discrete/modular version in which the individual project is the focus of assessment; the holistic in which the unit is assessed primarily as a whole; and the contextual, in which the unit is assessed within either its scientific or its policy context or both. Evaluation ranges from authoritarian/adversarial modes, in which the contest is, however, made more equal, to interactive modes where power and authority are tempered by mutual exploration. These modes and structures may be concerned with scientific quality or technical competence in work categorised as "policy relevant" science, "policy instrumental" science or "domain based" policy research. Such work may be centred in the traditions of scientific method or at the boundary between science and other forms of knowledge.

Epistomological issues in evaluation cannot be divorced from questions of authority and power. The predominant evaluative mode of Chief Scientist's visits worked well in many respects. But it is likely to be most acceptable when there is a consensus about criteria or equality of power and authority between assessors and assessed. Policy relevant research is too diverse to be subsumed under one method of inquiry, and there cannot be one authoritative view. These arguments may be rejected by those whose prime concerns are scientific standards, or with the authority of government and accountability. However, they can be further considered as we analyse the second stage of the review of units: that by the customers.

The Review of Policy Relevance

The guidelines drawn up by OCS for the review of units' work following the Chief Scientist's visits described an apparently simple, separate and internal exercise. Once the scientific standards of a unit were judged to be satisfactory, its "past and prospective" relevance to customers was reviewed so that its future could be determined.

Decisions were made by the policy makers and the OCS. The Chief Scientist would then authorise a revised or "rolled forward" contract with the unit, and a detailed programme would be worked out.

Expertise and accountability were asserted in the procedures. Relevance was the expertise of policy makers, and science that of advisers and researchers. Accountability for research commissioning rested firmly in the Department. Its exercise was not to be influenced by people external to the Department who might assert criteria other than relevance.

Policy makers might interpret the task of determining relevance variously. They might simply consider whether the unit's work had been useful to them in the past, and whether researchers' plans accorded with their needs sufficiently to extend the contract. If not, they might want to put different suggestions to them. Alternatively, they might undertake a more strategic exercise in determining the role of the research units. In the case of a large unit that might entail a major reappraisal of the customers' research policy. But review procedures denied a full strategic role for the Research Liaison Group, thus lessening the importance of collaboration between scientists and policy makers.

Did Policy Makers Reach Different Judgements from Scientific Advisers?

If the criteria applied by policy makers and scientists were not wholly separable, policy makers, nevertheless identified two specific areas in which they differentiated their approach from those of scientists. In doing so they exhibited a wide range of attitudes; government emerged from our study as anything but a monolith. Two made a distinction not explicit in Chief Scientist's visits: between research that is technically reliable and research that has scientific merit. Their concern was primarily with the former, but they assumed that the interest of the Chief Scientist was in the latter. Other policy makers discussed the problem of implementing research. They cited some research where the scientists' problems might be generalisability. They, however, feared that the research might be esoteric and large scale implementation impracticable.

Emphasis on the soundness and relevance of research was reflected in customer views of the function of units. Most customers took an instrumental view: that units should answer policy makers' questions, that their work should be structured round individually commissioned projects, and that it should be practical.

However, other policy makers gave thought to the degrees of freedom allowed to researchers. One was concerned that her division had managed to commission little research of direct use and that contracts with units should be tight and clear. But she both valued research and had liberal views about it, doubting whether government should be involved in its management at all. Another group wondered whether it had exercised too tight a control over its units and had thereby stifled initiative. A third, who had worked closely with one unit, believed that expecting a unit to meet the expressed needs of the Department need not encroach upon researchers' freedom, nor prevent units developing as centres of expertise, if not excellence. Linked projects and extended work could be extremely valuable to the Department. Structured collaboration could set up free and productive dialogue between policy makers and researchers. But in such circumstances, independent scientific appraisal could be a valuable safeguard againt collusive complacency.

Some policy makers actively welcomed an independent scientific appraisal of a unit's work to test the validity of their own views. One unit was newly launched by the policy makers themselves and they were reassured to have its value satisfactorily supported by scientific judgement. In a second case, the customers valued the unit concerned, but felt that it had acquired an unassailable but not altogether legitimate authority. They considered that the Chief Scientist's report had made possible a more critical approach. Some of their criticisms were similar to the scientific judgements; others were in direct conflict. Work that they considered esoteric was generally held by scientists to be of high quality. But the policy makers also stressed the importance of maintaining boundaries between research and policy making. They felt that in this unit, scientific and political authority has sometimes become confused.

So far, then, we have built up a picture of a narrow divide between scientists and policy makers. But judgements could not in all cases be aligned. In these cases, unless the scientific judgements were devastating, the policy makers would sustain approval of that which they thought useful.

The Chief Scientist consistently attempted to impose the principle of the separate assessment of scientific merit from policy relevance in place of compromises between scientific rigour and policy needs. In the end, however, policy needs could and sometimes did, win.

Authority, Influence and the Revised Review Procedures

By 1978, research management policies had emerged which assumed that policy makers and scientists belong to quite different systems and carry their respective roles best when clear divisions of expertise and tasks are maintained; that policy makers are well able to formulate their research needs, and that there is a strong, independent scientific community with the research capacity and experience to meet those needs under contracts with the Department. Pursuit of the principle that the authority of science depends upon adherence to the standards set and sustained through its own systems, would enable the Chief Scientist to establish the strength of his position in the Department. Further, just as scientific judgements ought not to be contaminated by the views of policy makers, so policy decisions should not be infiltrated by scientists. Policy makers too were to assert their proper role. Participants in the Chief Scientist's visits and the customer review clearly attempted to implement the principle of a separate assessment of scientific merit and policy relevance.

Thus, clear allocation of authority and responsibility within the Department was expressed. The Department had retained power over the review structure at key points. It was assumed that the centralised authority structure of the review was underpinned by a consensus about objectives and standards, and that procedures were best mediated through relationships and a common language rather than through rules or rights.

An Alternative Perspective

Are there other options for the process of review? The DHSS units were from their inception subject to multiple and changing expectations. They were engaged in research areas shaped by competing paradigms. Their work reflected problems in the relationship between the natural and social sciences and the conflict between positivist, interpretative and critical stances in social science.

The nature of the research raised questions about science as the sole yardstick against which it should be measured. Some work was shaped by and rooted in science, and this must continue to be reflected in evaluation; but some was rooted in the policy problems it sought to understand or resolve. Much of it could not realistically be assessed without reference to the policy field concerned. Some of these fields, such as nursing and social work research, hardly qualify as science but they entail and need disciplined inquiry.

In our view, an exclusive focus on scientific standards in the review processes distracted attention from an equally pressing concern. Much recent writing in policy research has been concerned not so much with scientific standards as with questions about the contribution that scientists can make to policy problems and the capacity of policy makers to use scientific knowledge.

This suggest that researchers wishing to contribute to policy problems must enhance their understanding of those problems and the way in which policy makers, administrators and practitioners address them. Some of the work assessed in the Chief Scientist's visits that tested the definitions of science can be seen as a response to these preoccupations. Action research may, as yet, be an underdeveloped form of inquiry. But it has been attempted because of perceived conflicts between scientific norms and policy needs that are not easily resolved. Many people believe that the primary problem for policy-relevant research lies in the understanding of the relationship between science and policy. They may in consequence perceive research policies aimed at divorce between the two as counterproductive.

The concept of a unified scientific community is an illusion. Research units work within different epistemologies and their networks are multiple. Scientific advisers vary in their views of the relationship between science and policy and of the means by which good policy relevant research is best promoted and evaluated. Their own judgements stand in complex relationship with those of the policy makers in the Department who, in turn, are often proxy customers for other members of the research unit networks, such as practitioners, administrators and consumers. This case study presents a picture of multiple authorities and multiple knowledge systems arguing for alternative approaches to evaluation. These might be based on beliefs in pluralism, greater participation in decision making and more exchange of knowledge. They might entail interactive modes of evaluation in which criteria and processes are geared to the objectives of units' research and its place on the policy-science continuum.

Current pressures on academic institutions to evaluate more rigorously the quantity and quality of their output are likely to be accompanied by a quest for more reliable and searching criteria and modes of assessment. This study shows that it is easy to underestimate the variety of academic research work and consequently to equate tightly defined and traditional norms of excellence with rigorous testing. Multiple and flexible frameworks may in the end provide clearer guides to value.

July 1986 Vol. 10 No. 2

REFERENCES

The empirical materials upon which this article is based are reported in:

Henkel, M. and Kogan, M. (1981). *The DHSS Funded Research Units: The Process of Review*, Brunel University, Department of Government,

Kogan, M. and Henkel, M. (1983). *Government and Research: The Rothschild Experiment in a Government Department*, Heinemann Educational Books.

Elzinga, A. (1986). "Research Bureaucracy and the Drift of Epistemic Criteria", in Wittrock, B. and Elsinga, A., *The University Research System. The Public Policies of the Home of Scientists*, Almqvist & Wiksell International.

Mulkay, M.J. (1977). "Sociology of the Scientific Research Community", in Spiegel-Rosing, I., and de Solla Price, D., *Science Technology and Society*, Sage Publications, London/Beverly Hills.

Mulkay, M.J. (1979). *Science and the Sociology of Knowledge*, George Allen & Unwin, London.

White Paper (1972). A Framework for Government Research and Development, Cmnd 5406, HMSO, London.

The Use of Bibliometric Data as Tools for University Research Policy[1]

H. F. Moed, W. J. M. Burger, J. G. Frankfort and A. F. J. van Raan
Research Policy Unit
State University of Leiden
The Netherlands

ABSTRACT

At the State University of Leiden a study has been performed on the potentialities of quantitative, literature-based (i.e. biblio-metric) indicators as tools for a university research policy. As a subject of evaluation we analysed the research performance of two large Faculties (the Faculty of Medicine and the Faculty of Mathematics and Natural Sciences), during the period 1970-1980. Publication and citation based indicators were calculated for all research groups, handling data on some 6 700 publications and 42 000 citations to these publications. Results were analysed and discussed with researchers from the Faculties involved. In this paper we will present the major experiences and conclusions from this study.

INTRODUCTION

The central issue of this study is the examination of the potentialities of quantitative, literature-based (i.e. bibliometric) indicators as tools for university research policy. As a subject of extensive investigation we analysed the research performance of two large Faculties of the State University of Leiden (Faculty of Medicine and the Faculty of Mathematics and Natural Sciences) for the period 1970-1980. In contrast to other recent studies in this field (e.g. Martin and Irvine, 1983) we focus on the (university) research group as the unit of analysis.

The study presented in this paper (a more detailed discussion is given elsewhere by Moed, Burger, Frankfort, and Van Raan, 1983) was actuated by the necessity for a large-scale project evaluation resulting from a drastic change in the allocation system at the State University of Leiden. The academic staff allocation system for teaching and research at Leiden was originally based almost entirely on student numbers. In fact, in the old allocation system there was a fifty-fifty ratio between staff time spent on the teaching and research, as is usual in Netherlands academia. This system, however, became increasingly unsuitable for financing research units on the basis of scientific merit. Furthermore, staff allocation for research should be protected against the financial consequences of the decline of student numbers. As a result of these considerations, the allocation system at Leiden was changed radically a few years ago (Van Raan and Frankfort, 1980) into a research project grant system. The establishment of a separate university research "financing channel" was achieved technically by a very considerable reduction of a proportionality factor which in the earlier allocation system coupled research financing (in terms of academic staff) with teaching capacity based on teaching-load calculations. The resources which thus became available could be "earned back" with current research projects if the Faculties and Departments concerned could demonstrate the quality of these projects. Therefore, university Departments were forced to develop research performance criteria and, subsequently, to apply these criteria in a sort of self-evaluation, in order to avoid a considerable decrease in research support.

Recently, the Netherlands government changed the national system for university financing into a system very similar to the Leiden system. Both the Leiden system and this recent policy of the national government expressed a need for more objective, quantitative, research performance indicators. The project presented in this report (started in 1981) arose directly from this need.

In this paper we are concerned with two important aspects of research performance: output and impact. Output refers to the extent to which the research creates a body of scientific results. Impact is defined as the actual influence of the research output on surrounding research activities.

A distinction is made between "quality" and "impact". It is assumed that publications must have a certain basic quality in order to generate impact (for a detailed discussion see Moed *et al.*, 1983). However, other factors can determine impact as well, factors like the state-of-the-art of the scientific field concerned, the visibility of journals or the extent to which researchers carry out public relations tasks. Impact is a relevant aspect of research performance since from a research policy viewpoint, one should not only require that researchers produce scientific results of some scientific quality, but also that they make their results known to colleagues.

The output indicators used in this study are essentially based on the numbers of publications within the international scientific literature. Impact indicators were constructed, on the basis of the number of times these publications were cited during a certain period by other articles published in the international scientific literature. We chose the research group as the level of aggregation, since a research group usually constitutes the "natural" unit of research activities (at least in the two Faculties involved).

Publication and citation data were obtained from the Institute for Scientific Information (ISI, Philadelphia). The Science Citation Index (SCI) covers several thousand scientific journals that constitute the core of the international scientific serial literature for many fields within the Natural and Life Sciences. In addition, the SCI contains non-journal material, such as published proceedings, multi-authored books, monographs and thematic collections of papers. Two important indexes are relevant for this investigation. First, the Source Index, which contains bibliographic descriptions of all articles published in the journals or books processed for the SCI. These journals (or books) are called source journals (or books). The articles published in them are called source articles. Secondly, the Citation Index, that lists all the references (i.e. citations) given in the source articles in a given year.

In this study we operated on all publications from the SCI Source Index that, according to their addresses, originated from the University of Leiden and that were published between 1970 and 1980. In addition, we obtained bibliographic data on all source articles published between 1970-1980 that cited any of the Leiden publications. Thus we operated on some

6 700 publications and 42 000 citations, the results of about 4 000 academic man-year research activities (12 500 man-year total personnel) and about 1 000 000 000 (400 million dollars) support from public resources. As far as we know it is the first time that a study of this kind, i.e. a bibliometric research performance analysis of two university Faculties — with a large research capacity and a long research tradition over a very wide range of different disciplines within the field of natural and life sciences — has been undertaken. At this moment we are updating our material for the period 1981-1983, so that eventually we will operate on about 10 000 publications and 70 000 citations. Apart from policy-oriented investigations, we also focused on underlying themes such as publication and citation characteristics in the various fields of science.

Bibliometric indicators — based on the ISI data — were calculated for all research groups in the Faculty of Mathematics and Natural Sciences, and in the Faculty of Medicine. An extensive software package (Moed *et al.*, 1983) was developed to carry out numerous tasks with respect to the data handling, which is in fact the combination of two large data clusters (bibliometric data and university data).

In this paper we shall focus our attention on the main points of our study: the construction of useful types of bibliometric indicators as tools for a university research policy; the specific problems of collecting and handling of the bibliometric and university data; the adequacy of the SCI data-base for past performance analyses; disturbing field-and time-dependent factors (publication and citation practices) that have little to do with impact as such; the comments of university researchers on the results of the analyses carried out in this study. Although this study is focused on a specific Dutch university (noting however that Leiden is generally recognised as one of Europe's major research institutions), the results of our investigation present in an illustrative way the typical problems arising in the use of bibliometric research performance indicators for university groups.

THE CONSTRUCTION OF IMPACT INDICATORS

We make a distinction between short-term impact and long-term impact. Short-term impact is indicated by counting the citations received by a publication a few years after publication (e.g. during the first three years, or only in the third year of a publication's life time). Long-term impact considers a much longer period of a publication's lifetime (some 10 years or more). This study deals with short-term impact. The rationale behind this is that the need was felt to assess the impact of recent work of research groups and to introduce a dynamic aspect (i.e. the trend of short-term impact over a longer period of time) in the assessment of past research performance. In this way, one can indicate groups that might have had considerable research success years ago, producing some high-impact papers, but whose production or impact has since declined. In addition the need was felt to assess groups that have not existed for longer than a few years and consequently do not (yet) have a large past performance. Of course, the influence of a publication cannot be fully determined by analysing its impact over the first few years after publication. One can however establish whether or not it is picked up, and whether it plays at least some part in the scientific debate — although it is hardly possible to assess the nature of the latter. Short-term impact-indicators are primarily considered as indicators of the visibility of a group at the research front: the extent to which it is active, its publications are known and picked up by fellow researchers.

We calculated indicators for each publication year during the decade 1970-1980 and analysed trends both in the annual numbers of publications and in the annual numbers of short-term citations received by these publications. An example of this trend analysis (for an arbitrary research group in the Sub-Faculty of Physics and Astronomy) is given in figure 1. In this figure, the left-hand panel gives: curve *(a)* (solid line): number of publications for each year (research output indicator); curve *(b)* (dots and dashes): number of citations received by these publications during the first three years of their lifetime, excluding in-house citations[2] (publication-impact indicator); curve *(c)* (dashed line): the ratio of these two above indicators, or the number of citations per publication.

The middle panel gives the same indicators as in the left-hand panel, but rather than calculating the values per annum, the year-average values for four-year publication blocks are calculated.

The right-hand panel also gives the same type of indicators but this time for a three-year publication block and a two-year citation counting scheme.

Our basic assumptions are that if the annual number of publications decreases (increases) the output of a group is declining (increasing). If the number of short-term citations decreases (increases) this is an indication that the impact of the group is declining (or increasing) and that the group is losing (achieving) the connection with the international research front.

A trend analysis alone is not sufficient to obtain a complete picture of the impact or output of a group, since in principle one cannot distinguish between an increase from "very low" to "low" and an increase from "average" to "high". Therefore, the trend analysis is supplemented with analyses that provide some indication of the output or impact level that a research group achieves. Probably the best way to obtain such an indication is to compare Leiden groups with other international groups working in the same field on the basis of their bibliometric scores. However, data on other groups outside Leiden were not available for this study, consequently such comparisons were not carried out. In this study, we approached the problem in another way. Citation counts of the publications of a group were compared with average citation scores of the journals in which the group itself had published. We assumed that this comparison of "expected" impact with "actual" impact provide an indication of the international impact level of a Leiden group. Therefore, apart from impact analyses based on citations of the publications of a group, the impact of the journals in which groups had published was assessed with the help of citation counts per journal, provided by ISI.

An example of this level analysis (for the same research group as given in figure 1) is presented in figure 2. Here, we see a comparison of "actual" and "expected" publication impact, or, in other words, a comparison of the citations per publication ratio for a research group with the same ratio for an "average publication" in the journals in which the group published. Only citations received by publications in the third year of their lifetime are counted, including in-house citations. Books are excluded as sources of publications and citations.

The solid line indicates the "actual" number of citations per publication; the dashed line indicates the "expected" number of citations per publication.

In this way, we obtained a large number of intriguing trend and level analysis results of research groups and departments in both Faculties. As discussed earlier, a detailed presentation of this method is given by Moed *et al.*, (1983).

DATA COLLECTION AND DATA HANDLING PROBLEMS

Obtaining complete publication and citation data was by no means an easy task. Several omissions, some due to programmatic or operational errors at ISI, were detected by us and completed at our request by ISI. The number of missing data amounted, in the first instance, to about 10 per cent of the total number of data involved. However, the nature of some of these errors was such that for several individual departments or research groups the bibliometric

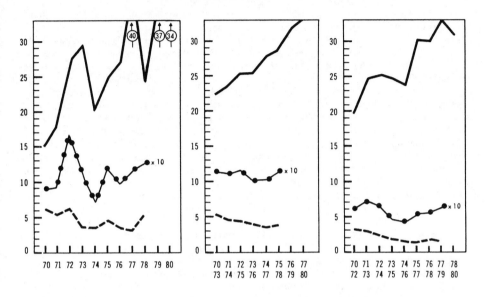

Figure 1 **EXAMPLE OF A TREND ANALYSIS**
(For explanation see text)

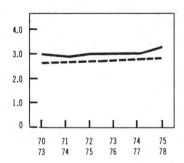

Figure 2 **EXAMPLE OF A LEVEL ANALYSIS**
(For explanation see text)

data were highly incomplete. The following may serve as an example. Due to some programmatic error, all citations to all publications of a number of journals were missing. These missing citations were about 3 per cent of the total number of citations. However, for a number of specific research groups namely those which published in these journals, 50 per cent of the citations were missing because of this error.

A complicating factor is that, generally speaking, most of the publications of a research group receive only a few citations, while a few particular publications can be highly cited. If one misses such a highly cited article, citation counts can be most incomplete. A striking example is the following. The Dutch National Survey Committee on Biochemistry evaluated the impact of a Leiden research group, and appeared to have missed one publication that was cited as many times as the total number of citations that the Committee had collected for this group.

We would like to emphasize the following problem. In regard to the relevance of impact analyses for university research policy, the research group seems to be the most adequate research unit. However, these units are rather small (2-10 researchers), and produce relatively few publications and citations. Consequently, bibliometric indicators are often based on relatively low numbers. Small errors or few omissions can lead to dramatic differences in results and interpretations. It follows that one should take considerable care in obtaining sufficiently complete bibliometric data. If a higher level of aggregation is chosen, for instance large Departments, Institutes or clusters of Departments, or even Sub-Faculties as a whole, thus operating on larger numbers, say a hundred publications and a few hundred citations, completeness becomes less important. However, bibliometric analyses on such high levels of aggregation are less relevant to research policy at university level.

Finally, we achieved a completeness percentage of 99 per cent with respect to publications with a Leiden address from the SCI Source Index. The search and selection techniques applied in this project hardly allow for a higher completeness percentage.

We propose 99 per cent as a standard rule with respect to the completeness of the publication data in impact evaluation studies of (small) university research groups. With respect to the citation data, a number of manipulations should be carried out in order to examine whether systematic errors were made when they were collected. Since such manipulations can actually only be carried out with the help of computer algorithms, all data should be on computer tapes.

Besides, it should be emphasized that complete university data are indispensable for bibliometric analysis at the research group of department level. In order to properly assign publications (and citations) to the research groups from which they originated, one needs complete data on research groups, either the names of all researchers who belong or have belonged to the group, or — even better — complete lists of publications per research group. Therefore, we conclude that a very crucial part of this type of university research performance analysis lies in a sophisticated combination of two data clusters: the (ISI) bibliometric data, and the university data. As stated before, automatic data handling is a prerequisite to carry out this work efficiently.

SPECIFIC PROBLEMS IN USING BIBLIOMETRIC DATA FOR PAST PERFORMANCE ANALYSIS

In order to gain an insight into the appropriateness of SCI source journals and SCI source books as an adequate tool for bibliometric analyses, we studied carefully the publications of each (Sub-) Faculty, listed in annual University Research Reports and determined the percentage of publications in SCI source journals or books (benchmark year 1979). The following results were obtained.

For the Sub-Faculties Chemistry, and Physics and Astronomy, 80 per cent or more of all listed publications are published in SCI source journals and books. The remaining publications are mainly contributions to international meetings and symposia. For the Sub-Faculties Pharmacy and Biology, and for a sample of four Departments in the Faculty of Medicine, the percentage of publications in SCI source journals and books is considerably lower: 33 per cent, 52 per cent and some 45 per cent respectively. The main reason is that some 25 per cent of all listed publications are written in Dutch. In addition, 26 per cent of the listed publications of the Sub-Faculty of Biology are written in English though published in journals not processed for the SCI. These are mainly publications of the Department of Taxonomy.

For the Sub-Faculty of Mathematics the percentage of publications in SCI source journals or books is the lowest of all the Sub-Faculties: 24 per cent. The main reason for this is that almost 40 per cent of all listed publications are research reports of the Sub-Faculty of the Mathematical Centre, a national research institute in Amsterdam. However, these are all published in English.

Therefore, in contrast to Mathematics, calculation of output and impact indicators based on SCI data presented no problems for research groups in the Sub-Faculties Chemistry, and Physics and Astronomy. Nearly all journals in which they publish are covered.

With respect to research groups in the Sub-Faculties Pharmacy and Biology, and the Faculty of Medicine (assuming that the four departments analysed with respect to this point can be considered as representative of the Faculty as a whole) the output in Dutch is not covered by the SCI source journals or books. In our opinion, this is not a serious problem. Since these articles are written in Dutch, they should not be considered as directed towards the international scientific community. From the point of view of university research policy, output and impact on the international research front are aspects in their own right, and this study deals with these aspects. On the other hand it is obvious that impact on a national level cannot be adequately indicated on the basis of SCI data. The fact that 26 per cent of the listed Biology publications are written in English though published in journals not processed for the SCI, is of more concern. Taking the language in which they are written as a criterion, these publications are directed towards the international research community, yet the SCI Source Index does not cover them. A field like Taxonomy (at least, we think, the European research efforts in this field) is probably not adequately covered by the SCI. Consequently, it is doubtful whether one can obtain reliable impact and output results based on SCI data alone.

Finally, the fact that almost 40 per cent of all listed publications of the Sub-Faculty of Mathematics are published in research reports, and are included in the SCI source journals or in books, constitutes a problem as well. Again, taking the language in which they are written as a criterion, they are directed towards the international scientific community, however the reports are not published in journals. Possibly the role of the serial (journal) literature for the communication of research findings differs from discipline to discipline. Further research into this problem is needed.

FIELD- AND TIME-DEPENDENT DISTURBING FACTORS

Dealing with impact indicators, i.e. variables determined (partly) by the impact level of a group, we should keep in mind that these indicators are also influenced by disturbing factors that have little to do with impact as such. In this study, we analysed disturbing factors related to specific citation practices within fields, and factors that are related to (changes in) the coverage of the SCI data base.

The main results of these analyses are:

1. Citation practices appear to differ significantly from field to field. In some fields, researchers tend to cite recent (for instance two-year-old) articles more frequently than in others. For example, an article in the *Journal of Differential Equations* (Mathematics) contains, on average, one citation of two-year-old journal articles. Yet, an article in the *European Journal of Biochemistry* contains an average of four citations of two-year-old journal's articles. It follows that the probability of a two-year-old article being cited, differs significantly within the two fields mentioned in this example. One should expect — and one actually observes — much higher (short-term) citation-levels in Biochemistry than in Mathematics. One of the analyses carried out by us (Moed *et al.*, 1983) provides an insight into these differences. This analysis is based on data such as those given in the example, for a number of fields (defined by the journals in which departments or research groups have published).
    We came to the conclusion that differences in citation counts for groups in different fields cannot be merely interpreted in terms of impact. In other words, one cannot establish relative impact by directly comparing citations counts for groups in one (Sub-) Faculty, or even in one Department. Disturbing factors due to differences in citation practices can, to a large extent, affect the numerical values of the citation-based indicators.

2. Citation practices within fields can also change during the decade. In fact, an analysis of the SCI data base between 1970 and 1980 brings to light that a journal article contains, on average, an increasing number of citations of 0-2-year-old articles during the decade. Hence, the increase of the average number of citations that 0-2-year-old Leiden articles receive during the decade should be directly proportional to this. We assume that this increase does not reflect an increase of the impact of the Leiden publications.

3. Considerable disturbances result from the fact that ISI has included more source journals during the decade and that, as from 1977, non-journal material (books) are also included. The following may serve as an example. Due to the inclusion of books in 1977, the number of Leiden publications increased by about 10 per cent, while some groups profited more than others. Moreover, the number of citations received by Leiden articles was affected as well. For some groups, the number of citations doubled, while for others it did not change at all.

We conclude that because of possible changes in citation practices or changes in the SCI source journals and books, one should be very cautious about interpreting trends in the numerical values of bibliometric indicators as trends in output or impact. It requires a considerable effort and knowledge to identify the effects of these disturbing factors, especially on the level of research groups. It should be noted however that we constructed bibliometric indicators (especially those used in the level analysis) that neutralise some of the disturbing factors mentioned above.

To investigate this important problem in the application of past bibliometric performance indicators, we are conducting further research on the distribution of the SCI source books over the various research fields and on differences with respect to communication practices between fields.

COMMENTS OF INTERVIEWED RESEARCHERS; CONCLUSIONS

Twelve researchers in the (Sub-) Faculties involved were interviewed. These interviews were meant as an "acceptance test", i.e. to examine whether our bibliometric results and interpretations differed or agreed with the ideas of scientists in the fields; whether we had overlooked hidden pitfalls and other problems with respect to bibliometric indicators, and whether the bibliometric results and interpretations provided a meaningful basis for the discussion of past research performance of research groups. During the interviews, the researchers saw our results for the first time. They expressed their personal views. So their comments should not necessarily be considered as representative of the view of any (Sub-) Faculty body or of the "scientific community" within the various (Sub-) Faculties. They made comments that were related to all the issues described above. Their comments dealt with matters like: what the constructed indicators actually indicate; the type of indicators chosen; the completeness of the bibliometric data; the coverage of the SCI data base; and disturbing factors that should be kept in mind in interpreting bibliometric results. We should discuss here the main points of their comments, for a detailed discussion the reader is referred to Moed *et al.*, (1983).

In our opinion, the most interesting general result of these interviews is the following. In many cases the researchers interviewed did not reject our bibliometric results and interpretations, but tried to find explanations for the observed output and impact of the research group. For example, they related a given low impact level of a particular research group to the low quality of the research performed by this group. Or they related the low impact to the fact that the researchers within the group are not fond of the limelight, or do not present their findings in an effective way. They mentioned causes that refer to particular events or circumstances within the groups, such as relational problems between staff members, changes in the permanent staff, or the fact that the group does not have a "second best man". In some cases, they thought the observed low impact of groups in experimental fields was related to the fact that they had fallen behind on a technological level. In addition, causes were mentioned that refer to characteristics of research fields, such as strong competition and complete lack of consensus, resulting in opposition from members of editorial boards of significant journals. So during the interviews, many policy-relevant factors were brought to light that otherwise would have remained undiscussed. Our indicators formed a sound basis for these discussions as they gave a concise indication of research performance over a relatively long period, up to recent years.

We therefore conclude that the type of bibliometric analyses carried out in this study can be a useful tool for a university research policy. It constitutes a "monitoring device" with which research groups can be "followed" over a long time up until quite recent years. In principle, bibliometric analyses provide a meaningful basis for discussion of the performance of research groups with scientists in the field, and possibly also with members of monitored research groups themselves. The analyses enable research policy-makers to ask relevant questions about research groups; to some extent the analyses provide an historical picture for those who are not familiar with the research performed by a group or with the field in which it works. Bibliometric analyses can, in principle, provide a basis for a dialogue between research policy-makers and the researchers of various university groups.

It should be emphasized however that there is no straightforward or simple relationship between the results of bibliometric analyses and the nature of future policy decisions. In order to make proper policy decisions, insight should be obtained into the factors or causes underlying the observed impact and output, and about the extent to which these factors can be expected to persist. Bibliometric analysis is not a substitute for background knowledge about these factors. Bibliometric analysis can, in fact, be used to bring these factors into the open through discussions about the analyses with the researchers concerned.

NOTES AND REFERENCES

1.   This paper was presented at the 6th European Forum of the Association for Institutional Research, August 22nd-24th 1984, Vrije Universiteit Brussels, and has been included in the proceedings of this conference.

2.   The concept of "self-citation", of "in-house citation" can be defined in various ways. The aim of these concepts is to identify citations by authors who work within the domain of direct influence of publishing authors. Clearly, each publication has its specific domain. How should such a domain be defined? In this study we used a rather broad conception of "in-house citation": the domain ("house") consists of all authors (both first and co-authors) of all Leiden publications. Generally speaking, these authors are researchers appointed for at least some years at Leiden University. In addition, there are researchers who are not affiliated to Leiden University, who nevertheless have published together with Leiden researchers.
     It follows that if such in-house citations are excluded, in fact only citations are counted from source articles of which the first author (from *citing* articles only the name of the *first* author is present in our Citation File) has never published a paper with a Leiden address during the period 1970-1980. In this way we are able to evaluate the impact Leiden publications have outside Leiden. The overall percentage of in-house citations amounts to approximately 31 per cent.

Martin, B.R. and Irvine, J. (1982). "Assessing Basic Research: Some Partial Indicators of Scientific Progress in Ratio Astronomy". *Research Policy*, 12: 61-90.

Moed, H.F., Burger, W.J.M., Frankfort, J.G., and Van Raan, A.F.J. (1983). *On the Measurement of Research Performance: the Use of Bibliometric Indicators.* Leiden: Research Policy Unit of the University of Leiden.

Van Raan, A.F.J. and Frankfort, J.G. (1980). "An Approach to University Science Policy: a New Research Funding System". *International Journal of Institutional Management in Higher Education*, 4: 155-163. Paris: OECD/CERI.

A Case Study on the Evaluation of Research at the Technical University of Denmark

Peter Rasmussen
Technical University of Denmark
Lyngby, Denmark

ABSTRACT

In the winter of 1983/1984 an evaluation was carried out of all research activities at the Technical University of Denmark (DTH). This paper describes the procedure and the experiences of the evaluation with emphasis on evaluation at the departmental level in the Chemistry and Chemical Engineering sector of DTH: input material (e.g. annual reports, department programmes); estimation of research activity and productivity (e.g. man-years spent on the different research projects, number of publications per man-year); evaluation of the research (e.g. relevance to the teaching activities, to international research, to society).

INTRODUCTION

During the first months of 1984 an evaluation of all research activities was carried out at the Technical University of Denmark (DTH) by a group of employees and students at DTH. This paper is an attempt to explain why and how the evaluation was done, and to describe some of our experiences from this in many ways interesting, but also frustrating exercise.

It should be emphasized that this text focuses on evaluation in the Chemistry and Chemical Engineering sector at DTH. It should also be emphasized that since the author is a teacher and researcher in a chemical engineering department, this means that his perspective is more or less fixed at the department level.

Finally, it should be stressed that the evaluation discussed here is an evaluation of the research carried out in each department. It is not an evaluation of the activity of any particular individual.

WHY EVALUATION ?

The activities at a technical university like DTH have a dual purpose. We have to teach and train young students to the highest possible level in the basic and applied sciences and in the engineering skills that are required to fill a job as a civil, mechanical, electrical or chemical engineer. Secondly, we have to do research partly to be able to provide the capability for teach-ing and partly to act as a centre for the highest technological knowledge in the country.

The teaching and research activities cannot, of course, be separated. It is impossible to teach at the highest level without the use of teachers who are fully aware of current knowledge and developments. The teachers therefore have to be personally engaged in research and the students have to train in active research environments. This is naturally true in general for any university. On top of this we have at DTH a special responsibility since DTH, for many disci-plines of applied and engineering science, is the only place in Denmark where such knowledge is publicly available. This means that we have to be especially careful in the distribution of the limited resources so that no mechanism will turn the allocation of resources away from re-search in these engineering and applied science activities.

The current procedure for fixing the number of staff members in each department may not be the best in this respect, since the procedure is almost totally rooted in the demands for teaching activity. This may make it difficult to start new research areas and to give special support to very active research groups. It may also be that some of the more special areas of applied science and technology may for some years not attract many students, and yet it is important for DTH as such to keep the activity. In this context one has to realise that there is a minimum size for a group to ensure an active research environment.

We have therefore good reason at DTH to make a continuous evaluation of research at each department of the university. Firstly, we have to make sure that there is a good research activity in each department for the sake of teaching. Secondly, the evaluation will help in locating especially strong and weak research groups and possibly in revealing areas where research has to be initiated or strengthened. The evaluation in itself gives an overview of the current research and may thereby help the administration in developing a procedure where the distribution of resources is not based on the teaching demands alone, but is also influenced by desired research activities.

Besides these reasons there is a side effect which comes just by doing the evaluation. That is the inspiration which the departments get from the knowledge that somebody looks into their research activity and judges the department relative to other departments.

WHO DID THE 1984 EVALUATION ?

Who can carry out an evaluation of research at an institution like DTH ? It would pro-bably be best for each department to appoint a group of well known and well respected re-searchers and specialists in the research areas of the department and to ask this group to make the evaluation. The group members should all come from outside the university and preferably also from outside the country to ensure a free and independent evaluation. This procedure has quite recently been used to evaluate Natural Science and Chemical Engineering in Sweden[1, 2].

This approach would, however, involve an excessive amount of effort in order to meet the stated objectives of the evaluation at DTH. An internal evaluation was carried out instead by employees and students from DTH:

Due to our administrative system the elected evaluation groups had to have representa-tives from various types of personnel groups at the university. This is illustrated in table 1 by the composition of the evaluation group, which had to look into the 13 departments within the Chemistry and Chemical Engineering sector at DTH.

Table 1

EVALUATION GROUP FOR THE CHEMISTRY
AND CHEMICAL ENGINEERING SECTOR

1 full professor 2 senior lecturers	2 craftsmen 1 student

It is obvious that there is a great difference between the composition of this evaluation group and the "ideal" external group described above. It could very well be that this internal group might end up with a judgment of a department which could be totally different from that given by an external group or another internal group for that matter. This partly explains why I think that the whole exercise was a little frustrating. I must also admit that I am so "undemocratic" that I believe that a worthwhile evaluation of research can only be done by experienced researchers.

Table 2 shows the types of departments and the number of employees at each department in the Chemistry and Chemical Engineering sector.

In total, six evaluation groups were formed: 1) Chemistry and Chemical Engineering, 2) Mechanical Engineering, 3) Electrical Engineering, 4) Civil Engineering, 5) Basic Sciences such as Physics and Mathematics, 6) Social Sciences. These groups reported to the central research committee of DTH.

Table 2

DEPARTMENTS IN THE CHEMISTRY AND CHEMICAL ENGINEERING
SECTOR AT DTH AND NUMBER OF EMPLOYEES

Department		Scientific Staff		Technical/ Administrative Personnel
		Permanent	Temporary	
A	Inorganic Chemistry A	23	18	37
	Inorganic Chemistry B	10	4	10
	Physical Chemistry	11	~ 6	14
	Organic Chemistry	15	~ 3	16
B	Microbiology	6	4	8.5
	Biochemistry	5.5	2.5	8.4
	Ecology and Environmental Chemistry	3	3	3
	Food Technology	4	6.5	10
	Technical Biochemistry	5	7	6
C	Metallurgy	5.5	6	7
	Ceramics and Mineral Industry	8	8	9
	Chemical Engineering	15.5	22.5	15
	Chemical Technology	10	11	16

A: "Basic Chemistry"
B: "Biosciences"
C: "Chemical Engineering and Materials Sciences"

INPUT INFORMATION TO THE RESEARCH EVALUATION

DTH is a state university which means that society has every right to demand documentation for the proper application of all kinds of allocated resources like money and personnel. This documentation must comprise research plans and results.

Each department at DTH therefore has to submit an annual report to the central university administration on the various activities in the department. These reports have been standardised and contain significant information of relevance to a research evaluation as shown in table 3.

Table 3

HEADINGS OF SECTIONS IN THE ANNUAL REPORTS
OF IMPORTANCE FOR RESEARCH EVALUATION

- Personnel (e.g. permanent staff members, technical, administrative personnel, PhD students, visiting staff, research fellows);
- Research projects;
- Publications from the past year;
- Participation in scientific conferences;
- Lectures given outside the department;
- Research collaboration with groups outside DTH;
- Membership of scientific committees, refereeing for international journals, membership of committees for the appointment of scientific personnel, etc.

In order to smooth out annual fluctuations evaluation is based on reports for a three-year period, i.e. the reports covering the years 1981, 1982 and 1983 were used for the recent evaluation.

Other important information can be obtained from the research programmes which the departments submit every third year. These programmes describe all the research projects in a department with the arguments and aims for the planned work. Comparisons between the research plans for a period and the annual reports for that period provide good information as to the ability of each research group to make reasonable plans which can be carried out.

Other relevant and important information might be:

1. The financial support to each department. How much money has the department received for research from sources outside DTH, e.g. from government or private funds or from companies or maybe from NATO, EEC or the like ? and
2. The facilities available for research in a department. Is there a good workshop, new equipment, easy access to computers and to support facilities ?

No attempt has been made to quantify this kind of information in the evaluation.

RESEARCH STATISTICS

Resources

There do not exist any unique and objective criteria for measuring research results relative to the applied resources. In order to make a relative study between various departments one can, however, develop some simple statistics indicating research activity and productivity.

From the annual reports one may easily extract information on the number of man-years spent during a given year at a given department by permanent staff members, PhD students, and visiting staff and research fellows. Table 2 gives such data for 1983. For visiting staff and other persons spending a short time in a department only periods of at least one month were counted and included.

Since the activity at DTH comprises both teaching and research, it is necessary to fix some general factors for the estimation of the time allocated to research. The factors which were chosen by the central administration at DTH are shown in table 4. These numbers were used by all evaluation groups.

Table 4

FRACTION OF TIME ALLOCATED TO RESEARCH BY SCIENTIFIC PERSONNEL

Permanent staff	0.4	
PhD students	0.6	
Visiting staff	0.6	Temporary staff
Research fellows	0.8	

The figures are empirical and average statistics which should closely reflect the actual situation. A senior lecturer is thus supposed to teach half the time, do administrative work in ten per cent of the time and forty per cent is left for research. I can assure you that these are average numbers, and I know of no-one who, as an individual, works accordingly. As an average for a department over a year the figure is reasonable.

For the other types of personnel in table 4 arguments about teaching obligations, time for learning about the activities in a department (visiting staff), participation in study-groups and informal seminar series led to the figures given here.

Table 5 shows the total number of man-years allocated to research for the three year period 1981-1983. The figures apply to scientific personnel only and are totals for the three "main" areas in the Chemistry and Chemical Engineering sector.

Table 5

MAN-YEARS ALLOCATED TO RESEARCH DURING THE
THREE-YEAR   PERIOD 1981-1983

	Total	Permanent staff	Total/ Permanent staff
Basic Chemistry	104.3	67.9	1.54
Biosciences	67.6	28.4	2.38
Chemical Engineering and Materials Science	123.5	44.8	2.76

The ratio between the number of man-years spent in total on research and the number of man-years spent by the permanent staff is an indicator of research activity. The ratio is an indicator of the scientific environment created by the permanent staff in the department. A large ratio will thus mean that many PhD students and guests have been attracted to the department.

One should, however, not stress this point too far as can be seen from table 5. Other explanations are obviously needed in order to explain the differences between basic science and engineering departments. Tradition and different degrees of contact with industry may explain part of it.

Results

The result of any research activity must be some sort of written contribution. If the results are presented via an oral presentation only, e.g. a lecture, it is not possible or at least not easy to reproduce and thereby verify the conclusions. It has been claimed that the most important benefits of doing research at a university are not the results of the research but the fact that by participating in research projects one becomes more qualified as a teacher. This is no doubt a good side effect, but the research project and the results must be described in a written publication in order to have any lasting value.

How can we otherwise on a systematic basis increase our stock of scientific and techno-logical knowledge and devise new applications ?

The annual reports contain information about publications which have been published during the last year. The publications are split into different categories as shown in table 6.

Table 6

CATEGORIES OF RESEARCH PUBLICATIONS IN THE ANNUAL REPORTS

1.	Dissertations;	4.	Other articles;
2.	Scientific monographs;	5.	Proceedings from conferences;
3.	Articles in journals with a referee system;	6.	Reports.

The number of publications in each category was counted for each department and totalled for the three-year period 1981-1983 according to the following criteria:

1. "Dissertations", "scientific monographs", and "articles in journals with a referee system" were counted according to whether the departments had presented the publications in the annual reports;

2. Some judgment was used as regards the category "other articles". Only articles which were found to have the same kind of lasting value as refereed articles were included;

3. "Proceedings from conferences" were only included if it was found that the con-tributions represented independent research work. Results which had been pre-sented almost identically in articles by the same authors were excluded as were review papers and contributions shorter than two pages (such contributions were consi-dered to be mere abstracts);

4. The critical selection of papers used for "proceedings from conferences" was also applied to the category of reports, and only reports available to anyone interested were included;

5. Some publications may represent the results of a joint effort between an author or a research group at the given department and someone from outside the depart-ment. The question then arises whether the publication should count as a full publi-cation or as some fraction given by the ratio between the number of authors from the department and the total number of authors. In our evaluation group we decided that it was such a positive thing to have co-operation that we gave full credit. Some of the other evaluation groups did only give partial credit accord-ing to the relative number of authors from the department.

It is obvious that this kind of critical counting of publications may lead to disagreements between the evaluation group and the departments. It turns out that even between departments in the Chemistry and Chemical Engineering sector at DTH there are great differences in the publishing traditions, e.g. a basic chemistry department like Inorganic Chemistry B does not seem to value publications for conferences and reports very highly while the Chemical Engineering Department has many original contributions presented at conferences and quite a few results in reports.

Our personal experience from this evaluation is that some dissonance could have been avoided if our evaluation group had had the necessary time to consult departments more closely during the evaluation process. The other evaluation groups at DTH did invest that time and avoided discussion afterwards.

Table 7 shows the publications calculated for the three-year period 1981-1983 split between the three main areas in our sector of DTH.

Table 7

NUMBER OF PUBLICATIONS FROM THE THREE-YEAR PERIOD 1981-1983

Publications	Basic Chemistry	Biosciences	Chemical Engineering and Materials Science
Dissertations	12	14	19
Scientific monographs	10	5	6
Articles	231	89	119
Proceedings from conferences	22	9	50
Reports	16	21	33
Total	291	138	227
Total / (Man-years for research)	2.79	2.04	1.84

In the calculation of publications no weighting has been applied for the different categories. The argument is that the number of publications is only a rough indication of the results of the research.

A weighting according to some more or less arbitrary criteria for the relative importance of the different categories did not seem justified to our evaluation group. This was not the conclusion by all evaluation groups and at least one group decided to use weight factors: dissertations, 1.0, scientific monographs with new results 2.0, articles 1.0, proceedings from conferences 0.3-1.0 depending on the applied reviewing system, reports 0.5. Other possibilities have been suggested 1) that one should not count the number of publications, but instead the number of published pages and 2) that one should only count the number of refereed articles and monographs, since all real valuable results from dissertations, conference papers and reports will end up as articles anyway.

Table 7 gives the ratio between the total number of publications and the total number of man-years spent on research. This number should be an indication of the effectiveness of the research, but from table 7 it is also obvious that the number discloses a difference in the publishing traditions between the fundamental and the applied disciplines of science and engineering. It should be recalled from table 2 that the group of departments in Biosciences comprises both fundamental and engineering departments.

Table 8

RESEARCH ACTIVITY AND PRODUCTIVITY IN THREE
DIFFERENT DEPARTMENTS 1981-1983

		Departments	
Publications	1	2	3
Dissertations	2	3	9
Scientific monographs	3	0	5
Articles	65	12	45
Proceedings from conferences	1	1	27
Reports	6	9	8
Total publications TP	77 (71)[1]	25 (16)	94 (86)
Total man-years of research TMY	23.8	15.1	59.2
Permanent staff man-years of research PSMY	19.5	6.0	18.6
TMY/PSMY	1.2	2.5	3.2
TP/TMY	3.2 (3.0)	1.7 (1.1)	1.6 (1.5)
Lectures/PSMY	3.1	5.5	5.7

1. The numbers in parentheses refer to the total number of publications excluding reports.

Table 8 shows the research statistics for three different departments. The table clearly indicates something about the research activity (TMY/PSMY) and also something about the effectiveness of research (TP/TMY) even though publishing traditions, the need for large and costly (also in terms of manpower) equipment and possibly other factors may blur the picture. The number of lectures presented outside the department by full-time staff numbers is also an indication of the activity concerning the communication of research results. These figures are also shown in table 8.

EVALUATION OF THE RESEARCH OF A DEPARTMENT

The final of the evaluation for each department was a short report (one to two pages)with a closing statement about the research activity;

A. above average;
B. average;
C. below average.

In order to get this final mark the evaluation group tried to combine the results of the research statistics with the general impression of the department gained from the annual reports and from the research programmes. The following topics were, for example, examined along with the statistics:

1. Did the research seem relevant with respect to the teaching activities and with respect to the kind of activities which one in general would expect at such a

department ? Was there an area where no research was done or was too much effort concentrated on one rather special area ?

2. Did all members of the permanent scientific staff participate in research ? It turned out that in quite a few departments one could find one or more persons who had not published in the three-year period. This question is to a certain extent related to the organisation of research in the department.

3. Was the research in any way part of an international cooperation exercise ? Could one for example find foreign authors in many of the publications ?

4. Could one find good progress and development compared to the previous evaluation ?

5. Did the members of the permanent staff take their share of the burdens of research administration such as acting as referees to international journals and being members of scientific committees, e.g. for the assessment of research projects, judgment of applicants for high-level research jobs and for organising conferences ?

We refrained from an evaluation of the need (national or otherwise) for the actual research were estimated as the number of man-years spent by permanent and part-time scientific of the research. At a previous evaluation one had tried to judge quality by using the Science Citation Index to find out whether the published papers were referred to and hence had been useful for somebody.

The final result for the departments in the Chemistry and Chemical Engineering sector at DTH was rather encouraging: 5 departments were judged to be above average, five to be average and only three were characterised as below average.

CONCLUSION

The goals of DTH are to create, maintain, and develop a high level of research and teaching, to produce new knowledge and to promote the practical application of applied and engineering science to the benefit of society.

In order to ensure that the departments at DTH live up to these high standards we have, at intervals, to evaluate the activities in each department. This paper has described an evaluation exercise carried out in the winter of 1984. During the evaluation the resources applied to research were estimated as the number of man-years spent by permanent and part-time scientific personnel alone, i.e. no account was taken of the contribution made by the technical/administrative staff or of financial support. The results of the research were determined as the number of publications. The annual reports and the research programmes from each department formed the basis for the final evaluation which was a mark: above average, average or below average.

It was planned to use the evaluation results to develop a procedure for separate allocation of resources to research and teaching in each department. The procedure which the central university administration asked us to use in the exercise described constituted only a very modest step in this direction. This means that the number of persons in the permanent scientific staff is still almost entirely fixed by the demands for teaching activity.

March 1985 Vol. 9 No. 1

REFERENCES

1. NFR Report (1981). "International Evaluations of Research Projects Supported by the Swedish National Science Research Council — Summary of Reports, Achievements and Criticisms, 1977-1980".

2. UHA Report (1984/85). "Chemical Engineering: Research and Evaluation in Sweden".

The Evaluation of Research: An Economic Process

Anne M. T. Rouban
Long-Range Forecasting and Evaluation Centre
Ministry for Industrial Redeployment and Foreign Trade
Ministry for Research and Technology
France

abstract
ABSTRACT

This paper discusses only a few of the more sensitive aspects of the relationship between research evaluation and resource allocation, i.e. the evaluation capability of the establishments concerned, the objectives as decisive factors, peer-group evaluation, and the search for new methodologies.
Research evaluation includes scientific evaluation and strategic evaluation, in which research workers and engineers are not the only people concerned. The integration of the evaluating process has to be worked out according to methods and criteria adapted to the economy of complex systems; in this both sociology and the economic and political sciences have a special role to play.

INTRODUCTION

The evaluation of research is vitally important, both for the management of research projects and as a tool for formulating and carrying out scientific and technical policies. The main difficulty in evaluating research lies in the absence of a common approach. For many authors, it is the *scientific evaluation* of research that is the most important. But the concept of evaluation should also cover the *regulating processes* related to the socio-economic spin-off of production activities and the transfer of knowledge thanks to feedback from the various information media.

Thus a seminar organised by the Long-range Forecasting and Evaluation Centre (CPE) in 1983 on the evaluation of research programmes in major French undertakings enabled two interesting aspects to be highlighted:

— The difficulty of evaluating research independently of its managerial structures (budget and programming);
— The transfer of evaluation activity outside some of the centres concerned.

It appears that a systemic approach to procedures for evaluating R & D activities could help to identify the main components, as these are used by enterprises, universities, institutes and research centres.

Various general aspects will be discussed here:

—   The evaluation capability of establishments;
—   The objectives as decisive factors;
—   Peer-group evaluation;
—   The search for new methodologies.

THE EVALUATION CAPABILITY OF ESTABLISHMENTS

Role sharing

Higher educational establishments have two main roles: to teach and to carry out research, i.e. to produce and transfer knowledge. But they are not the only groups involved: enterprises and research institutes are also concerned. However, whereas the former have to prepare people to cope with complex situations, the enterprises are concerned with employing these same people to design, manufacture and sell their products and processes (Archier and Serieyx — 1984).

Enterprises' role as a link in the transmission of knowledge should not be underestimated, and in some countries they are considered to be an integral part of the training system. Feigenbaum and Mc Corduck (1983) give a detailed description of the computer course taken by students at Tokyo University, where one of the principal responsibilities of the teachers is to select new graduates suitable for enterprises with job vacancies, which will undertake their further training.

The international aspect

There is no need to dwell on the extraordinarily complex network of non-university research institutes which, thanks to associative or co-operative contracts or sub-contracts, participate in R & D in the various countries.

Generally speaking, the more international the research is, the more essential it is to have the capability to evaluate it. The examples that can be mentioned here include the organisation of access to massive or large-scale exploration facilities in oceanology, nuclear physics or astronomy, as well as research programmes undertaken by international organisations.

The essentials

Faced with competition, the enterprise evaluates not only the share of the market represented by its production range, but also — for strategy's sake — the expedience of its investments, structures and production facilities, the skills of its staff and the soundness of its decision--making with regard to the goals sought, etc.

Similarly, higher education establishments not only have to evaluate their own research compared with that of other institutes, but also the sums invested and the structures providing an impetus for new research and educational capacities.

The evaluation capability of establishments will therefore depend on:

—   The control of scientific and technical *information,* and therefore of policies with regard to investment, for example, the hardware and software required, the improvement of statistics and the working out of methods for identifying and developing concepts;

- The *institutional* situation of the establishment with regard to the various governmental structures involved and thus the degree of independence enjoyed in negotiating the financing and programming of research;
  Evaluation of the results has indeed to be based on a precise analysis of the decision-making process affecting R & D, i.e. that used by the institutions concerned with planning, commissioning, and controlling and evaluating research.
- The capacity of the scientific community to *evaluate* the results of its own method of decision-making, given that establishments have to give due weight to *government policy* concerning employment and training;
- Their own outlets, which are conditioned by their physical location and by their fields of research.

The capacity to stop a programme

Stopping a research programme because it is ineffective or produces few results appears to have happened up to now only in enterprises, and more rarely in the context of a clearly targeted programme.

But this concern is now becoming a major one. As Cozzens emphasized during an international meeting organised by the CPE (1984), the most *strategic* way of evaluating a programme is to take the decision to launch or cancel it. This kind of decision implies the use of new evaluation methods.

Thus for the National Science Foundation (NSF), the main question raised in current evaluations concerns the NSF's degree of efficiency in maintaining its objectives, their value being estimated in comparison with other goals such as economic growth. So far, this principle had been applied only to fundamental research.

However, even in the context of enterprises, the cancellation of a project requires complex systems of reference. Balachandra and Raelin (1984) identify twelve factors influencing the decision whether or not to stop a project: support from directors, rate of introduction of new products, probability of technical success, the technological option, the role of the project director in promoting the project, the link between the marketing and the technical aspects, the targets sought, the efficiency of the person in charge, team motivation, the service life of the product, internal competition, and the financing programme.

The authors conclude their paper by saying that the financial and economic factors, such as return on investments (ROI), profit, the size of the market as a whole, or the market share do not appear to be decisive at the time the decision is taken to continue a project, since they are analysed before the R & D stage.

OBJECTIVES AS DECISIVE FACTORS

The specific weight of the criteria

The objectives focused on during an evaluation determine the very nature of the evaluation procedure selected and therefore the choice of experts, criteria and methods. If, very schematically, a gradient is imagined linking the researcher to an aggregate structure, it might seem trivial to note that the level of scientific expertise required increases the more the evaluation concerns the researcher only, and decreases as evaluation of aggregate structures (programmes, institutions, regions, States), and socio-economic and political criteria become preponderant. The scientific results should therefore be monitored first by the scientists themselves and by the scientific community.

In fact the complex reality that has to be managed at various levels of application requires evaluation procedures which, although they respect the same set of criteria, give them variable specific weights. Thus an industrial firm may use a set of scientific, production, marketing, financial or statistical criteria which will be weighted differently according to whether they are applied to cognitive or applied research or to R & D.

Is it desirable to correlate the evaluation procedure instead of the research ?

Generally, a clear distinction is made between the enterprise and the university, since industry's objective is profit. Any convergence between procedures for evaluating research and its programming and financing is therefore considered undesirable or at any rate irrelevant.

This view would appear to be more difficult to defend today in the case of high technology enterprises, which, with the help of associative contracts with universities, have to make a minimal research effort in order to be able to supervise, control and evaluate the scientific progress made outside the firm (Fundingsland – 1984).

At the same time, according to the country concerned, various projects and programmes can be found which we shall call "federative" insofar as research structures which are institutionally different may take part in developing research in a given sector, their objective being to become the instrument of a particular scientific and technical policy. In the case of these national and internationl programmes, the objective itself leads to an *ex-ante evaluation* procedure which involves the planning and budgeting of the resources to be used. Ad hoc committees are therefore set up by the decision-making bodies and evaluation has to take account of socio-economic requirements, research in progress, and R & D trends within the private sector. Thus, after various prior studies aiming at identifying the need for research and its feasibility have been carried out, the ad hoc committees will be in a position to choose the appropriate research structures, fix the objectives and draw up a plan (Yonekura –1984). The projects, in the form of completed applied research programmes, are then distributed among universities and enterprises.

Because of this, *new programming methods* for university research have to be worked out in the light of the commissions received from enterprises and government agencies. It is important to distinguish between two types of programmes: those of a strategic nature and those devoted to the study of specific themes (Chapman and Farina – 1983).

Defining objectives

Defining objectives before carrying out the evaluation is essential for any *on-going or a posteriori evaluation.* Scientific evaluation, specific to a given discipline, is carried out by the scientific institutions. But strategic evaluation, comprising economic, administrative, and policy aspects, receives an increasing amount of establishments' attention. Those responsible for research policy therefore have a decisive role to play by fixing the general objectives and specific sub-objectives of the scientific community.

PEER-GROUP EVALUATION

Rhetorical ambiguity

Research programmes and projects are evaluated by the peer group, not only in the context of evaluation units in research establishments, but also in ad hoc committees or auditing committees. The peer evaluation procedure is a general method used to assess research proposals and also the ultimate findings. The experts are sometimes asked to take only scientific considerations into account, not those of a financial or institutional nature.

Furthermore, it is generally accepted, if not always the practice, that experts should be totally independent of the project managers and directors. However, a certain ambiguity remains, particularly with regard to targeted programmes, for which the proposals may stem from scientists but where the decisions are taken by committees comprised of managers and representatives of industry and scientists (Chapman and Farina — 1983).

Ambiguity exists at two levels:

- The apparent passiveness of the decision-making committees, which "depend on" the proposals which are made to them, since the head of an establishment or an enterprise generally decides to submit the case to be reviewed to an examining group chosen by him.
- The absence of consideration for financial or institutional aspects is theoretical, since the system depends on the respect of the institutions whose work is under consideration and to which the experts are attached; and also on their reputation, which is another form of recognition, not only of the quality of the work but also the operational resources represented.

Many questions still have to be answered

The "conservative" nature of the peer evaluation system has been criticised by a number of authors. It is true, moreover, that scientific evaluation by peers cannot be applied exclusively at all levels of evaluation.

Programming based on commissions from an establishment have to be backed up by an evaluation of previous projects and the resources to be used for the objectives aimed at. There is *necessarily* a relationship between R & D policy, the institute's commissions and the financial and institutional backing for the research, and this in turn requires an evaluation to be made of the eventual spin-offs and the procedures applied, i.e. the decision-making process, the programming and funding and the legal and regulatory aspects.

So it is not possible to come to a decision concerning the quality of research (and thus of the financial backing that should perhaps be awarded for its continuation) without also considering the constraints imposed by the financing and the staff management systems, which vary from one establishment to another; and this, for a given scientific field. For example some establishments are able to set up subsidiaries or to ensure the mobility of tasks by a system of financial incentives, etc.

At the same time, the impact of scientific and technical policy has to be taken into account, as it may give added strategic weight to this or that discipline; so it is important to combine the study of scientific considerations with an analysis of the resources allocated.

Boundaries between the various officially listed disciplines are becoming increasingly blurred, as we see from the interdisciplinary programmes and evaluation groups set up in French research institutes.

Lastly, science and technology are closely associated, which means that the time lag between fundamental research and the technological application of the results has been considerably reduced in recent years. It should be added, too, that not only technologies but also services have become social and economic targets. So science policies cannot fix strategic targets on a long-term basis.

Scientists and non-scientists

From what has been said above it can be seen that complex evaluation systems, varying according to level and to the scientific fields concerned, require adequate communications to be established between professional people of diverse origins, both in the framework of the institutes themselves and in that of the consultancy contracts, so as to work out new methodologies.

Universities are evaluated both for the quality of their research work and for their ability to train researchers, the latter being in theory called upon to contribute to the production system. Whatever the type of evaluation procedure selected, it is certain that scientists have to take an active role in it, so as to introduce and apply their own criteria of scientific achievement. In return, the findings of the evaluation are all the more appreciated and the consequences all the more clearly understood in the sector concerned. However, without underestimating the contribution of peer evaluation, the impact of government policies aimed at producing useful short-term results should not be underestimated.

Chapman *et al.* (1982) have analysed the implications, for the financing of university research, of the concern to focus the latter on social and industrial requirements, a concern which, together with the falling growth rate of the research budget, has contributed to the selection of certain "centres of excellence". The authors took four components: the distribution of expenditure, the scale and growth rate of the organisations funded, the index of concentration based on the Lorenz coefficient, and the average levels of funding in a given field. These components determine the financial resources allocated to the universities through contracts which are evaluated by peers. This study shows that the relationship between the policies adopted and the allocation of resources is far from being a direct one, but that it depends mainly on the evaluation of the spin-offs from the funding and their general trend.

Over and above scientific evaluation, there are implications which the strategic evaluation of research can bring to light. Evaluation methods have to meet the numerous requirements of the eventual "consumers", whether or not they are scientists.

THE SEARCH FOR NEW METHODOLOGIES

The methodological tools and targeting criteria used for science policies respond very slowly to the programme requirements, for as Hellstern and Wollmann (1981) emphasize, the development of methodologies is still based on the scientific model of fundamental research.

Measuring research in the light of external objectives

There are several schools of thought concerning the assessment of research findings. For "critical rationalists", the scientific analysis of a finding should be independent of evaluation, which is considered to have arbitrary aspects. According to "critical theory", the socio-economic context is decisive where scientific evaluation is concerned — which makes it difficult to quantify the latter. Another way of putting the problem is to relate evaluation to the standards underlying scientific and technical policy options, not only for the distribution of governments funds between direct financing and subsidies, but also in order to improve the measurement of the interaction between research and the economy (Fundingsland — 1984). So current work focuses on the (micro and macro) effects of R & D on economic growth.

The criteria for scientific evaluation are worked out and "managed" by the scientific community itself and only have a relative influence on other levels of evaluation. But the weighting of these criteria has to be transparent, comprehensive and suitable to the level in question.

In the same way it is necessary to *evaluate the evaluation procedures.* As well as analysing the decision-making process, it is important to analyse the evaluation process itself, so as to make comparisons, where possible, and to establish a verifiable basis which can be used by those responsible for research projects.

In any case, there should be an on-going discussion about the criteria, methods, evaluation results and those responsible. For the relationship between programme managers and research structures is often all too loose. Those making the evaluation have generally never held administrative responsibilities, and the managers tend to consider evaluation merely in its statistical form, as a justification for the activity undertaken (Hellstern and Wollmann – 1981).

Integrating the evaluation process

Evaluation should result in findings that can be translated into concrete decisions, which means that it should be budgeted for, from the start of the programme, as a percentage that has to be estimated in the light of the expected value added.

According to the level and nature of the project concerned, evaluation criteria are integrated into R & D activities from the start. Where scientific evaluation is concerned, a system of criteria will have to be worked out with the scientific community concerned. When strategic evaluation focuses on the advisability of adopting a programme, it will be necessary not only to consult scientists but also to have long range *forecasting* methods.

Evaluation taking social, economic and political considerations into account will thus help to define implementation strategies. So it should be obvious that integrating the evaluation process is not only a specifically scientific approach; it also makes a more general contribution, in that it helps to involve science in the socio-economic processes. Understood in this way, and whatever the budgetary funds provided, evaluation results in economies for the system in question.

Methods

Apart from peer consultation, which we shall not return to here, many different quantitative methods have been worked out, mainly in the United States. They include risk analysis, scoring methods, ranking methods, etc.

For Krawiec (1984), for example, scoring methods associated with risk analysis enable research projects to be evaluated and selected in the solar and thermal energy sector. This author considers that although the methods of economics are widely used in applied research, they are not appropriate for every kind of research, and particularly for fundamental research. Risk analysis methods used for financial investments, marketing and the selection of R & D projects can be used in applied research where the projects have precise technical and commercial objectives. But these methods based on simulation techniques are very difficult to apply because of the complex nature of R & D. Optimisation methods enable the best set of projects to be selected, but they cannot be used for fundamental research, where the projects are less clearly defined and the spin-off effects may not be quantifiable. On the other hand, Krawiec (1984) considers that scoring methods have the great advantage of providing decision-makers with a target – i.e. to optimise the desired utility. These methods take a number of criteria into account, including non-economic criteria or even subjective aspects embodied in expert opinions. It seems as though these methods are best adapted to fundamental research and exploratory development, not requiring the mathematical formalism of the other methods.

On the whole, then, these works and those of many other authors show the opportuneness of the studies to be undertaken, particularly so as to optimise the various evaluation methods and find out which are the most appropriate.

CONCLUSIONS

Political, economic and sociological sciences are greatly in demand in connection with research evaluation, not only for studies based on the present situation and designed to propose short or medium term scenarios, but also, and above all, for research undertaken at the request of potential users which will help in working out new kinds of economic processes.

March 1985 Vol. 9 No. 1

REFERENCES

Archier, G. and Serieyx, H. (1984). *L'entreprise du 3ème type*. Paris : Seuil.

Balachandra, R. and Raelin, J.A. (1984). "When to Kill that R & D Project". *Research Management*, 4: 30-33

Chapman, I.D. and Farina, C. (1983). "Peer Review and National Need". *Research Policy*, 12 : 317-327.

Chapman, I.D., Farina, C. and Gibbons, M. (1982). "The Funding of University Research – a Comparative Study of the United Kingdom and Canada". *Research Policy*, 11 : 15-31.

Cozzens, S.E. (1984). "The Context of Program Evaluation in the National Science Foundation". *CPE Etude/Colloque international sur les méthodologies évaluatives de la recherche*. Paris : CPE (to be published).

Feigenbaum, E. and Mc Corduck, P. (1983). *The Fifth Generation*. Reading, Mass. USA: Addison-Wesley publishing company.

Traduction (1984). *La cinquième génération - Le pari de l'intelligence artificielle à l'aube du 21ème siècle*. Paris : Inter Éditions.

Fundingsland, O.T. (1984). "Evaluation of Federally Sponsored Mission Targeted Research and Development in the United States". *CPE Étude/Colloque international sur les méthodologies évaluatives de la recherche*. Paris : (to be published).

Garnier, P. (1983). *L'évaluation des programmes de la recherche scientifique*. Paris : CPE Étude 29.

Hellstern, G.M. and Wollmann, H. (1981). "The Contribution of Evaluation to Administration". In: R.A. Levine, M.A. Salomon, G.M. Hellstern and H. Wollmann (Eds.), *Evaluation Research and Practice – Comparative and International Perspectives*, 68-91. London: Sage Publications.

Krawiec, F. (1984). "Evaluating and Selecting Research Projects by Scoring". *Research Management*, 2: 21-25

Yonekura, M. (1984). "Research Program Evaluation in Japan". *CPE Étude/Colloque international sur les méthodologies évaluatives de la recherche*. Paris : CPE (to be published).

External Assessment of Dutch University Research Programmes: An Evaluation

Jack Spaapen
University of Amsterdam
The Netherlands

INTRODUCTION

In 1982 the Ministry of Education and Science introduced the so-called Conditional Finance System in the Dutch universities. Until that time, university research had been financed mainly through block grants to the institutions, and student enrolment was the determining factor. During the seventies, the idea developed that student numbers were not the appropriate criterion for the division of research money and that other criteria (scientific and social) should be taken into account.

Critical surveys of the Dutch Advisory Council on Science Policy (RAWB, 1971) and the OECD examiners (1973) may be seen as the initiators of a major change in science policy, which was officially announced in the government white paper on university research in 1979 (BUOZ-nota). It was the first white paper devoted exclusively to university research, and formed part of the new science policy which aimed at presenting an integrated view of research, education, planning and manpower questions. In 1984 this policy was published in a white paper entitled Nota Beiaard. In this article we will limit ourselves to the new system of research financing and especially to the assessment procedure that forms an integral part of it.

In the BUOZ-nota the following objectives of "conditional financing" were formulated:

1. To make university research visible as a distinct activity in terms of manpower involved, financing, accounting and evaluation;
2. To promote the cohesion of university research by stimulating groups of researchers to formulate research programmes;
3. To introduce independent external assessment of these programmes and their results;
4. To encourage socially relevant research;
5. To co-ordinate nationally allocation of research specialities and professorships among universities.

These objectives were in striking contrast with the fairly liberal science policy the Dutch scientists were used to. The state did not interfere because it was believed that the way science was organised — and especially the way assessment procedures played an important role in the development of the sciences — guaranteed the best results, scientifically and socially speaking. In the "nota Wetenschapsbeleid" (1974) the government expressed its confidence not only in the scientific but also in the social responsibilities of scientists.

As in most other western countries steady growth of the Dutch science budget was experienced during the sixties and beginning of the seventies. In the same period, as a matter of course, student numbers grew enormously. But then, in the same "nota Wetenschapsbeleid", the government reveals the first contours of the new science policy, for which it gives economic and social reasons. According to the "nota", science policy should aim at *(i)* relating research projects to societal priorities, *(ii)* improvement of quality, *(iii)* improvement of efficiency and *(iv)* democratisation, one of the last twitchings of the sixties. The former three points may be found in the "nota Voorwaardelijke Financiering" (Paper on Conditional Finance) of 1982. By the time this paper was published, *retrenchment* was the key word in all government policy, and reallocation was one of the alarming possible consequences. Conditional Finance was meant to protect good research against these consequences. Which research is good was to be decided by external assessors. Especially in the Dutch situation — where traditionally there existed an aversion to rewarding good work and punishing bad — this new system led to a great outcry.

CONDITIONAL FINANCE

The conditional finance system — introduced in 1982 — is part of a new finance structure for the Dutch universities, which differs quite a lot from the old one, based on student numbers. In this paper we will not go into details, but we will give some features of the new system. One of the most striking differences between the two finance structures is that in the new one the total amount of money is divided into two, more or less equal parts, one of which is allocated under certain conditions. This particular part, part B, is meant to contain all the qualitatively good research the faculties produce, provided it meets certain conditions set by the Ministry. The other part (part A) will contain teaching, societal tasks and some room for special research projects. This of course put an end to the unity of research and teaching being the fundamental characteristic of the old system. It also put an end, at least partly, to the autonomy of both researchers and university governors which may serve as one of the explanations of the outcry mentioned above. Our focus is on part B, the Conditional Finance System. When one states, as the Ministry does, that this part has to contain qualitatively good research, one of course has to find a way to assess what exactly is qualitatively good research. For that purpose the Ministry designed the external assessment procedure, which became our main research topic. But before we come to that, we will take a closer look at the Conditional Finance System itself.

One of the major motivations behind this system has been precisely to make explicit — subject to policy debate — the distribution of research effort. A second motivation was the desire to ensure that in the development of university research explicit attention be paid to criteria of scientific quality and social relevance. This derived from the view that student numbers were an inappropriate criterion for the division of research money and that other criteria should be taken into consideration. Another important motive was that qualitatively good research could be protected more easily in times of financial cuts if research was accounted for separately.

Research programmes to be financed conditionally should have a volume of 5 man-year scientific personnel (full time equivalents) per year and a duration of at least 5 years. In special cases a smaller volume would be acceptable. The procedure for the introduction of the new system is spelled out and characterised as "learning by doing". Universities are invited to submit programme proposals, which should include information on the goals of the programme, the reputation of the group, the possible social relevance of the research, the costs, the position of the group within existing networks of national research coordination, etc. Furthermore,

within the introductory period of the system no reallocations between universities were envisaged, under the assumption that every university would submit enough proposals to fulfil
its quota.

The policy document on conditional finance also referred to the consequences for personnel of the possible termination of programmes which are "conditionally financed". After
the introductory period the negative evaluation of a programme and its results would lead to
a decrease in the university budget, unless other positively evaluated new programmes compensated for the decrease. This would clearly have consequences for the personnel involved.
Most academic staff would be involved in a conditionally financed programme on the one
hand and in teaching work on the other. The policy document suggests that "part-time dismissal" of personnel should be investigated as a possible solution to the problems which might
arise with the termination of the programme.

After initial hesitation, the universities became very busy formulating and discussing
programmes. With more retrenchments in sight, conditional finance seemed to offer some pro-
tection. At this time (September 1984) many more programmes had been submitted than
expected. Some universities had already filled their total space for conditional finance, although
they were expected only to have reached 40 per cent by this time. With the hurried introduction, however, a number of problems came to the fore, notably:

<blockquote>

a) Establishing the division between student-related research and the volume of funds
for which programmes were to be submitted;

b) The degree of expertise of the academic community and the Ministry in evaluating
research programmes;

c) The criteria established for the duration and volume of the research programmes;

d) Bureaucratisation of research;

e) The formal consequences for personnel participating in a conditionally financed
programme.

</blockquote>

Programmes had been drafted and approved while these issues were still in the balance implying
the need for revision procedures at a later stage.

Of course, the introduction of the new system was widely seen in terms of power: a
changing balance of power between the Ministry on the one hand and the universities on the
other. But also within universities and within departments and faculties power relations were
seen as changing, giving more power to "coordinators" and "bureaucrats" at the expense of
the researchers. One of the domains in which researchers traditionally were able to monopolise
power, the evaluation of the scientific product, also felt the pressure of this changing relationship, in that the conditions research programmes had to meet to obtain a positive judgement
were set by the Ministry (in advance and for all disciplines alike), as were, partly anyway,
the committees which had to perform the assessment. During the negotiations for the introduction of the conditional finance system the Minister promised the universities that there should
be an independent investigation of the working of the external assessment procedure. The
Minister invited the vakgroep Wetenschapsdynamica of the University of Amsterdam to carry
out such a study and in the next section we will give an impression of our findings.

STUDY OF EXTERNAL ASSESSMENT

Evaluation processes of various kinds are fundamental to the working of the scientific
system. Therefore sociologists of science have had a great interest in these processes. The claim
was often made that science advanced (best) according to a norm of "universality": a scientist's
work should be evaluated only in terms of its intrinsic scientific significance (and irrespective

of the background, status, affiliation of its author). Other empirical investigations questioned whether it was indeed scientific quality alone that determined the acceptance of a particular piece of work. (These questions were stimulated partly by public accusations of cliquishness and bias levelled at the peer review system.) The focus was the various evaluation processes fundamental to the working of the scientific community, including appointment to scientific posts, refereeing of scientific papers by journals, and evaluation of proposals for research funds. They studied non-universal factors like the teaching and social background and institutional affiliation (Hargens and Hagstrom, 1967; Blume and Sinclair, 1973). A famous study by Cole and Cole (1967) dealt with the question whether quantity or quality of published work is the more important, a topic still alive today (for example the Science Indicator Project of the University of Leiden, 1983).

Most of these studies focus upon the individual scientist and the determinants of the "recognition" achieved by him or her. Broadly speaking the majority found that the various empirical indicators of scientific "quality" or "performance" were highly interrelated. For example close correlations were found between assessment of individuals by panels of peers and indicators of their output of scientific papers and citation profiles (Clark, 1957). Blume and Sinclair (1973) found, however, that "scientific quality" was poorly coorelated with "industrial relevance" of research. In these studies of formal evaluation processes, concern with the criteria of judgment merges with another set of issues within the sociology of science: processes of social stratification. The referees, it is argued, are mainly to be drawn from the scientific elite. Cole, Cole and Simon argue that much depends on an element of chance, i.e. on who is doing the assessment.

These studies have been criticised on a variety of grounds, but to discuss that here is beyond our intention. The point we want to make is that these investigations, originating from a sociological interest in the normative structure of science, subsequently became attached to practical considerations of planning within the area of science policy. Increasingly, as governments have become more interventionist in this area, evaluations are required which do not take as their unit of analysis the individual scientist or project, but the output of an institution or a national scientific community. From such interests have come the various attempts at developing science indicators; on the basis of which it should, hopefully, be possible to make allocation decisions objectively. Now it is possible to distinguish two kinds of evaluation process: *(i)* those which are fundamental to the working of the scientific community, carried out by "peers" and *(ii)* those which are designed for policy purpose, making use of analytical tools constructed by social scientists and statisticians. The external assessment procedure that goes with the Conditional Finance system may be seen as an effort to combine the use of quantitative (output) indicators associated with science policies with the traditional evaluation process (by making use of peer groups). Whether this effort is made to authenticate the process in the eyes of the scientific community or because there were doubts as to the objectivity and suitability of science indicators, is not unimportant, but the relevance for us in studying this process lies in the effects they have on the ways university scientists think about, plan and carry out their scientific work, and — ultimately — on the research process itself. However, these research topics require long-term investigations; for the time being our interest is focused at the assessment procedure itself.

This external assessment procedure differed in many ways from the work the evaluators (the members of the evaluation committees) were used to, as journal referees, ZWO (National Organisation for Fundamental Research) members, etc. In the first place, they had to judge proposals with a high aggregation level. The Minister set a minimum of 5 f.t.e. meaning 12-15 persons participating in an integrated project, preferably a programme. In the second place, since the criteria were imposed from the outside (by the Minister), they were very complex, open to various interpretations and, moreover, often had to be balanced one against the other. This was the more unpleasant to the assessors, because they were frequently uncertain about the consequences of their decisions. Finally, an important difference lies in the scale of the operation: by 1987 some 50 per cent of all university research has to be assessed.

It appeared not only that members of the evaluating committees (broadly speaking) felt insecure because of these differences, but also that arguments derived from these uncertainties played a role in the judgements: for example the importance of total acceptance/rejection rate for discipline as a whole or the possible consequences for colleagues (e.g. unemployment). Then there were differences which related to cognitive differences between the disciplines. For instance, many complaints were heard from the humanities and the social sciences (researchers and assessors alike) that the conditions would favour the natural sciences, which could have serious consequences in the future when reallocation decisions had to be made on a national scale. In these fields it is often difficult or uncommon to meet minimum criteria concerning the volume and duration of programmes. On the other hand, a criterion like *social relevance* seemed to reveal difficulties for some (fundamental) natural sciences as well.

Moreover, it appeared that there were differences between the *procedures* in the various disciplines, which could not be justified in terms of cognitive differences between the sciences, and had to do with the structuring of the procedure established in each specific discipline (for instance the extent to which interaction with the university community was possible). The differences in procedures were, at least in part, caused by the fact that the Ministry decided to work with various kinds of committees for the external assessment, according to their "learning by doing" motto. For several disciplines *international ad hoc groups* were set up, for others *national ad hoc groups* (both were constituted by the Ministry). The Royal Academy of Sciences and ZWO (National Organisation for Fundamental Research) were each asked to compose committees in a number of fields; a professional organisation did the assessment in the case of engineering. The various responsible bodies established somewhat different operating procedures.

However, we found three consequences which are not so easily justified:

1. The problem of institutional interests. The interests and the existing practices of the organisations involved influence the procedures they follow;
2. Social aspects of evaluation processes: the means by which members of evaluation committees interacted with each other in reaching their judgements, and the processes by which the judgements of the individual members became integrated into a decision varied;
3. Interaction with the research community: the interaction-variation not only influences, as we found, the assessment itself, but has another important consequence. Interaction − the possibility of the university (scientist) modifying the proposal in the light of a provisional judgement − seemed a much more *constructive* process. Disciplines in which it occurred (e.g. engineering, agriculture) were favoured over those in which it was not (e.g. political science, history).

It is clear that the various sciences were dealt with very differently because of the formal structuring of the decision-making process. Besides this there is the point of interpretation of criteria by the individual assessors: how to operationalise the norms set by the Ministry. Because of the many uncertainties which were left in the introductory period, the differences in assessing committees, the institutional interests, there appeared to be much room for individual interpretation. Broadly speaking we found two (apparently) opposed conceptions *(i)* one subjective: to cite one of the judges, "I know what my colleagues are worth, I don't have to count their publications or whatever", and *(ii)* one " objective ", for one reason to legitimise the final judgment and for another to prevent personal (or social) motives playing a role. Many times the two conceptions struggled in one committee or in one evaluator, sometimes leading to a very strict interpretation of the conditions of the Ministry (and it has happened that an excellent scientist was negatively assessed because the size of his programme was too small), sometimes leading to a very moderate judgement. However that may be, because of all this some scientists complained that a positive evaluation was a matter of luck.

Although we have not systematically analysed the role of university administrators, we do finally wish to comment on them. It relates to what their role has been during the introductory period of the conditional finance. There was no strong research policy tradition in most faculties – with the exception of one or two universities – and with the (rather sudden) introduction of the new finance system the influence of faculty level as well as central university administrators on the development of programmes may have been substantial. On the other hand, it is in the interest of the university to receive their legitimate share of the conditional finance funds, which can probably be best achieved with an integrated university (both at central level and at faculty level) research policy. The results a university scores as a whole in the conditional finance system then become significant. Generally speaking, one could say that the various results do indeed depend on the relationship between the central level and the faculties, and the existence of a (strong) research policy at the central level. On the other hand there is the tendency towards bureaucratisation which many scientists fear will lead to means for staff dismissal (instead of research policy) and to the steering of research towards more applied goals. This has been subject to extensive discussion, e.g. at an IMHE workshop in November 1981.

CONCLUSIONS AND RECOMMENDATIONS OF THE STUDY

One of the important goals of the Conditional Finance System is to "target" funds more effectively on research programmes of high quality (both scientifically and in terms of socio-economic relevance) and of probable success. To meet this goal, the Minister introduced the external assessment procedure. The question is, whether this procedure is likely to serve that goal. We did not interpret our findings as showing that it does so clearly and unambiguously. The work of the committees was far too uncertain, beset by doubts, ambiguities and variations between fields of science for ultimate funding decisions. Therefore we suggested that the Minister should avoid such decisions at this stage of the "learning process". Moreover, we indicated three areas in which the procedure could be improved. These were:

- *The efficiency* of the procedure (for example, ensuring that evaluators were provided with the information they considered necessary, and had adequate time for their task, etc.);
- *The fairness* of the procedure (so that, through greater similarity between the procedures as established in the various fields, disciplines would not be advantaged or disadvantaged with respect to each other);
- *The flexibility of the procedure* (so that, particularly with reference to the criteria on which the evaluations were to be based, greater appreciation of the cognitive differences between the sciences would be allowed for).

The modifications introduced by the Ministry in the 1984 procedure correspond, to a significant extent, with our recommendations and also with views expressed by members of the evaluation committees and university administrators and boards. Among these modifications are the following:

- Evaluators will have clearer instructions on their tasks and also more time to carry out their evaluations; proposals should, where possible, now indicate in their attached publication list which publications are clearly relevant to the programme and which are less so;

— Evaluators are asked, where appropriate, to make use of quantitative indicators of research programmes;

— Interaction between evaluating groups and universities and programme leaders is now formally proposed;

— Much greater scope for innate differences between the ways of working of the various sciences is now allowed (e.g. the 5 f.t.e. requirement may be reduced in fields where universities and evaluating groups feel this appropriate).

In presenting the modified procedure the Minister has indicated his intention once more to seek a scientific assessment of the external evaluation procedure. Within a few months we will present a report on the 1984 procedure in which we will try to answer the question whether the modified procedure is more suitable to serve the goals set by the Ministry.

March 1985 Vol. 9 No. 1

REFERENCES

Blume, S.S. (1982). "Research Excellence: the Importance of External Dialogue and Internal Management". *International Journal of Institutional Management in Higher Education*, 6:2, 159-168. Paris: OECD/CERI.

Blume, S.S. and Sinclair, R. (1973). "Chemists in British Universties: a Study in the Reward System of Science". *American Sociological Review*, 38:126.

Blume, S.S., Spaapen, J.B. and Prins, A.A.M. (1983). *De externe beoordelingsprocedure in de Voorwaardelijke financiering.* Amsterdam.

Clark, K.E. (1957). *America's Psychologists: a Survey of a Growing Profession:* Washington, D.C.

Cole, S. and Cole, J.R. (1967). "Scientific Output and Recognition: a Study in the Operation of the Reward System of Science". *American Sociological Review*, 32: 377.

Cole, S., Cole, J.R. and Simon, G.A. (1981). "Chance and Consensus in Peer Review". Science, 214: 881.

Hargens, L. and Hagstrom, W.O. (1967). "Sponsored and Contest Mobility of American Scientists". Sociology of Education, 40: 24.

Moed, H.F., Burger, W.J.M., Frankfort, J.G. and Van Raan, A.F.J. (1983). On the Measurement of Research Performance. Leiden.

OECD Examiners' Report (1973). *Reviews of National Science Policy: The Netherlands.* Paris: OECD.

Government White Papers:

Beleidsnotitie Voorwaardelijke financiering (1982). Den Haag.

Beleidsnota Universitair Onderzoek (1979). Den Haag.

Beleidsnota Beiaard (1984). Den Haag.

Nota Wetenschapsbeleid (1974). Den Haag.

Vervolgnotitie Voorwaardelijke financiering (1984). Den Haag.

Index

for evaluation113
for research 154, 155
results compared 196-8, 201
retrenchment 96, 211
and evaluation 102, 109-11, 128, 129
risk analysis 208
Robbins report 17
role sharing 203
Romney, L. C. 86
Roose-Andersen ratings 124
Rotem, A. 70
Rothschild reforms 23, 157-8, 159, 174
Rothwell, R. 158
Rouban, A. M. T. 22

Saxon, D. 130-1
scenario analysis 106-7
SCI *see* Science Citation Index
Science Citation Index (SCI) 184, 188-9, 201
science policy, Netherlands 210-11
scientific evaluation 12, 13, 144-5, 205
scientific merit, evaluation of 23, 176-82, 204, 212-13
and adversarial mode 179
and evaluation process 176-8
and policy relevance 174, 178-9, 181-2, 202, 206
scientists, policymakers compared 180-1
scoring methods 208
Scriven, M. 13
Selden, W. K. 97
Seldin, P. 142, 143, 144
self-citation 192
self-evaluation 11, 16, 19-20, 53
France 21, 117-21
managers of 112-14
portfolio analysis 107-12, 115
Sweden 20, 21, 74-83, 109
self-study *see* self-evaluation
Simon, G. A. 213
Sinclair, R. 213
Sizer, J. 19, 20, 113
small group evaluation 63-73
social relevance, and evaluation 149, 214
socio-economic importance of research 167, 168
Source Index 184
Spaapen, J. 23
specialized programmatic accreditation 97, 99, 100
staff, for evaluation studies 91
'standardization of skills' 58

Staropoli, A. 16, 21
'star' courses *108,* 109
state licensing 18, 98, 99
Stecher, B. 24
stopping research programmes 204
strategic evaluation 205, 207
strategic planning 111-12
Tennessee University 46, *47, 48*
strategic research 155-6, 157, 160
students
attitudes to evaluation 41, 42
evaluation by 15, 22, *40,* 51, 144
small group 63-73
Stufflebeam, D. 166
subject networks 136, 139
summative evaluation 13-14, 21, 150
Sweden
basic unit evaluation 21, 148-53
research evaluation 22, 161-5
self-evaluation 20, 21, 74-83, 109

Talbot, R. W. 22
task force, Tennessee University 44
teachers
evaluation of 21, 56-7
see also faculty evaluation
and research 149, 168, 183-4, 194, 210, 211
response to small group evaluation 69, 70
Technical University of Denmark 193-201
technology, and science research 155, 158, 203, 206
Tennessee Higher Education Commission 27-8, 31, 45
Tennessee State 20, 26, 27-32
Tennessee University, Knoxville 43-52, 53-5
theory, as evaluation criteria 150
timing evaluation 91, 144
trend analysis 186, *187*
'triangulation effect' 37 *38*

United Kingdom (UK) 17, 21, 113
research evaluation 157-8, 159, 173-82
see also CNAA; DHSS;
Loughborough University;
Rothschild reforms;
University Grants
Committee
United States (US) 18, 77, 85, 113
faculty evaluation 141-7
institutional evaluation 18, 95-104

performance funding 26-32
program review 122-33
value-added model 33-42, 53-5
see also California University;
North East Missouri
University; Tennessee
state; Tennessee University
University Grants Committee
(UGC) 17, 19, 112
'utilization crisis' 151
UTK *see* Tennessee University, Knoxville

validation *see* external validation
validity, of small group evaluation 64, 70
Value-Added model 53-5
NE Missouri University
Program 33-42
Tennessee University 43-52
Value-Added Tax system model 34, 53
visitations, academic 175-6
voluntary accreditation 18

Weldon, H. K. 86
withdrawal strategies 110, 111
Wollman, H. 207, 208
Working Party, Loughborough
University 107, 111

Young, K. 97, 99

Zegfeld, W. 158

.